WILLIAM GIBSON AND THE FUTURES

OF CONTEMPORARY CULTURE

THE NEW AMERICAN CANON
The Iowa Series in Contemporary Literature and Culture
Samuel Cohen, series editor

EDITED BY MITCH R. MURRAY AND MATHIAS NILGES

WILLIAM GIBSON AND THE FUTURES OF CONTEMPORARY CULTURE

UNIVERSITY OF IOWA PRESS, IOWA CITY

University of Iowa Press, Iowa City 52242
Copyright © 2021 by the University of Iowa Press
www.uipress.uiowa.edu

Printed in the United States of America

Design by April Leidig

No part of this book may be reproduced or used in any form or by any means without permission in writing from the publisher. All reasonable steps have been taken to contact copyright holders of material used in this book. The publisher would be pleased to make suitable arrangements with any whom it has not been possible to reach.

Printed on acid-free paper

Library of Congress Cataloging-in-Publication Data
Names: Murray, Mitch R., editor. | Nilges, Mathias, editor.
Title: William Gibson and the Futures of Contemporary Culture / edited by Mitch R. Murray and Mathias Nilges.
Description: Iowa City: University of Iowa Press, [2021] | Series: The New American Canon: The Iowa Series in Contemporary Literature and Culture | Includes bibliographical references and index. |
Identifiers: LCCN 2020021100 (print) | LCCN 2020021101 (ebook) | ISBN 9781609387488 (paperback; acid-free paper) | ISBN 9781609387495 (ebook)
Subjects: LCSH: Gibson, William, 1948—Criticism and interpretation. | Gibson, William, 1948—Influence. | Literature and Society.
Classification: LCC PS3557.I2264 Z94 2020 (print) | LCC PS3557.I2264 (ebook) | DDC 813/.54—dc23
LC record available at https://lccn.loc.gov/2020021100
LC ebook record available at https://lccn.loc.gov/2020021101

For Kevin Floyd

CONTENTS

ix Acknowledgments

　　FOREWORD . . . MALKA OLDER
xi Crime and Dislocation: William Gibson's Modernity

　　INTRODUCTION . . . MITCH R. MURRAY AND MATHIAS NILGES
1   Periodizing Gibson

PART I. GIBSON AND LITERARY HISTORY

　　CHAPTER 1 . . . PHILLIP E. WEGNER
21 When It Changed: Science Fiction and the Literary Field, circa 1984

　　CHAPTER 2 . . . KYLIE KORSNACK
49 No Future but the Alternative: Or, Temporal Leveling in the Work of William Gibson

　　CHAPTER 3 . . . MATHIAS NILGES
67 The Shelf Lives of Futures: William Gibson's Short Fiction and the Temporality of Genre

　　CHAPTER 4 . . . TAKAYUKI TATSUMI
81 *The Difference Engine* in a Post-Enlightenment Context: Franklin, Emerson, and Gibson and Sterling

PART II. GIBSON AND THE QUESTION OF MEDIUM

CHAPTER 5 . . . ANDREW M. BUTLER

97 "A New Rose Hotel Is a New Rose Hotel Is a New Rose Hotel": Nonplaces in William Gibson's Screen Adaptations

CHAPTER 6 . . . MARIA ALBERTO AND ELIZABETH SWANSTROM

111 William Gibson, Science Fiction, and the Evolution of the Digital Humanities

CHAPTER 7 . . . ROGER WHITSON

131 Time Critique and the Textures of Alternate History: Media Archaeology in *The Difference Engine* and *The Peripheral*

PART III. GIBSON AND THE PROBLEM OF THE PRESENT

CHAPTER 8 . . . SHERRYL VINT

153 Too Big to Fail: The Blue Ant Trilogy and Our Productized Future

CHAPTER 9 . . . AMY J. ELIAS

167 Realist Ontology in William Gibson's *The Peripheral*

CHAPTER 10 . . . ARON PEASE

179 Cyberspace after Cyberpunk

CHAPTER 11 . . . CHRISTIAN P. HAINES

195 "Just a Game": Biopolitics, Video Games, and Finance in William Gibson's *The Peripheral*

211 AFTERWORD . . . CHARLES YU

The World Implied

215 Notes

247 Bibliography

263 Index

ACKNOWLEDGMENTS

"Wintermute was hive mind . . . Neuromancer was personality." Hive mind and personality, common project and collective consciousness on one hand, individual thought and analytical impulse on the other, inseparable and irreducible to each other in William Gibson's groundbreaking 1984 novel *Neuromancer* and in *William Gibson and the Futures of Contemporary Culture*. This book is as much the result of the thoughtful input and collegial support of a large group of people who helped make the project possible as it is the result of the brilliant individual chapters our contributors have composed. We therefore see the acknowledgments section as an opportunity to thank all those for whose help we are immensely grateful and as a way to foreground the possibilities and complexities that make reading and editing collections of critical essays so intellectually and socially rewarding.

We begin with our wonderful contributors, and we thank them for their ideas as much as for their collegiality and professionalism. Special thanks go to Charlie Yu, whose words have been as inspiring to us as Gibson's. We are also deeply grateful for the support and guidance that we have received from the whole team at University of Iowa Press. Samuel Cohen has been an enthusiastic champion of this project from the very beginning, and he helped us navigate each step of the process leading up to this book's publication. We had the great pleasure of working with Ranjit Arab, whose enthusiasm matched Sam's own, and with Meredith Stabel, who brought this book to completion.

We thank a group of people who are part of the wider hive mind that made this book possible, people whose helpful input, encouragement, enthusiasm, and support contributed to the development of this project: Mark Bould, Madhu Dubey, Mark McGurl, China Miéville, Joshua Clover, Haerin Shin, Grace L. Dillon, Veronica Hollinger, Keren Omry, Kim Stanley Robinson, and Fredric Jameson. We thank Lee Konstantinou and an anonymous reader, both of whom provided helpful notes and their enthusiasm for this project. In addition, we thank the following colleagues and friends for their support and intellectual camaraderie: Rod Bantjes, Bret Benjamin, Bev Best, Tim Bewes, Kyle Bohunicky, Sarah Brouillette, Nicholas Brown, Jamie Owen Daniel, Alice Haisman, Susan Hegeman, Rafael Hernandez, Mitchum Huehls, Alyssa Hunziker, Caren Irr, Madison Jones, Helen Jun, Derrick King, Tim Lanzendörfer, Neil Larsen, Carolyn Lesjak, Walter Benn Michaels, Maureen Moynagh, Jason Potts, Mary Roca, Emilio Sauri, Malini Johar Schueller, Rachel Greenwald Smith, Paul Stasi, Matt Tierney, and Phil Wegner. We extend our thanks, too, to the Marxist Literary Group and the Marxist Reading Group.

Mitch R. Murray thanks his longtime best friend and now wife, Samantha Grenrock. Support from the University of Florida College of Liberal Arts and Sciences and from the Marston-Milbauer Eminent Scholarship, and the hard work of United Faculty of Florida—Graduate Assistants United made completing this book possible. Finally, he thanks Mathias and Phil, who taught him that science fictional worlds are possible.

Mathias Nilges thanks his wife, best friend, and favorite being across all timelines and dimensions, Maïca Murphy, his family, Mollie and Willow, and also Madhu Dubey for teaching him everything he knows about science fiction.

FOREWORD . . . **MALKA OLDER**

CRIME AND DISLOCATION

WILLIAM GIBSON'S MODERNITY

Rereading William Gibson thirty-five years after *Neuromancer* was published, it's easy to get stuck on the startlingly accurate predictions, even those that haven't come true yet, or to be caught in the scintillating micro-images of many possible futures. Indeed, my memories of the novels before going back for this reread were mainly vivid details: mirrored glasses fused to ocular bones and spit from rerouted tear ducts; 3D holograph vagina tattoos on the wrists of young women skittish as giraffes; fake tans on fake French teenagers; an idoru spun out of a device like a cocktail shaker; a customizable, beautiful computer that looks nothing like my laptop, although I'm not sure exactly what it does look like; River Phoenix dying invisibly and continuously on the street where he collapsed.

I am not sure whether this retrospective reduction of complexly plotted books to a few anecdote-level, non-load-bearing details is a function of how my brain works or of the way Gibson's writing works, and it's possible that the difference is academic in any case, because they may both be symptoms of a mutual condition: modernity.

These moments feel unprecedented and inevitable because they anticipate the technology they require but nail the human nature that is going to use that technology to create them as soon as it becomes possible. Of course nonverbal flirtation and increasingly risqué physical accoutrements are eventually going to evolve to the point of 3D vagina tattoos.

It's a kind of science fiction rooted in sociological observation along with technological savvy. The story is less about the amazing kinds of technology we will invent—and when I say "amazing," try to cast your mind back to the world before the sea-change that is the internet, making *Neuromancer*'s matrix no less amazing than space travel—than the bizarre ways we use those technologies. Corrupt, hedonistic, bad-ass, ritualistic, artistic, self-aggrandizing, righteous, mystical: Gibson shows us the range of human motivations through technological appropriation, from the elite who make their own innovations to the marginal who bricolage the unexpected by-products.

Many of these insights, like the ones I mentioned at the outset, come across not as revelations or turning points but as non-plot-bearing character details or pure asides with no relevance to the rest of the story other than thickening the world it takes place in. Yet those scintillating details, with their precision and prescience, often stick in the mind and captivate even in the moment, even as the movement of the story draws you unfailingly from one to the next. The sense is of a net of tangentially connected images—or in the more current parlance, GIFs or Vines—held together by the strands of an unerring, action-driven plot. It's tempting to use the image of a kaleidoscope or a collage, but consider a page, maybe the fourth or fifth page, of Internet search results: windows into different landscapes, some commercial, some artistic, some nonprofit, many only loosely connected to the original terms and all liable to change over time and with tweaks to the algorithm, yet all together offering a multidimensional compilation image, possibly incomplete and wrong but still powerful.

On rereading more of Gibson's books en masse, the details are still arresting but it is easier to see their overall, collective effect and refocus on the persistent theme of the author's work: dislocation, disorientation, disubication. This sense of upheaval and disconnection, more than Gibson's acuity for technical speculation, is what makes his books so apt for the modern world. They inhabit our feelings of change and uncertainty, the awareness of always being slightly behind the curve of innovation, the thrilling and relentless proliferation of perspectives that is the modern experience. Yet they manage to hover on the cusp of modernity without tipping over into postmodernism, the dislocation in time, space, class, humanity, scale, identity, culture, and reality tempered by our awareness of being safely strapped into the confines of that most modern of plots, the suspense novel, mystery, or thriller.

When I say "modern" here, I'm using it in a broad sense, for the age of speed and change rather than just the Internet age. The railroad and the telegraph, when they appeared and then rapidly became normal in certain contexts, compressed time and space in much the same confusing way that the airplane and the Internet have, and dissociative fugue states surged (in documentation, at least). The sense of being slightly unhinged from the self, if not from reality, evolved as the concept individual became disassociated from social roles, much at the same time that science fiction emerged to look at the present through the lens of the future.

Dislocation of self as a function of modern movement and introspection is a theme hardly limited to science fiction. Take this passage from Proust's *Swann's Way*:

> For me it was enough if, in my own bed, my sleep was so heavy as completely to relax my consciousness; for then I lost all sense of the place in which I had gone to sleep, and when I awoke in the middle of the night, not knowing where I was, I could not even be sure at first who I was . . . For it always happened that when I awoke like this, and my mind struggled in an unsuccessful attempt to discover where I was, everything revolved around me through the darkness: things, places, years. My body, still too heavy with sleep to move, would endeavour to construe from the patterns of its tiredness the position of its various limbs, in order to deduce therefrom the direction of the wall, the location of the furniture, to piece together and give a name to the house in which it lay. Its memory, the composite memory of its ribs, its knees, its shoulder-blades, offered it a whole series of rooms in which it had at one time or another slept, while the unseen walls, shifting and adapting themselves to the shape of each successive room that it remembered, whirled round it in the dark.[1]

How many Gibson characters wake up this way: in an unfamiliar room, unsure of where they are and who they are? Whether because air travel has left their souls floating behind, or because their professional identity has become suddenly fluid, or because someone has modified their face into someone else's as they slept, Gibson's characters regularly find themselves in a partially understood, fragmented world that reflects their inner confusion. Internal and external conditions can change while they are unconscious; the past, present, and (unevenly distributed) future are all available options when they wake.

This unexpected change is the experience of modernity. We wake up and check our phones (phones!) to find out what kind of world we are living in today, aware that nations may fall, new colors may be discovered, and aliens may visit while we sleep. Our waking hours are often fragmented into bits of information from scattered sources: an email from work, a message from a friend, a conversation with the person across the table, a tweet from the other side of the planet, a photo from a celebrity. Our identities have become fragmented or fluid or both, and when we wake in the night we are likely to have many more remembered rooms to choose from than Proust did, from dorm rooms to Holiday Inns to Airbnbs.

Asked about the sense of temporal dislocation in his work in a 2012 interview with *The Verge*, Gibson responded,

> I think that part of my experience of growing up in the American South in the early '60's was one of living in a place unevenly established in the present. You could look out one window and see the 20th century, then turn and look out another window and see the 19th.... It provides a sort of parallax. If you only have one eye, you don't have depth perception. If you're able to look at things with one eye in the 21st century and the other eye in the 20th century (or possibly even the late-19th), it provides a kind of perspective that otherwise wouldn't be available.[2]

The dislocation we feel through Gibson's fiction is both a reflection of the dislocation we feel in modernity and a kind of tool for dealing with it, or for comprehending it more broadly. Our times are too precarious and changeable to be understood in isolation or—one of the risks of seeing them without that perspective—assumed to be permanent.

The dislocation in Gibson's novels is not limited to the temporal. It is multiple, iterative, and complex. In addition to time, his characters tend to suffer from cultural dislocation. This comes most obviously from international travel, most often in Japan. In *Mona Lisa Overdrive*, Kumiko flips that, viewing the West from an (imagined) Japanese perspective.

Naturally in this postmodern, self-reflective world, perspective is mirrored back and forth for further disorientation: "The decor of the bar induced a profound sense of cultural dislocation: it managed to simultaneously reflect traditional Japanese design and look as though it had been drawn up by Charles Rennie Mackintosh."[3]

In *Pattern Recognition*, Cayce finds mirror worlds in London and Russia as well as Japan. For her, the small physical-industrial differences are both confusing and anchoring, confirmation that one is elsewhere; she is reminded that the kind of globalization practiced by companies like Blue Ant, "more post-geographic than multinational," threaten that "no borders, pretty soon there's no mirror to be on the other side of. Not in terms of the bits and pieces, anyway."[4]

In some cases, the act of movement itself triggers disorientation, as with Cayce's soul-delaying jet lag. On her arrival in London, "in spite of the Jaguar's speed, Kumiko felt as if somehow she were standing still; London's particles began to accrete around her" (*Mona Lisa Overdrive*, 5). In *Spook Country*, Tito's trip across the country in an anachronistic plane, literally under the radar of modernity, is entirely different from his personal, traumatic definition of air travel.

Gibson reminds us that geographical travel is not the only way to encounter culture shock. Different classes within the same city can be oceans apart: their experiences of life incompatible, their reference points unmatchable, identical words holding entirely different meanings:

> "'It's not the Ritz,' he said, 'but we'll try to make you comfortable.'
> Mona made a noncommittal sound. The Ritz was a burger place in Cleveland." (86).

Mona might as well be in a foreign country: meaning is slipping by and she is disoriented by incentives, artifacts, and behaviors that make no sense to her.

The disorientation of the characters is typically paralleled by that of the readers, as the quick-cut scenes and multiple point-of-view characters yank them into a dislocation that mirrors that of the plot. For many readers, it may not be easy to separate what is science fiction and what are unknown but current details in, for example, Case's descriptions of Japan early in *Neuromancer*. But Gibson's books also manufacture their own culture shock or jet lag in the reader with their jumps among settings and points of view. We move between perspectives, registers, knowledge bases, and cultural framings constantly and without warning or explanation. As with Kumiko and Mona in *Mona Lisa Overdrive*, most of the books toggle between extremely wealthy segments and the quite poor. Most of our points of view are confused, but they are confused about different things, as in *Spook Country*, with the case of Hollis, confused about Blue Ant and her career; Tito, who is completely sure about his role but faces mysteries about his history and his future; and Milgrim, lost in addiction and at the mercy of a stranger. Shuttling between such viewpoints enforces that disorientation on the reader while giving us a sense for the immense variety of existences in the world.

We occasionally get landmarks for navigating these worlds, but the landmarks have to be recognized through their different perceptions by different characters: the New Suzuki Envoy in *Mona Lisa Overdrive*, the critical building in *The Peripheral*, Tito's room, the bridge. These touchpoints offer some orientation for the reader and remind us that real artifacts are subjective and changeable.

Modern dislocation goes far beyond culture shock. Many of Gibson's characters—often the ones we most identify with—are lost in ways that have nothing to do with the people around them. Some, like Case and Milgrim, are distracted by addiction. Case and Hollis struggle with losing a part of their identities. Most powerfully, Cayce offers a picture of a person deeply affected by an indirect trauma that goes unmentioned for half the book and is eventually contrasted with the direct physical trauma experienced by Nora, the maker of the footage. Cayce wonders whether the strangeness she experiences during the story is because "the world had gone in such a different direction, in the instant of having seen that petal drop, that nothing really is the same now, and that her expectations of the parameters of how life should feel are simply that, expectations, and increasingly out of line the further she gets from that window in the SoHo Grand" (*Pattern Recognition*, 195). The world around Cayce—and around the rest of us—has changed so profoundly that it is little wonder we have trouble finding our bearings.

These characters all suffer from a disconnection to others, whether because of addiction, trauma, or simply changing their professional lives. We learn of largely absent friends, reconnections after long gaps, and isolation in the midst of crowds. Technology sometimes seems to worsen this, but for the most part it mitigates it, often in direct contrast to unmediated contact. In the opening scene of *Pattern Recognition*, for example, the "real" environment is sterile and empty: "Damien's new kitchen is as devoid of edible content as its designers' display windows in Camden High Street.... Very clean and almost entirely empty.... Nothing at all in the German fridge, so new that its interior smells only of cold and long-chain monomers" (1). "Whatever faintly lived-in feel the place now has, Cayce knows, is the work of a production assistant" (2). The space is beautiful but anonymous, devoid of character and contact to the point that even the smell of a nonlover's body in the sheets is welcome: "it's not unpleasant; any physical linkage to a fellow mammal seems a plus at this point" (2).

But if Cayce can't, at that moment, get a closer physical linkage than a fading smell, she can get warmth and connection on the Internet. "The front page opens, familiar as a friend's living room.... She enters the forum itself now, automatically scanning titles of the posts and names of posters in the newer threads, looking for friends, enemies, news." The Internet, and for Cayce specifically this chatroom, "is a way now, approximately, of being at home. The forum has become one of the most consistent places in her life, like a familiar café that exists somehow outside of geography and beyond time zones" (4). Later in the book we are treated to a creepy physical variant of that concept in the form of a London Starbucks with "exactly the same faux-Murano pendulum lamps they have in the branch nearest her apartment in New York" (207). Unlike the dynamic and interactive familiarity of the Internet forum, this version is static and sinister. The Starbucks is part of the global flattening that Cayce senses from Blue Ant, a calculated erasure of difference and anger alike: "The decor somehow fosters emotional neutrality, a leveling of affect" (207). For all its personality snags and even spies, the virtual world is not stale in the same way as corporate replicas.

None of this is science fiction—Internet forums and identical Starbucks were common when the novel was released in 2003—but Gibson captures the very modern feeling of living in a futurized present, in which change has occurred too quickly and along too many axes to be fully assimilated or known. The book is crammed with the disorienting weirdness of living in the present, from the unevenly distributed nature of technology to the all-too-believable catfishing (before that term was popularized) of an *otaku*, to the collision of virtual and real effects. This gets supercharged with prose even more truncated than usual and a point-of-view character still occasionally in the throes of traumatic dissociation, adding to the sense of disorientation.

In the more futurist novels, the dislocation gets more existential. Gibson chips away at our concepts of identity, first through cyberspace and then, as avatars and online personalities became part of our mundane present, through peripherals. He challenged the reader's ideas on what is human with Kumiko's ghost and the idoru. With *The Peripheral*, he mind-bends reality with the idea of stubs.

Although Gibson's books are an experience of disorientation for characters and readers, they are never formless or directionless. In fact, the novels tend toward the most plot-driven of literary forms: the mystery, detective story, or thriller. Gibson has said in an interview with *Salon* that "Detective fiction and science fiction are an ideal cocktail, in my opinion."[5] This is fitting, as detective stories are also the most modern of genres, coming into existence—if you take Poe as the originator—some two decades after *Frankenstein*. Gibson agrees with the interviewer that crime fiction is one way to follow a prescription he heard from Samuel R. Delany: "If you want to know how something works, look at one that's broken."[6]

Indeed, while *The Peripheral* is the exception in being a literal murder mystery (and still more of a thriller than a mystery in Todorov's typology[7]), most if not all of Gibson's novels contain not only mysteries but strong elements of crime fiction. There are smugglers, assassins, Mafia families of various nationalities, and of course the more respectable and devastating crime of the rich and powerful. In fact, almost anyone with any significant power in the books is, if not an outright criminal, certainly comfortable with the shady side of the law. If the kleptocracy of twenty-second-century London described in *The Peripheral* is unusually explicit, it is echoed in what we see of the hierarchies in the other books.

The primary function of the detective story is the search, and many of Gibson's characters are driven by something specific, if undefined: a mystery they need to solve. Cayce follows the mystery of the footage. Laney, particularly in *All Tomorrow's Parties*, is driven to guide or catalyze a moment of change that he cannot define. In *Mona Lisa Overdrive*, Gentry is searching for a shape that defines cyberspace in some coherent way. None of these characters are certain there is meaning in what they are doing, much as Flynne is unsure of the reality of the murder she saw for a long time.

These characters often act through means that they don't fully understand: Cayce's brand sensitivity and Laney's drug-triggered obsession, its specific origins lost to his powerlessness as the child subject of testing. Tito understands his relationship to the Orishas but cannot explain why they do what they do. Nora Volkova creates in ways that the ones around her cannot explain or decipher, yet her creation resonates with thousands of others. The method is almost as much a mystery as the objective. Notably, for Nora and Laney, and in a more oblique way, Cayce, their special ability or insight is a side effect of the violence of modernity. The way to this abstract insight, Gibson suggests, is nonlinear and possibly requires a different sort of intelligence, a reliance on the intuition that often derives from the very damages committed by the modern world.

Even when the characters don't fully understand what, why, or how they are seeking, they feel compelled to continue the search; those actions, directed toward something, push the plot forward. Todorov's "second story, the story of the investigation"[8] pulls us unerringly along with the books. Something has happened, changed, been broken, and we, along with the characters, need to understand why, or how, or at least what. For all the dislocation in the world we are asked to inhabit, the need to figure out what happened is enough to give shape to the unnerving, perspective-shifting narrative. Like the characters, we are searching for something that might or might not be interpretable, might or might not provide meaning for the whole experience.

It is reminiscent of how a character in A. S. Byatt's *Possession* explains their fascination with literary criticism: "I suppose one studies—I study—literature because all these connections seem both endlessly exciting and then in some sense dangerously powerful—as though we held a clue to the true nature of things?"[9] Gibson's characters study technology, and its intersections with art and celebrity and commercialism, subtextually, searching for the unstated, unintended, improbable connections that hint at the shape of the society and maybe the species that created them.

Many of Gibson's characters are sensemaking, in Karl E. Weick's sense: in the crisis that is modernity—a time of confusion, dislocation, and crime—they struggle to find a narrative or an image that will re-create a worldview of some kind, even if it isn't the same one they started with. Moreover, this is enacted sensemaking: "To sort out a crisis as it unfolds often requires action which simultaneously generates the raw material that is used for sensemaking and affects the unfolding crisis itself."[10] Perhaps the clearest example of this is Laney, working to bring about a crisis moment without understanding what that moment is or will mean until it happens (and, Moses-like, not even then). Cayce's leap-of-faith flight into Moscow is similar: she doesn't know what she will find, and her presence there and contact with Stella changes the situation she has come to explore. In the Sprawl trilogy, those who seek to understand the matrix must enter it and, necessarily, affect its overall shape and evolution.

Readers are asked to follow the plots of the novels in almost the same way: confused, not quite understanding the connections we are being asked to make, but possibly trusting that there is a meaning behind it all. It might be a meaning of our own collective or individual making, or an illusion created by the author. It might help us understand something we already know about the world we live in. As has been suggested, if reading literature builds the skills needed for empathy,[11] then Gibson's work provides us with the relief of seeing our peripatetic modern experience represented in prose and with a kind of practice in continuing that existence more aware and more alert to the new ways we fall apart and fit together.

WILLIAM GIBSON AND THE FUTURES
OF CONTEMPORARY CULTURE

MITCH R. MURRAY AND MATHIAS NILGES

INTRODUCTION

PERIODIZING GIBSON

On the cusp of the new millennium, *The Guardian* considered William Gibson "in terms of concrete influence probably the most important novelist of the past two decades."[1] Gibson's groundbreaking 1984 debut novel *Neuromancer*, for instance, was a tremendous global success. It sold close to eight million copies, received numerous awards, was translated into dozens of languages, and was adapted (among other media) into films, a graphic novel, a radio play, and an opera. A major film adaptation, directed by Tim Miller, was announced in late 2017, underscoring the continued significance and renewed importance of Gibson's early work in the context of our current return to a brand of "cyberpunk 2.0."[2] Yet as Tim Adams notes, ten years passed before the *New York Times* mentioned *Neuromancer*.[3] There exists a notable temporal lag between the rise in popularity and influence of Gibson's work and its critical reception. Despite his rapidly growing global influence, mainstream commentary has registered the significance of Gibson's work with substantial delay. Literary and cultural criticism lags further behind. To date, there exists no collection of essays tracing the wide-ranging influence and cultural importance of Gibson's work. In the volume of the Cambridge

American Literature in Transition series dedicated to the 2000 to 2010 decade (the same decade in which Gibson made the dramatic shift from cyberpunk to a new kind of realism in *Pattern Recognition*, widely known as the first novel to directly address the terrorist attacks of September 11, 2011), for example, Gibson garners only two passing mentions.[4] *William Gibson and the Futures of Contemporary Culture* aims to address this long-standing and in many ways baffling problem: Gibson is one of the most well-known and globally influential North American authors in recent decades, yet his work remains underexamined and its reach and significance underappreciated. Together, the essays we gather here highlight the scale of Gibson's work by trading in localized readings of select works for large-scale explorations of the implications and significance of Gibson's work for the development of recent literature and culture and for literary and cultural criticism.

Before we turn to an outline of and introduction to this volume's critical project, it is useful to survey the notable breadth and richness of Gibson's creative output to illustrate the immensely productive archive it provides for critical interrogation. Born on March 17, 1948, in Conway, South Carolina, Gibson moved to Toronto, Canada, in 1968, relocating later to the West Coast. In 1977, he graduated from the University of British Columbia with a degree in English literature. Although Gibson is most well known as a novelist, he began his career writing short fiction. In 1977, he published his first short story, "Fragments of a Hologram Rose," which emerged out of his undergraduate work. Although Gibson has remained a prolific writer of short fiction in his career, the late 1970s and early 1980s saw the publication of what arguably became his most significant series of short stories. These stories, which were collected in the volume *Burning Chrome* (1986), remain relatively underexamined yet significant insofar as they establish Gibson's voice as one of the key authors of the cyberpunk genre (including Pat Cadigan, Rudy Rucker, Masamune Shirow, and Bruce Sterling, among others). *Neuromancer*—the first volume in his Sprawl trilogy, which also includes *Count Zero* (1986) and *Mona Lisa Overdrive* (1988)—was soon established as one of the ur-texts of cyberpunk. Several essays in this volume return to this formative stage in Gibson's work and outline how his early short stories lay the groundwork for developing his stylistic and formal constants and some of the foundations of cyberpunk in general. Most of Gibson's short stories remain uncollected and have been published in a wide variety of venues. No doubt, some editing work remains to be done to make this crucial and understudied facet of Gibson's work more accessible to readers. Gibson is also a prolific essayist and writer of nonfiction, contributing frequently to publications like the *New York Times* and *Wired*. Some of this work has been collected in the volume *Distrust That Particular Flavor* (2012). As Kylie Korsnack shows in her contribution to this book, Gibson's nonfiction not only provides us with an invaluable resource for contextualizing and understanding his larger oeuvre, but much of it remains underappreciated as a source of striking ideas and critiques of our historical present.

After the Sprawl trilogy and *Burning Chrome* established him as one of the "godfathers" of cyberpunk and one of the key voices in the rejuvenation and innovation of science fiction in the 1980s, Gibson transitioned into a particularly productive period. During the 1990s, Gibson published a second trilogy, the Bridge trilogy, consisting of the novels *Virtual Light* (1993), *Idoru* (1996), and *All Tomorrow's Parties* (1999). In addition, Gibson collaborated with fellow science fiction writer Bruce Sterling to publish *The Difference Engine* (1990). Bafflingly enough, some of these 1990s works are often understood as Gibson's least interesting output. Yet as Takayuki Tatsumi, a foremost critic of cyberpunk's transnational flows between the United States and Japan, illustrates in his chapter, *The Difference Engine*'s alternate history—particularly its constant movement between Western Enlightenment and the development of Western and American modern social and political structures on one hand and the rise of Japanese modernity on the other—enables Gibson and Sterling to develop their particularly rich version of steampunk, which deploys the same speculative blend of the historical and the political that characterizes cyberpunk. Strikingly reconfiguring steampunk into another innovation on the level of cyberpunk, Tatsumi gives us a new way of understanding this apparent outlier among Gibson's works as "hardcore cyberpunk in the disguise of steampunk." In fact, the 1990s may be considered among the most formally and medially experimental periods in Gibson's career. Given that Gibson, as the essays in this book together show, was fundamentally dedicated to formal and generic innovation based on interrogating the relationship between historical change and generic conventions, this is a significant statement.

In addition to charting new generic territory in steampunk, in the 1990s Gibson also branched out into screenwriting. He adapted his short story "Johnny Mnemonic" into a screenplay of the same title in 1995, and he wrote two episodes of the TV show *The X-Files*: "Kill Switch" and "First Person Shooter," which aired in 1995 and 2000, respectively. Andrew M. Butler's chapter sets into play these underexamined screenplays as key moments in Gibson's rich and evolving artistic project. Gibson struggled to replicate his success as a science fiction author in his screenwriting. Nonetheless, Butler shows, Gibson's work as a screenwriter marks a significant stage in his development as a writer on par with his stories and novels. Butler reads Gibson's scripts in Marc Augé's terms as attempts to represent "the nonplaces of supermodernity" and thus "the ongoing alienation of the individual in the world (non)place of late capitalism" that continues to subtend his fiction. Because these scripts demand a struggle with different cultural mediums such as film and television, we must also understand this aspect of Gibson's work as central to his later attention to the artistic and political differences between mediums.

On December 9, 1992, in a performance titled "The Transmission," author, musician, actor, illusionist, and free-market advocate Penn Jillette read portions of a poem that stands at the center of the multimedia artwork *Agrippa (A Book of the Dead)* (1992), produced collaboratively by Gibson, artist Dennis Ashbaugh, and publisher Kevin Begos Jr. *Agrippa* consists of a 300-line poem by Gibson, stored on a 3.5-inch floppy disk, held inside an artist's book created by Ashbaugh.[5] The disk with the poem is programmed to automatically encrypt itself after a single use. The pages of the artist's book are chemically treated to cause a gradual (and ultimately complete) fading after the book's first exposure to light. Although *Agrippa* remains one of Gibson's least frequently studied works, it is notable in its attention to precisely those questions that his writing explores in his larger body of work. *Agrippa* asks, for instance, how we should understand the relation between those artistic media that are brought into connection and possibly seamlessly intertwined in the digital era. For instance, what is the status of the text, writing, and literature in the digital era, and where do traditionally established boundaries that separate mediums end in this new historical context? In other words, *Agrippa* highlights that Gibson's work, in addition to striving to innovate science fiction, is fundamentally wedded to his attempt to probe the historically changing status and function of art in general and of literature and writing in particular. This self-reflexive component of his work, we would argue, lends it notable complexity and richness and makes it particularly salient for critical inquiry and as a form of critique in its own right: Gibson's work, this volume seeks to illustrate, contains a critical archive of the historical—which is to say social, political, and material—development of literature and culture after the 1970s.

In 2003, Gibson shocked his fans and critics alike with what was widely understood to amount to another significant generic and formal innovation: the publication of *Pattern Recognition*, the first novel in what came to be called either the Blue Ant trilogy or the Bigend trilogy. What shocked readers who had come to associate Gibson centrally with cyberpunk was that *Pattern Recognition* is a realist novel. Although readers wondered if he had abandoned cyberpunk (with whose invention he had often been credited), Gibson himself insisted this was not the case. He was still writing cyberpunk, he suggested, tongue significantly in cheek, but history had changed such that what used to look like cyberpunk now simply looked like our present. What underlies this remark is one of Gibson's fundamental and sincere convictions to which *William Gibson and the Futures of Contemporary Culture* returns time and again: science fiction, if it can serve as a form of critique of and interrogation into the historical conditions of the present, must be self-reflexively attuned to the dialectical relationship between historical and generic change at every moment. What happens, Gibson's work asks, when history renders genre conventions or established images of the future obsolete? How may science fiction answer the call to constantly innovate to maintain its vital connection to history and its critical function as an interrogation of our historical present? As several essays in this book show, *Pattern Recognition* and the two novels that complete this trilogy, *Spook Country* (2007) and *Zero History* (2010), together ask precisely these questions, and Gibson's turn to realism should be understood as yet another crucial development in science fiction, one that marks a new stage in his work that is aimed at historicizing and exploring the historical limits of cyberpunk.

The 2010s have been marked by a further stage in this project to examine what critics are beginning to describe as, and what this book understands as, a postcyberpunk era. Gibson's 2014 novel *The Peripheral* blends some of the trademark strategies of his cyberpunk period with their reformulation during the "realist" period in a turn to examinations of multidimensional time-travel narratives. Yet Gibson anchors his time-travel narratives not in the long and often lowbrow history of time travel tales but in the crucial attention to matters of time and temporality that his work, beginning with *Pattern Recognition*, understands as central to our ability to historicize our present and its attendant aesthetic, political, and philosophical crises. Likewise, *Agency*, published in January 2020, just as we were finishing this volume, extends this most recent project.[6] In addition, the 2010s mark yet another stage in Gibson's exploration of different mediums. From 2016 to 2017, he published a five-issue limited series comic book, *Archangel*, and in 2018–2019, his rejected *Alien III* screenplay (1987) was adapted into a miniseries by Dark Horse Comics.[7]

Given the rich, innovative, and multifaceted nature of Gibson's work, we are astounded that much editing work remains to be done to gather and make more accessible aspects of his work and critical responses to it. Of course, by pointing out the absence of a collection of critical essays dedicated to the historical significance of Gibson's work and the general lag between his rise to global success and the beginning of a wider critical engagement, we do not mean to question the significance of the important work that some critics have been producing since the 1980s. Although several aspects of Gibson's work remain strikingly under-explored (one may point toward the Bridge trilogy as an example), there certainly exists some notable critical work on Gibson. Yet it must be said that existing criticism on Gibson is decidedly uneven: it ranges from well-researched and intricately argued gems of science fiction criticism to approaches that struggle to transcend reverence or the desire to pinpoint what exactly his innovative creative output truly means for science fiction in particular and contemporary culture in general. A comprehensive bibliography of existing criticism on Gibson is available elsewhere and lists available critical sources and a full list of Gibson's work.[8] Here, we wish to foreground some sources that we consider particularly helpful for beginning readers and scholars of William Gibson. In addition, these sources are formative for the essays we gather in this book. In some cases, we are fortunate to be able to include work by critics who revisit some of their own earlier engagements with Gibson's work that have since become notable in their own right.

There exist two excellent book-length studies of Gibson's life and work, which include biographical detail that many readers will find helpful: Gerald Alva Miller's *Understanding William Gibson* (2016) and Gary Westfahl's *William Gibson* (2013). In addition, Neil Easterbrook's contribution to the volume *Fifty Key Figures in Science Fiction* offers a concise and accessible overview of Gibson's biography and works.[9] Given that interrogating the era of globalization is a crucial aspect of Gibson's work, it is not surprising that some critics have examined this aspect in some detail. Notable essays in this field include Fredric Jameson's "Fear and Loathing in Globalization," Tom Moylan's "Global Economy, Local Texts: Utopian/Dystopian Tension in William Gibson's Cyberpunk Trilogy," and Lee Konstantinou's "The Brand as Cognitive Map in William Gibson's *Pattern Recognition*."[10] Critics like Sherryl Vint and Timo Siivonen have produced important studies of how Gibson's work offers us striking reexaminations of the relationship between the body and technology.[11] A number of excellent critical essays by Lauren Berlant, Veronica Hollinger, Lisa Swanstrom, and Robert Briggs explore the relation between genre, time, memory, and history in Gibson's work, a particular focus of recent critical approaches.[12] Darko Suvin, Jaak Tomberg, Vint, and Phillip E. Wegner have generated some of the most notable examinations of Gibson's generic and formal innovations and of his significance for the historical development of science fiction.[13] Finally, some of the earliest critical work on Gibson includes essays by critics like Easterbrook, Larry McCaffery, Claire Sponsler, and Hollinger, which examine Gibson's significance in the context of the rise of literary and philosophical postmodernism.[14]

With this gloss on Gibson's oeuvre and some of the most valuable critical engagements with it in mind, allow us to emphasize the goals, scope, and interventions of this volume. We understand Gibson's long career, spanning from the height of postmodernism to the contemporary, as not just central to some key developments in recent science fiction and its subgenres but also as a privileged microcosm in which to develop and test the kinds of literary and cultural criticism that help us grasp the unfolding present of globalization or full postmodernity. Gibson's works, we maintain, not only attempt to narrativize the ungraspable totality of a contemporary history still in process, they also offer models of thought and criticism adequate to this historical development—a claim further borne out in the chapters that follow by their diversity of approaches, from digital humanities and critical finance studies, game studies and media archaeology, to the ontological turn. With this wide array of approaches—necessitated by the expansiveness and internal heterogeneity of Gibson's corpus—we have organized this book according to three overarching questions or problematics: Gibson and literary history, Gibson and the question of medium, and the problem of the present. To be up front about it, these categorizations are porous and somewhat artificial. Many of the contributions to this collection could have appeared under two or all three sections. To engage with an author such as Gibson, who is deliberate in his treatment of these questions and many more besides, as well as the historicity of his own oeuvre, demands such porousness, "as though you could not say one thing until you had first said everything; as though with each new idea you were bound to recapitulate the entire system."[15] We hope, then, to give our readers some indication of our contributors' major themes and interests while inviting them to proliferate the connections among them and, in the spirit of this collection, produce their own recapitulations of Gibson's rich contribution to recent literature and culture.

Bringing together a wide range of critical accounts of Gibson's significance and making legible the large-scale influence of his writings on contemporary literature and culture, this book argues that a fuller exploration of this author's work can yield compelling models for practicing literary and cultural criticism today. Indeed, Maria Alberto and Elizabeth Swanstrom show provocatively that Gibson's fiction, through its parallel relation with science fiction studies and through specific tropes and strategies like cyberpunk's elision of the distinctions between human and computer that characterized mid-century science fiction, gave critics new vocabularies and problematics that presaged the kind of cultural critique that came to define what we now call the digital humanities. For Alberto and Swanstrom, Gibson's work offers an opportunity to cross digital humanities' most pressing disciplinary divide: between the computationally literate and the sociopolitically astute. Moreover, they signal a claim central to this collection as a whole: namely, that Gibson's fiction is especially amenable to enabling such intra- and interdisciplinary jumps.

We begin the work toward such an interdisciplinary project of literary criticism when we consider some key tendencies in contemporary criticism, at least two of which take on especial importance here and underwrite to some degree all the chapters to follow: periodizing "the contemporary" and the "genre turn." Let us begin with the latter. In recent years, literature and criticism alike (it is perhaps now cliché to note) have been undergoing a "genre turn," which Andrew Hoberek suggests is one of the key developments in the Anglo-American literary field since 1999. Literature of this so-called post-postmodern period, Hoberek notes, might be located "in the embrace of the long-neglected storehouse of genre models built up over the years when experimentalism and realism were understood, to varying degrees, to constitute the literary."[16] Gibson's modulations of science fiction and other genres (steampunk, detective, time travel, the "geopolitical novel"[17]) would seem to put him well ahead of the curve. One might reasonably expect that Gibson would find a good fit among contemporary critics' revitalization of genre theory. But still, the absence of a full engagement with his oeuvre indicates a rather conservative and nostalgic vision of literature and literary criticism in the present. In conversation with Adams, Gibson recalls the allure of science fiction around the time of his writing *Neuromancer*: "The best thing about science fiction was always its lack of legitimacy. It was like, 'Fuck it, I've run away and joined the circus.' You couldn't, for example, if things got tight, go and teach at Harvard like 'real' novelists."[18] Although things have somewhat changed in this regard—and for the better, we would argue—Gibson implies here that our thinking about science fiction, about genre, and about what literature is and does is still largely molded by the institutional biases and power relations within which most academic labor is performed in North America.

In a clarifying account of the genre turn, Jeremy Rosen argues it is most properly understood as an "embrace [of] *the genres of* genre fiction, not genre fiction as such."[19] Authors such as Michael Chabon, Jennifer Egan, Kazuo Ishiguro, Emily St. John Mandel, Cormac McCarthy, and Colson Whitehead "deploy such genres in ways that are marked as literary, both in their internal features and in the manner in which they are marketed and received in the literary field. Thus, *certain* works using these genres are marked as high-status while the bulk of popular production utilizing them gains no status boost whatsoever."[20] Rosen helpfully foregrounds the fact that the recent raiding of the genre storehouse in the literary field does not amount to the disappearance of distinction nor of literary regimes of value (and certainly not the end of their classed underpinnings). In short, the genre turn can be understood as yet another iteration of literary canonization. Carl Freedman, writing in 2000, just before Gibson made his leap to a more mainstream-able kind of realism, explains: "if science fiction has rarely been a privileged genre, this means that the literary powers-that-be have not wished science fiction to function within the social prestige that literature in the stronger sense enjoys." Science fiction's relatively rare inclusion among the ranks of great literature "results from a wholesale *generic* dismissal of a kind organic to canonization as a practice."[21] In other words, the genre turn is as much a product of a literary criticism that perceives itself as losing its grip on its most prized object—the literary as such—as it might be any genuine interest in the affordances of genre fiction. Gibson is nothing if not a master literary stylist, and it is perhaps his strong footing in both "literary" genre fiction and straight-up science fiction that can account for some of the ambiguity with which his oeuvre is approached, even as his work puts pressure on the structural integrity of this division.

Meanwhile, science fiction and the field of science fiction studies also risk the institutional and disciplinary codifications that would reinstate and fortify the immutability of oppositions like genre/literature. Gibson often laments his identification with cyberpunk because it has enabled readers and critics to distance his work from science fiction as such, prizing it instead as a literary/genre blend while allowing what he considers science fiction's most regressive tendencies to go unchallenged. "That label [cyberpunk] enabled mainstream science fiction to safely assimilate our dissident influence, such as it was. Cyberpunk could then be embraced and given prizes and patted on the head, and genre science fiction could continue unchanged," with commitments to what Gibson saw as a "triumphalist, militaristic ... folk propaganda for American exceptionalism."[22] In criticism, genre and literary fiction may no longer be seen as determinate others,[23] but they are nonetheless in danger of sliding (back) into reified niches of specialized knowledge with their agenda and concerns. As Wegner explains: "Science fiction studies often undertakes the quest for legitimacy under the aegis of a sociological or popular culture studies inclusiveness that flies in the face of conservative disciplinary retrenchments such as those of the new formalists or surface readers."[24] To adapt Gibson's words, the best part of science fiction studies was always its lack of legitimacy. But you couldn't, if things got tight, go teach science fiction at Harvard like a "real" literary critic. Wegner goes on, cautioning, "in disciplining, reifying, and isolating science fiction studies in this way we risk, as other once vibrant interdisciplinary projects such as film and American studies seem at times to have done, reinforcing the walls of our ghetto in the larger academic field."[25] Wegner's contribution here likewise establishes Gibson's historical significance for the development of science fiction, and he makes strides toward a claim central to this collection's understanding of the current recomposition of the literary field, of which the genre turn is symptomatic: namely, with *Neuromancer*, Gibson fundamentally rewrote the rules not only of science fiction but also of the Anglo-American literary field more broadly speaking. Gibson's work is an early indicator of what Wegner argues "we are only really coming to understand in the last decade or so: the crack up of what Mark McGurl identifies as the program era in American literature, the moment of the hegemony of a 'literary' writing style largely defined by MFA programs."

Close attention to Gibson's oeuvre, we maintain, gives us solid footing on a third route toward an understanding of the genre turn, one that harnesses the strengths of criticism of both "proper" literature and science fiction without making evaluative and moralizing claims about one over the other. Indeed, there have been several developments that make it increasingly difficult to dismiss the necessity of dissolving these hierarchical distinctions and polarizing critical commitments. To name just a few key instances in recent years, consider Gibson's turn to a more hardcore science fiction with his take on the time travel subgenre (*The Peripheral*, *Agency*); the massive popular and academic interest in N. K. Jemisin's science fiction/fantasy the Broken Earth trilogy; the migration of "serious" authors to comics writing, including Ta-Nehisi Coates's takeover of *Black Panther* and *Captain America*; the increasing influence of literary science fiction authors on television writing and production, such as Charles Yu's work on HBO's *Westworld* (2016–) and FX's *Legion* (2017–2019); and the turn to fantasy by major authors including Marlon James, Mohsin Hamid, and David Mitchell. Though still committed in some ways to the distinction of the literary, Hoberek nonetheless concludes that in its mixture of "postmodernism's interest in alternative realities [and] realism's commitment to accessibility and social impact, the genre turn opens up the possibility of a fiction capable of broadcasting visions of life not as it is, but as it might be."[26]

We find in such work—both creative and critical—a vitalizing development for the kind of criticism that this collection forwards. In its most radical promises of cognitively mapping emerging post-postmodern realities and even in its most conservative reinstantiations of older literary institutions and values, today's renewed attention to genre creates the preconditions necessary for a totalizing (if still incomplete) reckoning with Gibson's place in the contemporary literary and critical scenes. That is, the willingness to take seriously previously maligned genres, especially speculative fictions like science fiction—whether as a liberatory potentiality or as a threat to the unsure status of proper literature—puts us today in a position to finally understand Gibson's literary trajectory as not just a landmark in the territory of science fiction but also as a particularly important test-bed for the development of literature over the past four decades. In *Postmodernism*, Fredric Jameson found a vocabulary for the moment "when it all changed" by turning to Gibson's *Mona Lisa Overdrive*, and he registers his regret of not including a chapter about cyberpunk, which he named "the supreme *literary* expression if not of postmodernism, then of late capitalism itself."[27] Since then, Gibson has been often pegged as a quintessential "postmodern" author. Yet this designation has been reified into its own style of late or has otherwise come to be a synonym to describe a novel as "globe-trotting," "psychedelic," "genre bending," or whatever. In Gibson's case, "postmodern" flattens the internal heterogeneity that has always driven his fiction forward. But his work provides a self-aware vocabulary that undercuts such a homogenizing take on his fiction. In *Idoru*, for instance, we meet Colin Laney who—in ways that very much presage Cayce Pollard's allergy to brands that make her such an effective "cool hunter" in *Pattern Recognition*—discerns "patterns of information: of the sort of signature a particular individual inadvertently created in the net as he or she went about the mundane yet endlessly multiplex business of life in digital society. . . . Laney was the equivalent of a dowser, a cybernetic water-witch."[28] Laney calls these patterns of information "nodal points," the experience of which is "like seeing things in clouds . . . Except the things you see are really there" (158). Or consider the idoru itself—a synthetic Japanese idol named Rei Toei—which literalizes what Gibson performs in narrative: "the tip of an iceberg, no, an Antarctica, of information. Looking at her face would trigger it again: she was some unthinkable volume of information. She induced the nodal vision in some unprecedented way; she induced it as narrative" (190–91). We thus seek to surpass disciplinary divisions—both institutionalized and interiorized—and to move not toward a definitive account of Gibson's career but toward models for a literary criticism with all the dialectical plasticity adequate to the unfurling historicity of the contemporary moment.

The situation we've been sketching, in which the genre turn's internal tensions may be productively rethought and rearticulated, brings us to a second critical tendency with which Gibson's work has always been centrally concerned, namely, the task of "historicizing the contemporary."[29] In what appears to be a corrective to the missing chapter on cyberpunk in *Postmodernism*, Jameson has argued that *Neuromancer*, more than any other work of science fiction, rose to the occasion of "the new incommensurabilities of that greatly enlarged and as it were post-anthropomorphic totality which is that of late or third-stage capitalism" and generated a "new and post-realistic but also post-modernistic way of giving us a picture and a sense of our individual relationships to realities that transcend our phenomenological mapping systems and our cognitive abilities to think them."[30] In this sense, "literature can serve as a registering apparatus for historical transformations we cannot otherwise empirically intuit, and in which *Neuromancer* stands as a precious symptom of our passage into another historical period."[31] In *William Gibson and the Futures of Contemporary Culture*, by thoroughly examining Gibson's career-long interrogation of genre, history, and changing notions of literariness, we show what his work can be understood to have always shown: it is not *the* genre turn but *genre's turning* that is central to literature's capacity to register and mediate historical change and, via narrative, make that change apprehensible by human thought. Gibson's career full of genre turns foregrounds what we find to be a critically and politically useful way to approach his work: as a microcosm in which to track, on one hand, like the migrations of endangered species, the disappearance and historical exhaustion of genres, cultural imaginaries, and futures. On the other hand, just as important, these genres, imaginaries, and futures emerge under particular historical conditions in the context of which they allow us to respond to and, Gibson's work shows, make sense of the world that is developing before our eyes. Gibson's fiction, that is, instantiates a methodology for apprehending his work within its immanent progression and repetitions of (sub)genres.

In fact, Gibson's fiction has always been strikingly aware of genre's historical flux as a driver of artistic practice and possibility. *Spook Country*'s Hollis Henry, for instance, is the lead voice of a defunct "early-nineties cult" band called The Curfew, which, in her words, "just ended. It stopped happening, at some essential level, though I never knew exactly when that happened. It became painfully apparent. So we packed it in."[32] It is suggestive to read The Curfew as a postpunk or grunge band that, as Gibson's cyberpunk fiction, was made inessential by the onset of what becomes increasingly and just as painfully apparent throughout the Blue Ant novels: the onset of globalization. Mathias Nilges returns to Gibson's short fiction to show that the historical ebb and flow of genres have been methodological and formal constants from the very beginning. "The Gernsback Continuum," for instance, outlines the historical and political stakes of cyberpunk as the necessary departure from outdated literary and epistemological forms of futurity. We find the same methodological commitment in later formal shifts, such as the one from cyberpunk to realism beginning with *Pattern Recognition*. By understanding Gibson's earliest stories as methodological blueprints according to which later novels are built, we gain a deeper understanding of Gibson's attention to the relation between history, our temporal imagination, and literary form. Focusing similarly on the tension between realism and science fiction, Sherryl Vint argues that *Pattern Recognition* should be read as a convergence of the two through which Gibson generates an "estranged vision of living in the present." Through this vision, Vint shows, the Blue Ant trilogy mediates the hegemony of neoliberal capitalism and the temporal foreclosure resulting from what she describes as our "productized future." But even as neoliberalism names a structure without an apparent outside, by examining the opposition between art and advertising, Vint traces a palpable sense of nostalgia in Gibson's work: a nostalgia for the power of art to "resist capitalism's infiltration of social and political life." Aron Pease addresses this productized future we inhabit by routing a discussion of Gibson's landmark literary invention (cyberspace) through Henri Lefebvre and the revolutionary "invention" of linear perspective with Brunelleschi in fifteenth-century Florence. Pease shows that space (cyber- or otherwise) is also always a mediation of historically specific "scenes of accumulation." If Gibson's cyberspace was able to figure the internet as an emerging site of "prosumption" (in which consumption becomes a new kind of production). Understood as such a figure for space, Pease argues that Gibson has never really left cyberspace behind. Rather, cyberspace finds updated articulations in the Blue Ant trilogy, in the textures of the Gibsonian sentence, and in novelistic form, that key into the new realities of the global market.

Just as Gibson's fiction provides new figurations and expressions of the ever-shifting contemporary, several contributors set aside the particularities of his individual works and foreground how they anticipate or provide new vocabularies for emerging disciplinary approaches to literature and culture. Amy J. Elias notes that Gibson's time-travel fiction ratchets up his interest in ontology at precisely the same time literary and cultural criticism are swept up by movements like object-oriented ontology, new materialisms, and Anthropocene studies. Yet, Elias argues, what these new methods and disciplines do at their best—even if, at their worst, they miss while Gibson himself is on the mark—is shuttle us back to the fundamental historical mutability of human sociality. What goes "often unacknowledged in theoretical discussions about realist ontology, object-oriented ontology, thing theory, and some versions of posthumanism," Elias maintains, is the fundamental "problem of relation, for though we may be in relation to all other things in a flat ontology, we still have the ability to act according to our abilities, to enact power over others."

Similarly, Roger Whitson argues, reading *The Difference Engine* and *The Peripheral* as case studies, that Gibson's works have never just been "about" historical, cultural, and technological transformations. Rather, they are fundamentally tied to what is made materially allowable and historically thinkable. With the rise of computational technologies during Gibson's lifetime, the "untold textures of history blur into various data storage techniques," which are far from politically neutral, themselves saturated with what Walter Benjamin called "anonymous forced labor" or the barbarism subtending all documents of great culture. If in these novels media archaeology shows us how nonhuman technological actors aid the "remak[ing of] the world in line with a logic that may regard human beings with complete indifference," Gibson and Sterling also importantly make visible that otherwise invisible maker's mark imprinted on all technological development: the past, present, and future history of class struggle.

Christian P. Haines's Marxist critique of *The Peripheral* foregrounds Gibson's increasing interest in perhaps the preeminent medium of financialized capitalism: video games. Gibson has often spoken of his fascination with arcade games and the micro-communities that emerged around them, but today, Haines argues, gaming is not only suitable content for science fiction but a key logic through which capitalism cultivates financialized subjectivities. *The Peripheral*, Haines argues, "transposes the register of finance into the domain of digital games." Far from merely depicting the contemporary moment, Haines understands this transposition as precisely what enables us to forward a critical account of the reticulations of financial speculation and risk, militarism, digital technology, and precarious labor.

Confronted, it would seem, with an epistemologically insurmountable capitalism, Kylie Korsnack's essay traces the problem of what she calls "temporal leveling" through Gibson's work and shows how historically specific temporal crises that make the future unavailable to thought, culture, and politics constitute one of Gibson's central concerns. Korsnack shows that Gibson's examination of time and futurity that mediate moments of historical transition are always bound up with provocative reflections on the status and possibility of art. In a "sustained reflection on the relationship between art, temporality, and human experience in contemporary culture," Gibson's fiction does more than just point to the present's contradictions and foreclosures: it provides us with a hopeful orientation toward, a way of optimistically inhabiting, a time marked by severe crises.

Much like Gibson himself—born in South Carolina, raised in Virginia, and self-expatriated to Canada—we write this with a weird polyspatial and -temporal perspective from Canada and the US South. It is difficult, from such a perspective, to not register our own cultural, historical, and political disjunctions and continua that Gibson's fiction has always sought to capture. To quote Malka Older's foreword, Gibson "provides us with the relief of seeing our peripatetic modern experience represented in prose and with a kind of practice in continuing that existence more aware and more alert to the new ways we fall apart and fit together." In dark times such as these—afflicted by the rise of neofascisms around the world, climate crisis, and capitalism's stranglehold on our imaginative and material lives—if literary criticism is to mean anything it must, we maintain, enact a sustained critique of all the ways we fall apart. Without being too naive, just dialectical, it must also attune us to the emergence of alternative visions of contemporaneity without which there is no "now" on which possible and better futures can stand. We thus end with a final word from Charles Yu, one of the most compelling new voices in science fiction to emerge after Gibson. Reading Gibson with equal parts bewilderment and exhilaration, Yu suggests that what makes his oeuvre so monumental—when you get right down to it—is that it enacts the fundamental labor of all good fiction: worldbuilding "at the level of fundamental particles, in the language itself. Realities built word by word." This collection and its contributors ultimately stride toward this rich, utopian possibility of language, literature, the arts, and reading itself.

PART I . . . **GIBSON AND LITERARY HISTORY**

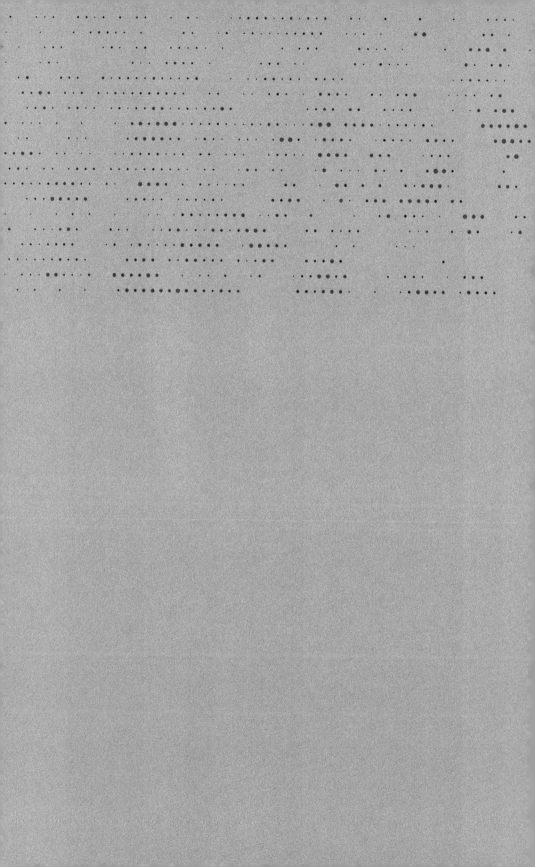

CHAPTER 1 . . . **PHILLIP E. WEGNER**

WHEN IT CHANGED

SCIENCE FICTION AND THE LITERARY FIELD, CIRCA 1984

I am confident many readers will recognize that my title is taken from one of the great works of New Wave science fiction, Joanna Russ's Nebula Award–winning short story "When It Changed" (1972), the precursor to her landmark "critical utopia" *The Female Man* (1975).[1] Russ's story focuses on the arrival of a group of aliens—men from Earth—on the planet of Whileaway, a former Earth colony where six centuries earlier all human males died off as the result of a plague and the surviving women built a flourishing society without them. At the conclusion of the story, the narrator acknowledges that this event will alter their lives irrevocably, fearing that the result will be the reinstallation of the hierarchies and oppressions they had lived without for more than a half millennium: "Men are coming to Whileaway. When one culture has the big guns and the other has none, there is a certain predictability about the outcome."[2]

At the same time, in a far more affirmative sense, Russ's title also could be understood as referring to her story's publication, as well as that of the anthology in which it appeared—the Harlan Ellison–edited collection *Again, Dangerous Visions*, which also included Ursula K. Le Guin's Hugo Award–winning antiwar novella *The Word for World Is Forest*, the latter a direct influence on the original *Star Wars* franchise and James

Cameron's *Avatar*.³ These works had a profound effect on the field of science fiction, inaugurating a vibrant new wave of feminist and militant utopian science fiction. In terms of the practice of science fiction, then, 1972 should also be understood as one of those years when things changed.

In this essay, I focus on another year of equally significant literary and cultural transformation. The year 1984 has long been of singular importance in the history of science fiction, largely because it was chosen by George Orwell as the fictional setting for his grim masterpiece, the anti-utopian dystopia *Nineteen Eighty-Four* (1949).⁴ However, 1984 also proved to be of great significance within the genre, as it witnessed the publication of three novels—Samuel Delany's *Stars in My Pocket Like Grains of Sand*, William Gibson's *Neuromancer*, and Kim Stanley Robinson's *The Wild Shore*—which, as I suggest here, at once mark the past, present, and future of the practice of science fiction and notions of the literary more generally.

The year 1984 was one of extraordinary ferment and change in cultural production writ larger, so much so that in an earlier essay on Gibson's *Pattern Recognition* (2003) I advance the claim that 1984 stands to postmodernism as 1922 does to modernism.⁵ Not surprisingly, a number of the works released in that year—Martin Amis's satirical novel *Money*, Michael Radford's film *Nineteen Eighty-Four*, Ridley Scott's legendary Apple Macintosh commercial, and Nam June Paik's experimental multimedia broadcast *Good Morning, Mr. Orwell*—directly take up and respond to themes and concerns in Orwell's fiction, all working to show, as the final title card of Scott's commercial declares, "Why 1984 won't be like '1984.'" Among other significant texts appearing that year were J. G. Ballard's *Empire of the Sun*; Julian Barnes's *Flaubert's Parrot*; Thomas Bernhard's *Holzfällen*; Anita Brookner's *Hotel du Lac*; Angela Carter's *Nights at the Circus*; Don DeLillo's *White Noise*; Anita Desai's *In Custody*; Marguerite Duras's *L'amant*; Alasdair Gray's *1982, Janine*; Milan Kundera's *The Unbearable Lightness of Being*; David Lodge's *Small World: An Academic Romance*; Pratibha Ray's *Yajnaseni*; Rudy Rucker's *Master of Space and Time*; and Madath Thekkepaattu Vasudevan Nair's *Randamoozham*. The year saw the publication of debut novels by Iain Banks (*The Wasp Factory*), Sandra Cisneros (*The House of Mango Street*), Tom Clancy (*The Hunt for Red October*), Louise Erdrich (*Love Medicine*), Keri

Hulme (*The Bone People*), Jay McInerney (*Bright Lights, Big City*), and Neal Stephenson (*The Big U*); and the release of such influential films as James Cameron's *The Terminator*; the Coen brothers' directorial debut, *Blood Simple*; Francis Ford Coppola's *The Cotton Club*; Brian De Palma's *Body Double*; Jonathan Demme's *Stop Making Sense*; Jim Jarmusch's *Stranger Than Paradise*; Robert Mark Kamen's *The Karate Kid*; David Lynch's *Dune*; Rob Reiner's *This Is Spinal Tap*; John Sayles's *The Brother from Another Planet*; and Wim Wenders's *Paris, Texas*. In 1984, the second and third volumes of Michel Foucault's groundbreaking *Histoire de la sexualité* were published, as was the expanded English-language edition of Jean-François Lyotard's *The Postmodern Condition*. Philip Johnson's iconic AT&T Building in New York City (whose open pediment crown one critic recently suggests "may be the single most important architectural detail of the last fifty years"[6]) and PPG Place in Pittsburgh were completed that year. Michael Azerrad, using a phrase that recalls Harry Levin's celebrated characterization of the modernist year 1922, notes that for punk music 1984 "yielded a spate of bona fide classics: the Meat Puppets' *Meat Puppets II*, Hüsker Dü's *Zen Arcade*, the Minutemen's *Double Nickels on the Dime*, the Replacements' *Let It Be*, and Black Flag's lesser but no less influential *My War*. It was an annus mirabilis for indie"; and *Billboard* magazine similarly names 1984 "pop music's best year ever."[7]

The year also witnessed the publication of a series of essays by literary and cultural theorist Fredric Jameson that brought to new prominence the notion of "postmodernism." The most significant of these essays first appeared in the summer in the pages of *New Left Review*, under the title "Postmodernism, or the Cultural Logic of Late Capitalism."[8] Perry Anderson points out that this essay "redrew the whole map of the postmodern at one stroke—a prodigious inaugural gesture that has commanded the field ever since."[9] Near the conclusion of his essay, Jameson characterizes postmodernism—or what he now refers to as postmodernity—as involving fundamental mutations in global space:

> What we must now affirm is that it is precisely this whole extraordinarily demoralizing and depressing original new global space which is the "moment of truth" of postmodernism ... postmodern (or multinational) space is not merely a cultural ideology or fantasy,

but has genuine historical (and socio-economic) reality as a third great original expansion of capitalism around the globe (after the earlier expansions of the national market and the older imperialist system, which each had their own cultural specificity and generated new types of space appropriate to their dynamics). The distorted and unreflexive attempts of newer cultural production to explore and to express this new space must then also, in their own fashion, be considered as so many approaches to the representation of (a new) reality (to use a more antiquated language). As paradoxical as the terms may seem, they may thus, following a classic interpretive option, be read as peculiar new forms of realism (or at least of the mimesis of reality), at the same time that they can equally well be analyzed as so many attempts to distract and to divert us from that reality or to disguise its contradictions and resolve them in the guise of various formal mystifications.[10]

(The significance of the latter part of this statement for a discussion of *Neuromancer* will become evident shortly.) Such an expansion involves, Jameson maintains, "a new and historically original penetration and colonization of Nature and the Unconscious: that is, the destruction of precapitalist third world agriculture by the Green Revolution, and the rise of the media and the advertising industry."[11] The reason Jameson does not use "globalization" to describe these spatial transformations is that this concept-term was not yet available; as Doug Henwood demonstrates, it did not rise to prominence until the mid-1990s.[12] Jameson's direct engagement with the notion of globalization begins in earnest with his essay, "Notes on Globalization as a Philosophical Issue," first presented at a conference in 1994.[13]

Jameson claims in the original "Postmodernism" essay that as a consequence of this transformation of space, contemporary or postmodern culture is "increasingly dominated by space and spatial logic."[14] A little earlier, he notes, "We have often been told, however, that we now inhabit the synchronic rather than the diachronic, and I think it is at least empirically arguable that our daily life, our psychic experience, our cultural languages, are today dominated by categories of space rather than by categories of time, as in the preceding period of high modernism proper."[15]

In the final section, Jameson moves beyond the diagnostic or denotative mode and into the performative, with a call for developing an original aesthetic practice: "the conception of space that has been developed here suggests that a model of political culture appropriate to our own situation will necessarily have to raise spatial issues as its fundamental organizing concern. I will therefore provisionally define the aesthetic of such new (and hypothetical) cultural form as an aesthetic of *cognitive mapping*."[16]

Few notions in Jameson's project have been more misunderstood than that of cognitive mapping. I argue in *Periodizing Jameson* (2014) that what he calls for here is not the invention of cognitive mapping per se—it already exists on the scale of the city, as demonstrated in Kevin Lynch's *The Image of the City* (1960), from which Jameson takes the term. I maintain that the great breakthrough of Thomas More's *Utopia* (1516) is to begin to articulate a cognitive mapping for the emerging social and cultural scale of the nation-state, with all the political and cultural consequences that follow.[17] Rather, what Jameson demands in "Postmodernism" is a dialectical reinvention—not merely a quantitative but a qualitative change—of cognitive mapping for our original situation of globalization or postmodernity. He concludes the essay in this way:

> The new political art—if it is indeed possible at all—will have to hold to the truth of postmodernism, that is, to say, to its fundamental object—the world space of multinational capital—at the same time at which it achieves a breakthrough to some as yet unimaginable new mode of representing this last, in which we may again begin to grasp our positioning as individual and collective subjects and regain a capacity to act and struggle which is at present neutralized by our spatial as well as our social confusion. The political form of postmodernism, if there ever is any, will have as its vocation the invention and projection of a global cognitive mapping, on a social as well as a spatial scale.[18]

Moreover, in his most recent book, *Allegory and Ideology* (2019), Jameson emphasizes that such a labor of cognitive mapping will always be allegorical in nature: the crucial allegorical questions concern "the relationship of the levels to one another, and whether any proper allegorical reading exists in a situation in which there is, if not a contradiction, then at least a disjunction between the anagogical (or world-political) level and the literal or domestic-political levels. Allegory thereby serves as a diagnostic instrument to reveal this disjuncture, which is itself the cause of political aimlessness and apathy."[19]

Many of the works I mentioned already were similarly marked by or even deeply involved in remaking cultural and social space—the lived and the conceived respectively, to use Henri Lefebvre's terms—and especially that of the dominant US metropolises of New York City and Los Angeles. One of the most influential of these was McInerney's *Bright Lights, Big City*, which participated in a reorganization of the city's literary establishment and a reconquest of the spaces of Lower Manhattan by the increasingly powerful class fraction known as the yuppies. (*Newsweek* magazine proclaimed 1984 to be "The Year of the Yuppie" in its year-end issue, graced with a cover by *Doonesbury* creator Garry Trudeau.) Jameson points out that although the yuppies do not represent anything "like a new ruling class ... their cultural practices and values, their local ideologies, have articulated a useful dominant ideological and cultural paradigm for this stage of capital."[20] Amis's *Money* similarly attests to the rise of this middle-class social fraction and their role in the reorganization of the London–New York–Los Angeles cultural and spatial axes. The transformation of LA's film industry and the city's spatial map are also at work in the unlikely film diptych of Cameron's *The Terminator* and De Palma's *Body Double*, both released on Friday, October 26, 1984, the same day as Michael Jordan's debut in the NBA.[21] Conversely, two novels that look toward and educate our desire for the utopian potential in the older urban fabric of the city, especially New York City, are Kathy Acker's first major experimental work, *Blood and Guts in High School* and Samuel Delany's *Stars in My Pocket Like Grains of Sand*.

Delany's novel was overshadowed by the publication of a debut work in the influential New Ace Science Fiction Specials series edited by Terry Carr: Gibson's *Neuromancer*. Nowhere is the triumph of postmodernism over an older modernist sensibility, with "its innovative and indeed subversive power," more clearly evident than in the couple of Delany's and Gibson's novels.[22] *Stars in My Pocket Like Grains of Sand* stands as the last great monument of science fiction's extraordinarily rich and diverse period established in the 1960s and known as the New Wave, which I describe in *Shockwaves of Possibility* as a modernist formation within the specific institutional situation of science fiction; *Neuromancer* represents the first major work in the singular postmodern movement known as cyberpunk.[23] Indeed, Veronica Hollinger claims, "Science fiction 'officially' became postmodern in 1984, with the publication of William Gibson's now-classic Cyberpunk novel."[24]

Delany's novel marks an ending of another sort: although originally intended as the first book of an extended two-volume narrative, it turned out to be his final major science fiction work, at least until 2012's quasi-science fictional *Through the Valley of the Nest of Spiders*. Although *Stars in My Pocket Like Grains of Sand* has always had its champions—Carl Freedman refers to it as "the most intellectually ambitious work in the entire range of modern science fiction," an assessment with which I would not disagree, and Steven Shaviro offers a rich and stimulating engagement with the novel—it has largely languished among science fiction and more general readers alike, a massive achievement whose greatness is often attested to but more rarely visited.[25] Gibson's novel, on the other hand, quickly attracted an immense readership, not only among science fiction fans but, even more interestingly, among literary scholars and critics, who in the past would have rarely engaged with the genre.

As a result, cyberpunk—with its poaching from and pastiche of a wide range of styles and genres, including noir detective fiction, its affirmative portrayal of virtual reality and new informational technologies, and its low-affect "mirror shades" cool—quickly came to be recognized as a privileged symptom of postmodern cultural production more generally. Jameson testifies to the rapid rise of the work's significance in one of the only three additions he makes to the 1991 republication of the original "Postmodernism" essay: cyberpunk, he later claims, "is fully as much an expression of transnational corporate realities as it is of global paranoia itself: William Gibson's representational innovations, indeed, mark his work as an exceptional literary realization within a predominantly visual or aural postmodern production."[26]

Gibson's cyberpunk contributed to a significant reorganization of not only science fiction but also the literary field more generally. The transformation to which the work will contribute is indicated only four years after its publication, in Larry McCaffery's contribution, "The Fictions of the Present," to the *Columbia Literary History of the United States*. McCaffery writes of the current moment:

> Crucially, however, that "daily world" was frequently portrayed as an ambiguous construct in constant flux, a mass of information, words, and images whose "meaning" was deferred, whose very "reality" was suspect, unknowable. In short, this daily world was a shifting, fabulous entity greatly resembling the poststructuralist text, a world whose depiction required a definition of "realism" flexible enough to accommodate the claims to "realistic aims" made by writers as different as Robert Coover, Raymond Carver, Larry McMurtry, Joyce Carol Oates, Walter Abish, Toni Morrison, William Gibson, Max Apple, and Leslie Silko.[27]

McCaffrey even uses the celebrated opening line of *Neuromancer*—"The sky above the port was the color of television, tuned to a dead channel"—as his essay's epigraph.[28]

Like all such lists, McCaffrey's is partly an exercise in canon formation, a performative speech act aimed to convince his readers what they should spend their time reading. Brian McHale is correct in his engagement with McCaffery's essay to point out that "the myth of the collapse of hierarchical distinctions in postmodern culture is just that, a myth, and the institutions for the production, distribution, and consumption of high culture continue to be distinct from those for popular culture."[29] What McHale misrecognizes, or perhaps is not yet in a position to realize when he formulates his insights, is that McCaffery's inclusion of Gibson among the celebrated writers of the later twentieth century contributes to reorganizing the larger literary field, the consequences of which we are only really coming to understand in the past decade or so: the crack-up of what Mark McGurl identifies as the "program era" in American literature, the moment of the hegemony of a "literary" writing style largely defined by MFA programs, which privileges Jamesian psychological realism and precludes "the shoddy inauthenticity of genre fiction of all kinds" as the hallmarks of "good" or "serious" fiction.[30] The transformation signaled here is illustrated in figure 1.

This indicates an opening of the literary field that occurs on or about 1984, such that science fiction and other generic texts begin to be taken

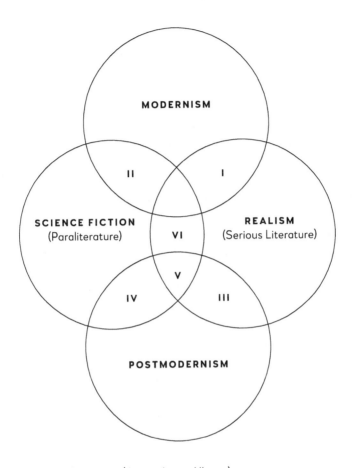

I   Modernist Literature (James Joyce, *Ulysses*)
II New Wave SF (Samuel Delany, *Stars in My Pocket Like Grains of Sand*)
III Postmodern Program Era Literature (Raymond Carver, Toni Morrison)
IV Cyberpunk SF
V   William Gibson, *Neuromancer*
VI Literary Dystopia (George Orwell, *Nineteen Eighty-Four*)

Figure 1: The literary field, circa 1984. Courtesy of Phillip E. Wegner.

seriously by the critical establishment. This is very different, I should add, than the practice of "literary" writers drawing on the conventions and tropes of genre fiction, as was the case from modernism onward. It is one thing to say that James Joyce's *Ulysses* (1922) uses science fictional tropes and quite another to identify it generically as science fiction, let alone value it for the latter fact, as do McCaffery, McHale, Jameson, and others in the case of *Neuromancer*. What is also useful about such a representation is that it can help us better grasp the differences between Gibson's achievement in *Neuromancer* and that of many of the other writers associated with cyberpunk and the position of *Stars in My Pocket* in the literary field in its original moment. The latter is understood to share attributes of the great experimental modernist fiction of the likes of Joyce, Virginia Woolf, or John Dos Passos, but it still is identified by most readers as unfolding within the generic or "paraliterary" ghetto of science fiction.[31] If New Wave writers like Delany, Russ, and Le Guin transform the field of science fiction, it is only because Gibson's cyberpunk novel and others like it unleashed a revolution such that the walls of the ghetto begin to come down and these writers come to be celebrated as producers of serious literature in their own right.

Also significant is McCaffrey's unexpected characterization of Gibson's cyberpunk fiction as "realism." Jameson similarly notes in *Postmodernism*, "Under those circumstances, where a formerly futurological science fiction (such as so-called cyberpunk today) turns into mere 'realism' and an outright representation of the present, the possibility [the great proto–New Wave science fiction writer Philip K.] Dick offered us—an experience of our present as past and as history—is slowly excluded."[32] What this might mean is borne out in Jameson's essay, "A Global *Neuromancer*," published in his 2015 collection *The Ancients and the Postmoderns*. Here Jameson argues that the representational achievements of Gibson's novel are twofold. On one hand, we have Gibson's most well-known figure, that of cyberspace, which is not, Jameson maintains, a representation *avant la lettre* of the informational space of the world wide web, as some hasty readers assumed it to be (Gibson was largely computer illiterate at the time and composed the manuscript on a typewriter), but "an abstraction to the second degree."[33] Jameson further observes,

> Here, on this new level, what can be imagined and mentally grasped is the new dimension of sheer relationship—what Le Corbusier began to theorize as the "trajectories" through space—now intensified to an incalculable degree. What looks here like some stereotypical postmodern lapse into visual representation is on the contrary a complex mapping of the incalculable connections—Spinoza's *rerum concatenatio*—between all the multiple powers and vectors of the real world, that is, the underlying and invisible one, that we cannot see with our normal bodily senses. It is a totality, but a totality in constant movement, evolution, and metamorphosis.³⁴

Jameson further argues that "this unrepresentable totality, which until now only science fiction has uniquely possessed the representational means to designate, is that of finance capital itself, as it constitutes one of the most original dimensions of late capitalism (or of globalization or of postmodernity, depending on the focus you wish to bring)."³⁵ He significantly concludes this section of the essay in this way:

> My argument has been that in the face of the impasses of modernism, which proved unable to handle the new incommensurabilities of that greatly enlarged and as it were post-anthropomorphic totality which is late or third-stage capitalism, science fiction, and in particular this historically inventive novel of Gibson, offered a new and post-realistic but also post-modernistic way of giving us a picture and a sense of our individual relationships to realities that transcend our phenomenological mapping systems and our cognitive abilities to think them. This is the sense in which literature can serve as a registering apparatus for historical transformations we cannot otherwise empirically intuit, and in which *Neuromancer* stands as a precious symptom of our passage into another historical period.³⁶

Three things are worth stressing in the argument being advanced here. First, I suggest that what Jameson calls postrealism should be understood more precisely in McCaffrey's terms as something beyond a restrained program era definition of realism: in the new realities of postmodernity, science fiction may prove to be the most effective realism available, an argument Jameson further advances in the concluding chapter of *The Antinomies of Realism* (2013). Second, it is significant that Jameson refers to Gibson's global aesthetic not as a full realization of cognitive mapping, as we might assume, but as a symptom of transformations then under way. The Althusserian notion of the symptom is the privileged diagnostic operation of Jameson's *Postmodernism*, a way of registering what is most original and characteristic of the condition of postmodernity or globalization—and as in the medical procedures from which this figure is derived, one must be exceedingly careful not to come to too rapid a diagnosis based on too limited a set of such symptoms (i.e., if you have a cough, you must have cancer).

Finally, although this may sound like the essay's climax, Jameson does not end here but immediately takes up that other great innovation in Gibson's novel, "simstim": the technologically mediated capacity to project one's consciousness into someone else's body. For Jameson, simstim stands in the novel as a figure for the symptomatic bodily experience in postmodernity: "another testimony to our unreal life in Guy Debord's society of the spectacle, our life among what Jean Baudrillard calls simulations (a term significantly preserved in the very term simstim). Here then we have a second and different type of abstraction from the real; and indeed what is essential is to see that in Gibson these two abstractions are dialectically related."[37] In his essay's penultimate paragraph, Jameson queries,

> Global versus local? This is indeed the form expressed by the twin presence and opposition between the exploration of cyberspace and the utilization of simstim; but it projects this rather glib contemporary formulation as what it is, namely a contradiction rather than a simple alternation or even a choice of perspectives. The limits of our thinking, of our capacities for cognitive mapping, of our possibilities of imagining and representing, these "our real conditions of existence" are then dramatized by the poverty of the formula as well as by the richness of Gibson's novel. The two poles are two dialectically linked dimensions which structure our daily lives in this society, and confirm the paradoxical proposition that we are both too abstract and too concrete all at once.[38]

That is, *Neuromancer* fails in its attempts at realizing an aesthetic of cognitive mapping precisely because of its inability to construct the mediating links between these poles, the global and the local/bodily. Keep in mind that in Jameson's 1984 formulation, cognitive mapping is all about the constructions of these kinds of mediations. Jameson notes that at the basis of Althusser's formula for ideology as "the imaginary relationship of individuals to their real conditions of existence," we find at work a reformulation of

> an older and henceforth classical Marxian distinction between science and ideology, which is still not without value for us. The existential—the positioning of the individual subject, the experience of daily life, the monadic "point of view" on the world to which we are necessarily, as biological subjects, restricted—is in Althusser's formula implicitly opposed to the realm of abstract knowledge, a realm which as Lacan reminds us is never positioned in or actualized by any concrete subject but rather by that structural void called "le sujet supposé savoir", "the subject supposed to know", a subject-place of knowledge.[39]

Jameson goes on to point out, however, that the Lacanian system on which Althusser draws in developing his formula "is three-fold and not dualistic. To the Marxian-Althusserian opposition of ideology and science correspond only two of Lacan's tripartite functions, the Imaginary and the Real, respectively . . . what has until now been omitted was the dimension of the Lacanian Symbolic itself."[40] The Symbolic is the mediation that ties together these other two poles: neither the embodied phenomenological subject nor the evacuated place of the subject is supposed to know, the Symbolic in this formulation is another name for the languages and other collective realities we produce and share. Indeed, elsewhere Jameson reminds us that one of the "other basic philosophical underpinnings" of his formulation of the practice of cognitive mapping is Georg Lukács's notion of collective standpoint epistemology, "according to which 'mapping' or the grasping of the social totality is structurally available to the dominated rather than the dominating classes."[41]

It is precisely in its representation of these collective dimensions of contemporary existence—specifically in terms of work and urban space—

where Gibson's vision slips into ideology in Althusser's specific sense of formulating imaginary resolutions to real contradictions. Jameson suggests that in the novel's "heist plot"—a plan to break into the highly secure orbiting palazzo of the unthinkably wealthy and corrupt Tessier-Ashpool clan and free the artificial intelligence they control, enabling it to achieve its full autonomy—we might find "a distorted expression of the utopian impulse insofar as it realizes a fantasy of non-alienated collective work."[42] However, the narrative labor undertaken in the novel more readily exemplifies what Jameson identifies in his earlier essay "Reification and Utopia in Mass Culture" (1979) as a stirring up of utopian desires only to recontain them "by the narrative construction of imaginary resolutions and by the projection of an optical illusion of social harmony."[43] *Neuromancer* projects its utopian vision of labor as deeply preferable to the one it could perhaps still imagine in 1984 to be the dominant: "The crowd, he saw, was mostly Japanese. Not really a Night City crowd. Techs down from the arcologies. He supposed that meant the arena had the approval of some corporate recreational committee. He wondered briefly what it would be like, working all your life for one zaibatsu. Company housing, company hymn, company funeral."[44] The collective in which the protagonist Case works is decidedly without the deadening day-to-day monotony of those employed by the classic postwar corporations; but then, it is also a life without the securities such employment made available—lifetime employment, housing, high wages, guaranteed recreation time, and health insurance. Case's labor is already fully contingent and flexible—freelance and temporary. In an earlier critical reconsideration of the limits of *Neuromancer*'s utopianism, Tom Moylan notes:

> Three categories of workers can be identified in this flexible economy: a declining number of skilled industrial workers who hold relatively high paying and secure jobs in large corporate structures and who are still protected by union contracts; a growing number of minimum-wage, part-time workers who are hired as needed and fired with short notice and who have no union protection and consequently no job security; and a smaller, but growing, number of skilled professional-managerial-technical workers who individually contract with corporations (and governments) for limited term,

relatively high-paid tasks. It is in this last category that the protagonists (and indeed many of the readers) of Gibson's cyberpunk world can be found—albeit at the lower end of that sectors' pay scale.[45]

Moving ahead three decades, it becomes even more evident that the romance of Case's labor might best be represented today by the adjunct university instructor, or one of those 15,000 employees now trumpeted at the end of any blockbuster film.[46] The price of failure in such an environment (again one not unlike the contemporary university) is also made clear early on: "Night City was like a deranged experiment in Social Darwinism . . . Biz here was a constant subliminal hum, and death the accepted punishment for laziness, carelessness, lack of grace, the failure to heed the demands of an intricate protocol."[47] The utopia of *Neuromancer* thus turns out to be that of what had in 1984 only just been named post-Fordism, what Yanis Varoufakis later calls the "reign of the Global Minotaur," or what William Davies more recently periodizes as "combative neo-liberalism: 1979–1989."[48]

Similarly, the novel's imaginary of the collective "meat" spaces of the contemporary city are made apparent in this description of Case's subway journey across BAMA (Boston-Atlanta-Metropolitan Axis, known more informally as the Sprawl):

> The local came booming in along the black induction strip, fine grit sifting from cracks in the tunnel's ceiling. Case shuffled into the nearest door and watched the other passengers as he rode. A pair of predatory-looking Christian Scientists were edging toward a trio of young office techs who wore idealized holographic vaginas on their wrists, wet pink glittering under the harsh lighting. The techs licked their perfect lips nervously and eyed the Christian Scientists from beneath lowered metallic lids.[49]

A little later Gibson writes of Case's journey on another train journey across "a blasted industrial landscape:"

> The landscape of the northern Sprawl woke confused memories of childhood for Case, dead grass tufting the cracks in a canted slab of freeway concrete.
>
> The train began to decelerate ten kilometers from the airport.

Case watched the sun rise on the landscape of childhood, on broken slag and the rusting shells of refineries.[50]

Andrew Ross notes that cyberpunk, like a more generally domesticated suburban punk scene from which it arises,

> offered an image-repertoire of urban culture in postindustrial decay for white suburban youths whose lives and environs were quite removed from daily contact with the Darwinist street sensibility of "de-evolved" city life. It is perhaps no coincidence that none of the major cyberpunk writers were city-bred, although their work feeds off the phantasmatic street diet of Hobbesian lawlessness and the aesthetic of detritus that is assumed to pervade the hollowed-out core of the great metropolitan centers. This urban fantasy, however countercultural its claims and potential effects, shared the dominant, white middle-class conception of inner-city life. In this respect, the suburban romance of punk, and, subsequently, cyberpunk, fashioned a culture of alienation out of their parents' worst fears about life on the mean streets.[51]

In what could very well serve as a plot summary of *Neuromancer*'s influential contemporary work of fiction, McInerney's *Bright Lights, Big City*, Ross goes on to point out that "All through the 1980s, this romance ran parallel with the rapid growth of gentrified Yuppie culture in the 'abandoned' zones of the inner cities, where the transient thrills of street culture served up an added exotic flavor for the palates of these pioneers in their newly colonized spaces."[52] Given this linkage, it becomes evident how much Gibson's novel, and cyberpunk more generally, contributes to remapping the urban landscape as it does to reconfiguring the collective spaces of work.

Delany, on the other hand, was "city-bred": he was born and raised in Harlem, on 7th Avenue between 132nd and 133rd Streets, and he has lived the majority of his life in various parts of the city. Thus, as we might anticipate, the urban and collective imaginaries found in *Stars in My Pocket* are radically different than those in *Neuromancer*. This is especially the case in the novel's great utopian vision of southern Velm, the home of the protagonist, the interplanetary traveling industrial diplomat Marq Dyeth. Velm is a world co-inhabited by two radically different species:

the humans to which Marq belongs, and the three-sexed Evelmi. The intermingling of these different communities allows a wild proliferation of identities to develop, far beyond the binaries of male and female and straight and gay, as well as truly queer kinships:

> Though I was sure he listened as intently as anyone else could possibly listen (as intently as I knew I listened to him), still, before his still face, to believe it was all faith. "I was adopted by the Dyeths when I was a baby—from some infant exchange in the north; but most of my sisters [in the novel, all citizens, regardless of biological gender, are referred to by feminine pronouns, the masculine reserved exclusively for the object of one's desire] come from even farther south. Small Maxa was semisomed from some neuroplasm that an evelm grandmother of mine, N'yom, donated to a bioengineering experiment many, many years ago and that was just taken out of suspension about a decade and a half back—though of course most of Maxa's chromosome sequence was taken from humans. But in the genetic sense she's part evelm. Still, there is no egg-and-sperm relation between any of our parents and any of this generation of children, nor between any of my sisters—human or evelm—and each other."[53]

Of his home and family, Marq observes late in the novel,

> Perhaps the greatest generosity of my universe is that in so much it's congruent with the worlds of others, which I suppose is finally just one with the generosity of my evelm parents, who thought my unique position among humans quite charming and were proud of it, and my human parents, who from time to time worried if, as distinct from more usually sexually oriented males, gay or straight, I might not encounter some social difficulty, say, of the same sort as I might have had in some societies had I been a nail-biter myself. But both spoke, both agreed on who I was, that I was a ripple that shored their stream, so that their universe, with all its idiosyncratic wonder, unique to my eyes, has still, always, seemed a part of mine.[54]

This combination of difference and congruity of "universes" makes the utopia of this world one of unexpected encounters. Crucially, these encounters are enabled by the very texture of the collective urban spaces themselves:

Tingling heels drying, we walked down the resilient woven flooring of the shadowy tunnel. Here and there along the arched ceiling or the curved wall, a meter-wide vent, or sometimes a three-meter-wide vent, let in light. . . .

The hollow-eyed face looked down. "This is where you come for sex?"

"And sculpture." I nodded for him to follow me between two high vegetal shapes of plastic with a ring of taste plates at licking level. . . .

"Excuse me." The hand on my shoulder, from weight and heat and texture, was not his. I glanced back; so did Korga. The other hand was on Korga's shoulder. The male (human) said, mostly to me: "Could I interrupt you two long enough to take your friend to my friend . . ." He gestured with his tongue at a purple-black evelm, standing a few meters down the run, foreclaws off the ground; darting long and short tongues from his jaw, creating no sound in anticipatory lust.

I said: "You must ask my friend."

Korga said to me: "Will you watch if I go? Please?" And to the human: "Is it all right if Marq watches?"

The human, surprised, smiled and shrugged at once: "Yes. Certainly. Of course." And to Korga: "You have come from very far away, am I right?"

Korga glanced at me.

"But that's no matter." The human hand dropped from my shoulder but remained on Korga's.[55]

This scene resonates with the equally utopian set piece at the heart of De Palma's *Body Double*—a music video of Frankie Goes to Hollywood's "Relax," a song that was "one of the most controversial and most commercially successful records of the decade," banned by the BBC throughout 1984 but still topping the charts for five consecutive weeks and returning to number two later that year.[56] The scene in question begins with the film's *Rear Window* (1954) pastiche hero, Jake Scully (Craig Wasson), telling the porn actress Holly Body (Melanie Griffin), "I like to watch."

As I hope this passage makes evident, the spaces in Delany's novel represent a transfigured vision of the urban and especially queer communities in which Delany lived and thrived in the New York City of the

1960s and 1970s. Delany later reflects that it was precisely such mediatory spaces that encouraged "interclass contact and communication conducted in a mode of good will."[57] The world we are presented with in the novel similarly fulfills the criteria of all the great modern utopias, from Le Guin's *The Dispossessed* (1974) through Kim Stanley Robinson's *2312* (2012) and Karen Lord's *The Best of All Possible Worlds* (2013) in that it stresses how these utopian spaces encourage and enable "evental encounters," in Alain Badiou's sense, to occur in the four conditions of politics, science, art, and love.[58]

Given the immensity of his achievement in this work, why does Delany not complete the project? Over the years, a range of possible answers have been suggested, including a number by Delany himself: the full onset of the AIDS crisis, the end of his eight-year-long relationship with Frank Romeo, and the general neoliberal remapping of the Manhattan cityscape—the last documented in Delany's extraordinary nonfiction book *Times Square Red, Times Square Blue* (1999)—made the project feel increasingly out of step with an emerging reality. However, there may be something in the nature of the project that made its completion impossible.

Throughout his novel, Delany stresses the precarity of the utopian collective spaces achieved on Velm. First, on the most universal intergalactic plane, it is threatened by the rising tide of the fundamentalist political alliance known as the Family: soon after allying themselves with the Family, former allies of the Dyeths violently denounce the collective's queer kinships: "a disease is not innocent, and this equation of unnatural crime with innocence is, in itself, a disease, which can only be cured by the most primitive means: quarantine, fire, prayer."[59] The Family no doubt figures the deeply homophobic Moral Majority—also mentioned early on in *Times Square Red, Times Square Blue*—founded by Jerry Falwell only five years before the novel's publication, and influential in Reagan's two presidential victories. Second, Delany raises the possibility that Velm itself be on the verge of what he calls "Cultural Fugue": "For a *world* to go into Cultural Fugue—for the socioeconomic pressures to reach a point of technological recomplication and perturbation where the population completely destroys all life across the planetary surface—takes a *lot* of catastrophe. There are more than six thousand worlds in the Federation of Habitable Worlds. And Cultural Fugue is *very* rare."[60] Finally, there is the international "tragedy of the north" on Velm, a situation in the planet's northern environs where the relationships between humans and Evelmi regularly explode into violence.

The narrative problem that Delany would have to confront in composing the book's second volume would involve resolving satisfactorily (for himself and his readers) the various crises that emerge by the conclusion of *Stars in My Pocket*, such that the pocket utopian community of Marq's home would be able to reproduce itself.[61] Such problems, considered in spatial terms, are fundamentally ones of scaling: how to translate the successes of the local, urban communities onto wider and wider national and global scales. As Jameson points out in the concluding section of *Postmodernism*, these questions are the same as those that in the latter part of the 1960s confronted successful radical political formations: "since the crisis of socialist internationalism, and the enormous strategic and tactical difficulties of coordinating local and grassroots of neighborhood political actions with national or international ones, such urgent political dilemmas are all immediately functions of the enormously complex new international space in question."[62] Jameson's case study is the rise and fall in the late 1960s and early 1970s of Detroit's League of Black Revolutionary Workers. The challenges the movement faced and the ultimate reason for its failure were quite similar to those faced by Delany, albeit on different scales: "how to develop a *national* political movement on the basis of a *city* strategy and politics."[63]

Before this can happen, Jameson suggests, a new collective narrative, or cognitive mapping, is necessary to allow these collectives to position their local experiences in relationship to the larger, discontinuous scales they also occupy. Unable to effect such a movement across scales—in the political sphere as much as in Delany's novel—such projects lose their momentum and ultimately stall: "Having acceded to a larger spatial plane, the base vanished under them: and with this the most successful social revolutionary experiment of that rich political decade in the United States came to a sadly undramatic end."[64] Unlike the history of the league, Delany leaves us with an open-ended vision, where neither success nor failure are predetermined. However, without a figure of the new mediations between the collective lived spaces so brilliantly imagined in the novel and the more abstract "global" contexts in which they suddenly find themselves, the novel, for all its tremendous emotional and intellectual power, comes to take on the bittersweet nostalgic tone of a paean to the radical cultural and political possibilities made available by the 1960s and seemingly exhausted by the mid-1980s. Such a conclusion seemed to be reconfirmed by another monumental event that occurs late in 1984: the landslide reelection of the arch-neoconservative and fierce opponent of 1960s political mobilizations Ronald Reagan. Reagan's reelections signals the "second death" of the 1960s, the deferred symbolic closure of a situation whose real conclusion had occurred more than a decade before.[65] Revealingly, the ascendance in 1984 of the problematic of postmodernity was accompanied by a number of other significant looks backward to the 1960s: notable among them is the *Social Text* double issue "The 60s without Apology," which also included Jameson's essay "Periodizing the 60s"—an essay originally intended, Jameson announces in another work published in 1984, as part of "a book-length study of the 1960s."[66]

The shared ground and differences between *Neuromancer* and *Stars in My Pocket* can be located in their respective attitudes toward the political, social, cultural, and spatial experiments of the 1960s and 1970s: a rejection in Gibson's case, and cyberpunk more generally, of these older experiments and the development of new strategies for surviving, negotiating, and flourishing in an emergent present; and in Delany's unfinished work, the refusal of such an emergent present and an affirmation of a fidelity to the past.

Jameson concludes *Postmodernism* with a call to arms: "'We have to name the system': this high point of the sixties finds an unexpected revival in the postmodernism debate."[67] Although this evocation would at first glance appear to be akin to that implicit in Delany's project, I want to suggest that Jameson's abandonment sometime in the mid-1980s of his 1960s book in favor of an extended engagement with the present situation—the period of the contemporary—points toward another very different project only then just beginning. In a discussion of the most effective relationship between any prior and current radical project, his case study being Lenin's life work, Slavoj Žižek develops a productive distinction between what he calls "return" and "repeating." Allow me to paraphrase Žižek here, replacing his name, "Lenin," with that of the "sixties":

> As a result, *repeating* the sixties does not mean a *return* to the sixties—to repeat the sixties is to accept that "the sixties are dead," that its particular solution failed, even failed monstrously, but that there was a utopian spark in it worth saving. Repeating the sixties means that we have to distinguish between what the sixties actually did and the field of possibilities it opened up, the tension in the sixties between what it actually did and another dimension: what was "in the sixties more than the sixties itself." To repeat the sixties is to repeat not what the sixties *did* but what it *failed to do*, its missed opportunities.⁶⁸

It was precisely such a repeating of the 1960s New Wave that Carr hoped would be accomplished in his New Ace Science Fiction Specials series. Indeed, Carr maintains in his editor's general introduction:

> most of the science fiction today is no more advanced and imaginative than the sf stories of the fifties, or even forties: basic ideas and plots are reworked time and again . . . when authors are constrained to writing nothing but variations on the plots and styles of the past, much of the excitement of science fiction disappears. Science fiction is a literature of change; more than any other kind of writing, sf needs to keep moving forward if it is to be exciting.⁶⁹

Although *Neuromancer* and cyberpunk did spark the kind of excitement Carr refers to here and thereby contribute significantly, as I suggested earlier, to a general reorganization of the literary field, it ultimately accomplishes a postmodern recontainment of 1960s New Wave energies rather than repeating them, which Carr calls for. Indeed, in an outstanding study of the place of *Neuromancer* in the context of contemporary science fiction publishing practices, Sara Brouillette points out that the success of the novel teaches its readers the decidedly postmodern ideological lesson that "corporate culture" can "effortlessly assimilate any creative intelligence that wants to critique it." Rather than educating the desire of its readers for something radically other, *Neuromancer* shows them "the future they are already living in. It is, finally, that community's canonical text, a text that explains and codifies what they see themselves as having lost at the hands of their corporate others."⁷⁰ This is borne out in *Neuromancer*'s conclusion, whose literal deus ex machina brings Gibson's science fiction narrative to a happy ending in the kind of wish-fulfilling fantasy that will be characteristic of so many subsequent techno-determinist celebrations of the "liberatory" power of the new informational technologies. The successful freeing of the AI by Case and his colleagues enables an unanticipated first contact with an alien intelligence from the "Centauri system."[71] This seemingly closed antinomy formed by the pair of *Neuromancer* and *Stars in My Pocket* is beautifully captured in one of the hit songs of 1984 (also released on October 26), Don Henley's "The Boys of Summer." The song at once stages the deadlock of the inevitable recuperation of all subcultures—"I saw a Deadhead sticker on a Cadillac"—and the impossibility of a return to the past—"Don't look back, you can never look back."

However, such closure is always imaginary or ideological. The couple of an emergent cyberpunk and the residuals of the New Wave do not exhaust the range of possibilities in this moment. I conclude this essay by briefly touching on another practice, one that opens toward the possibilities of the "new political art" Jameson calls for in his "Postmodernism" essay. Interestingly, this occurs in a work that was, along with *Neuromancer*, one the first novels to be published in the New Ace Science Fiction Specials series. Unlike Gibson's novel, its significance was not fully recognized for a number of years. I am referring to Kim Stanley Robinson's debut novel, *The Wild Shore*. One of the greatest of the New Wave writers, Le Guin—whose breakthrough *The Left Hand of Darkness* (1969) was published in the original Ace Specials—proclaims on *The Wild Shore*'s cover, "There's a fresh wind blowing in *The Wild Shore*. Welcome back, Ace Specials, and welcome Kim Stanley Robinson." With *The Wild Shore* in hand, we can complete our survey of the science fictional field circa 1984 with the diagram in figure 2.[72]

The Wild Shore is set in a postapocalypse Southern California, sixty years after thousands of neutron bombs had been exploded across the United States, reducing the nation to a scattering of isolated agricultural communities. The novel focuses on two such communities, those occupying the remains of Southern California's coastal San Onofre Valley and San Diego (the wonderful original cover image, recalling Madelon Vriesendorp's paintings for Rem Koolhaas's *Delirious New York* [1978], is a

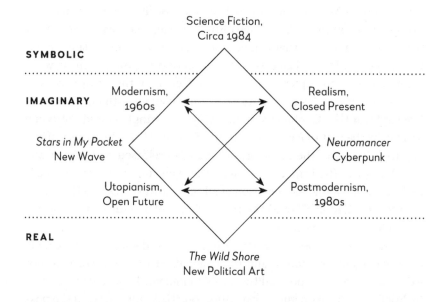

Figure 2: Science fiction, circa 1984. Courtesy of Phillip E. Wegner.

representation of a scene in the latter location), and the contacts between the remaining Americans and the Japanese military who patrol the coast to prevent any breaking of a UN-imposed quarantine. The novel is a first for Robinson in a number of other ways. It is the opening novel in his Three Californias trilogy and was soon followed by what Moylan identifies as the "critical dystopia" of *The Gold Coast* (1988) and the marvelous green utopia of *Pacific Edge* (1990).[73] In this trilogy, Robinson allegorically reverses and retraces the chronology of modern science fiction. He opens by reproducing a classic Cold War science fiction subgenre, the nuclear postapocalypse story—a subgenre also regularly mined to great effect by Philip K. Dick, another California-based writer who deeply influenced Robinson and on whom the latter wrote his doctoral dissertation (also published in a revised form in 1984).[74] With *The Gold Coast*, Robinson moves further backward to the late-nineteenth-century precursor to modern science fiction, the fusion of the literary utopia and naturalism that produced what became the dominant middle-brow expression of literary science fiction, especially in Great Britain—the dystopia.[75] Finally, Robinson brings the trilogy to a rousing climax with a contemporary version of the practice Darko Suvin retroactively identifies as science fiction's great sociopolitical subgenre: the narrative utopia. The utopia of *Pacific Edge* is a throwback to this older literary practice in another way, in that its utopian imaginary remains constrained to the spatial scale of the nation-state. The next dialectical step in Robinson's project will involve the arduous labor of constructing a vision of new collective spaces appropriate to truly global realities. This is exactly the labor he undertakes in his masterpiece of the 1990s, the trilogy of *Red Mars* (1993), *Green Mars* (1994), and *Blue Mars* (1996).

Yet to tell the story in this way ignores all the ways *The Wild Shore* already recognizes the challenges that must be surmounted in the extended and still incomplete project the novel inaugurates. The limits to the imagination and political action imposed on us by the older cognitive mapping of the nation-state are at the heart of *The Wild Shore*. The fantasy of returning to an imaginary past of American greatness—of restoring what, in 1984 at least, would readily be understood as a Cold War US global hegemony—is voiced by the imperious leader of San Diego (a stronghold then of neoconservatism): "'You tell them they can make this country what it used to be. They can help. But we all have to work together. The day will come. Another Pax Americana, cars and airplanes, rockets to the moon, telephones. A unified country.' Suddenly, without anger or whispery passion, he said, 'You go back up there and tell your valley that they join the resistance or they oppose it.'"[76] This passage not only prefigures George W. Bush's chilling words to a joint session of Congress on September 20, 2001—"Either you are with us, or you are with the terrorists"—it calls to mind another, more recent postapocalypse fiction set in Manhattan, Colson Whitehead's *Zone One* (2011): "It was a new day. Now the people were no longer mere survivors, half-mad refuges, a pathetic, shit-flecked, traumatized herd, but the 'American Phoenix.'"[77] The adventurism and voluntarism encouraged by the mayor and his allies ultimately results in the senseless death late in the novel of one of the protagonist's companions. Robinson's vision here thus gives effective voice to the anxiety then provoked by the increasingly vociferous saber-rattling of the Reagan administration and its desire to bury the shames of the Vietnam War in some new glorious military conflict (a fantasy even more evident in John Milius's 1984 film *Red Dawn*).

Even more significantly, the fantasy of being able to live in the enclosed and bordered totalities of the nation-state, and thus move through the world according to the dictates of obsolete cognitive mappings, is also one shared by those who first launch the attack on the United States. This fact is revealed to the reader through the device of the book-within-the-book, a perhaps authentic, perhaps fictionalized travel narrative, Glen Baum's *An American Around the World: Being an Account of a Circumnavigation of the Globe in the Years 2030 to 2039*:

> I asked him if he could tell me why the weather had become so much colder on the California coast since the war. This was several hours into our trip, and the Soviets around us filled the compartment with an air of utter boredom; at the prospect of talking about his specialty, Johnson's face brightened somewhat.
>
> "It's a complicated question. It's generally agreed that the war did alter the world's weather, but how it effected the change is still debated. It's estimated that three thousand neutron bombs exploded on the continental United States that day in 1984; not too much long term radiation was released, luckily for you, but a lot of turbulence was generated in the stratosphere—the highest levels of air—and apparently the jet stream altered its course for good."[78]

A little further on, the conversation continues:

> "It sounds as if California's weather has changed most of all," I said.
>
> "Oh no," Johnson said. "Not at all. California has been strongly affected, no doubt about it—like moving fifteen degrees of latitude north—but a few other parts of the world have been just as strongly affected, or even more so. Lots of rain in northern Chile!—and my, is that washing all that sand off the Andes into the sea. Tropical heat in Europe during the summer, drought during the monsoon—oh, I could go on and on. It has caused more human misery than you can imagine."[79]

This marvelous passage offers a full-blown announcement of what will become years later an even more effective figure of our global situation and the imperative to think on a planetary scale: the Anthropocene, or the transformation of the entire planet wrought by human-made global climate change.

In the end, Robinson's first novel offers less a set of solutions than an articulation, no less provisional than that found in the latter parts of Jameson's "Postmodernism" essay, of the fundamental project that will not only be at the center of Robinson's subsequent literary output but also a fundamental aspect of all contemporary radical politics: an allegorical mapping of the concrete relationships between the individual, the local, and the global; and the development of the ability to "think globally," as the slogan goes, and to think the new spatial forms—collectivities and urban mediators—necessary before "we may again begin to grasp our positioning as individual and collective subjects and regain a capacity to act and struggle which is at present neutralized by our spatial as well as our social confusion."[80] That *The Wild Shore* is no more than a beginning of such a project, oriented toward what still remains our collective future, is indicated in the novel's final lines, which signal that the book is an example of another great utopian genre, the *Künstlerroman*, or the story of the artist: "The damp last page is nearly full. And my hand is getting cold—its getting so stiff I can't make the letters, these words are all big and scrawling, taking up the last of the space, thank God. Oh be done with it. There's an owl, flitting over the river. I'll stay right here and fill another book."[81] That Robinson did and continues to do so is something for which we can all remain grateful.

CHAPTER 2 . . . **KYLIE KORSNACK**

NO FUTURE BUT THE ALTERNATIVE

OR, TEMPORAL LEVELING IN THE WORK OF WILLIAM GIBSON

Today, just as yesterday, the tension of living in several
times at once remains unsolved. —Jacques Rancière[1]

Halfway through William Gibson's 2003 novel *Pattern Recognition*, the protagonist, a New Yorker named Cayce, reflects on the early days after the September 11, 2001, terrorist attacks on the World Trade Center towers. She recalls sitting on a bench in Union Square, surrounded by the burning candles of newly erected monuments to the dead and the missing: "She remembered sitting there, prior to her tears, looking from the monument that was still taking shape at the base of Washington's statue to that odd sculpture across Fourteenth Street, in front of the Virgin Megastore, a huge stationary metronome, constantly issuing steam, and back again to the organic accretion of candles, flowers, photographs, and messages, as though the answer, if there was one, lay in somehow understanding the juxtaposition of the two."[2] Whereas Gibson offers a thorough description of the emerging, memorial art forms taking shape in Union Square, the "odd sculpture" across the street is suspiciously understated, especially considering it is "one of the largest private commissions of public art in New York's history."³ Designed by Kristin Jones and Andrew Ginzel, *Metronome* was installed in 1999 on a building that stands just south of Union Square. Composed of eight separate elements with names like "the vortex," "the infinity," "the passage," and "the phases," *Metronome* presents an overwhelming array of temporal signifiers. The artists describe the work as "an investigation into the nature of time" that "references the multiple measures of time that simultaneously inform and confound our consciousness of the moment."⁴ *Metronome* also serves a functional purpose. In a review, artist and critic Robert C. Morgan commented: "It is questionable whether Metronome is less pragmatic than other utilitarian aspects of the building. After all, it does tell the time. Not only does it give the exact time of day in the most literal sense, it also extends the concept of time into geology and astronomy; in essence, it projects time from what is literal to that which is metaphysical—time beyond measure."⁵ In this sense, Morgan's review seems to align with the artists' hopes for the project as a catalyst for temporal rumination, inviting viewers to contemplate, "geological, solar, lunar, daily, hourly, and momentarily, revealing the factions of seconds in the life of a city—and of a human being."⁶ What neither of these perspectives takes into account is the fact that this "public art wall" adorns the outside of a building owned by the private company that funded its construction. What lies within that building? A luxury apartment complex with a website that proudly invites prospective residents to "Live Luxuriously in a Work of Art."⁷

I begin with this somewhat indulgent elaboration on a single reference in *Pattern Recognition* because it captures a fundamental predicament that haunts Gibson's fiction. On one hand, *Metronome* embodies the utopic ideal of the possibilities and potential of art. In full display, accessible to all, *Metronome* demonstrates art's intervention into a labor-driven culture of postmodernity. The piece disrupts the fast-paced, forward-moving bustle of city life while simultaneously inviting viewers—free of charge—to slow down and contemplate those measures of temporal experience that exist beyond the dominating logic of the second hand. In its dual status as artwork and art wall, as an aesthetic intervention and a commodified aesthetic form, *Metronome* epitomizes the particular struggle faced by the artwork in the culture of late capitalism. In contrast to the "organic accretion of candles, flowers, photographs, and messages" of Gibson's memorial art forms, this commissioned work seems too permanent, too curated, too reproducible. Indeed, it is precisely the ephemerality of the memorials that seem to distinguish them from that "odd sculpture" across the way. This juxtaposition highlights a central thread that exists throughout Gibson's work: a sustained reflection on the relationship between art, temporality, and human experience in contemporary culture.

In this chapter, I trace Gibson's long engagement with the concept of temporal multiplicity to highlight the importance of the framework to his narrative thinking. Across his work, we can identify a variety of narrative approaches that foreground his interest in temporality. Whether in the form of alternative history (*The Difference Engine*), psychological movement through time ("The Gernsback Continuum"), multiverse (*The Peripheral*), or machine-powered time travel (*Archangel*), it is often through overlapping or multiple timelines that Gibson explores the relationship between art, aesthetics, and culture. Although it might seem too obvious to suggest that time is important to Gibson's aesthetic, I want to explore the possibility that there is something very particular about how Gibson thinks about, represents, and problematizes temporal experience, especially in his most recent fictional works. With his 2014 novel *The Peripheral*, the comic book series *Archangel* (2016), and *Agency* (2020), Gibson's fiction, perhaps more explicitly than ever before, foregrounds multiple simultaneous registers of time. To borrow a question from Fredric Jameson: "Has the author of *Neuromancer* 'changed his style'?"[8] Not exactly. Although questions of temporal multiplicity have infused his work from the beginning, in his most recent work, Gibson's emphasis on temporal simultaneity has stretched beyond the content of his work, infiltrating its very form.

Important to my reading of Gibson's work are several theoretical paradigms that link the concept of simultaneity to the temporal experience of modernity. In the introduction to *Time: A Vocabulary of the Present*, Joel Burges and Amy J. Elias identify multiplicity and simultaneity as dominant terms defining "our sense of the present."[9] As they put it:

> Over the course of modernity, and with continued momentum in our time, the present has emerged as an experience of simultaneity in which temporalities multiply because they are synchronized as

simultaneous on economic, cultural, technological, ecological, and planetary registers. Thus while simultaneity is often understood as a reduction of that multiplicity, creating a singular time beholden to capital, the present is actually animated by a tension between the simultaneous and the multiple, variously contracting and protracting a sense of contemporaneity in which times conjoin.[10]

For Burges and Elias, the postwar present can best be described as an "experience of simultaneity," an occurrence that captures and resists the dominating temporal logic of contemporary capitalism. In their view, capitalist contemporaneity constructs the illusion of simultaneity, a singular notion of time that aligns itself with the demands of an accelerating and expanding global market. This "illusion of simultaneity" resembles what French philosopher Jacques Rancière has referred to as the "time of domination." In the opening lecture of a 2011 conference on "The State of Things," Rancière posits:

> There is a dominant form of temporality, for sure, a "normal" time that is the time of domination. Domination gives it its divisions and its rhythms, its agendas and its schedules in the short and long run: time of work, leisure, and unemployment; electoral campaigns, degree courses, etc. It tends to homogenize all forms of temporality under its control, defining thereby what the present of our world consists of, which futures are possible, and which definitely belong to the past—thereby indicating the impossible.[11]

Like Burges and Elias's theorization of simultaneity, Rancière categorizes modern experiences of temporality as conditioned by a single, dominating temporal structure. The "time of domination" captures the consensual and forced ways that social and economic structures support the illusion of homogeneous time, a force that controls and governs how individuals, societies, and global markets move through and experience temporality in contemporary culture. In actuality, modern temporality functions "according to the regulation of the convergence and divergence of times."[12] In other words, simultaneous or homogenized time is a fiction produced by the logic of capitalism.

Interestingly, Burges and Elias's insistence on the illusionary quality of capitalist temporality and Rancière's attention to the fictionality of homogeneous time create a vision filled with space and potential for cultural resistance. For Burges and Elias, capitalism's contemporaneity captures an experience where multiple temporalities are synchronized according to a variety of temporal registers. Rather than work in service to postmodern culture, this synchronicity creates a tension, a contradiction that by its very existence threatens to disrupt capitalism's insistence on a singular notion of contemporaneity. In other words, the antidote to capitalist contemporaneity is breaking apart the illusion of simultaneity by exposing the multiple and simultaneous forms of temporality that structure the present.

Rancière identifies other forms of temporality—what he calls intervals and interruptions—that exist in and threaten to disrupt the dominating logic of homogeneous time. "[A] way out of that logic," he writes, "should be a way out of its time."[13] Whereas intervals capture moments when individuals or groups of people "renegotiate the ways in which they adjust their own time to the divisions and rhythms of domination," interruptions are "moments when one of the social machines that structure the time of domination break down and stop."[14] In both cases, the fictionality of homogeneous time is exposed, making visible the actual existence of multiple and competing forms of temporality. Thus, for Rancière, this proliferation of competing temporalities creates disruptive potential.

With this theoretical background in mind, we can begin to explore the multiple and simultaneous temporalities that categorize much of Gibson's fiction. As we will see, although there are traces of temporal multiplicity throughout Gibson's oeuvre, his more recent work reconfigures the novel form, disrupting its tendency toward progression and linearity in favor of simultaneity. With this shift from content to form—especially in *The Peripheral*—Gibson crafts an artistic form capable of interrupting the so-called time of domination or illusion of contemporaneity that categorizes the temporal experience of the postwar present.

Traveling through Time with Gibson

Often credited with helping establish the foundations for cyberpunk and steampunk, Gibson's work has routinely framed the conventions for new subgenres of science fiction or pushed past previously established parameters to propel science fiction forward and in new directions. Although

Gibson's turn to simultaneity may seem new, his interest in alternative temporalities has spanned the majority of his literary career, and he even cites H. G. Wells's *The Time Machine* as providing his first exposure to and subsequent interest in science fiction.[15] It may not come as a surprise to discover that throughout the nonfiction collection *Distrust That Particular Flavor*, watches, clocks, and time machines routinely inhabit Gibson's reflections on his life and work. From his early exposure to Wells to his brief fascination with mechanical watches and his often-quoted speculation that "the end-point of human culture may well be a single moment of effectively endless duration, an infinite digital now," Gibson has been consistently drawn to literature, commodities, and theorizations that consider how humans understand, experience, and narrate the temporal quality of living in the present.[16]

This temporal thinking extends to how Gibson understands his own aesthetic. Buried within a parenthetical of the essay "Dead Man Sings," Gibson describes the "central driving tension" of his work as a "perpetual toggling between nothing being new ... and everything having recently changed."[17] Here, he identifies a temporal tension in his writing between an ever sameness of the now and a rapid acceleration into the future; such tension manifests even in his reflections on the first time he tried to create a new world with his writing. Of that initial attempt at narrative creation, Gibson recalls: "I began to imag[ine] that the deserted (recently deserted?) office building in which Graham/Bannister reviewed film had in its atrium a fountain, and in this fountain, submerged, along with the usual coins, were dozens of wristwatches, some of them very expensive. Time had ended, perhaps, or the awareness of its passage had become somehow undesirable. And that was as far as I went."[18] This unresolved confrontation between an indeterminate protagonist and a vision of submerged wristwatches could be read specifically in terms of stalled technological development or a lapse in historical progress; however, we might also consider it a general statement on the unstable, ungraspable quality of temporality. Even more significant, this early scene—Gibson's first fictional attempt to capture and explore a person's relationship to temporal experience—haunts much of what would become his most well-known fictional works.

Gibson's first two novelistic trilogies—the so-called Sprawl trilogy in the 1980s and the Bridge trilogy in the 1990s—imagine futuristic settings that are chronotopic visions in the Bakhtinian sense. Recall that for Bakhtin, literary chronotopes are often places—the road, the castle, the salon—infused with temporal meaning. Time becomes visible in these settings because they are sites of encounter or structures that preserve the past and represent it in the future.[19] In Bakhtin's vision of the chronotope, spatial and temporal categories fuse together into "one carefully thought-out concrete whole."[20] Such a collapse of time and space can be seen in the prominent sites of Gibson's early fiction. For example, return to that well-known description of cyberspace from *Neuromancer* (1984): "A consensual hallucination experienced daily by billions of legitimate operators, in every nation, by children being taught mathematical concepts.... A graphic representation of data abstracted from the banks of every computer in the human system. Unthinkable complexity. Lines of light ranged in the nonspace of the mind, clusters and constellations of data. Like city lights, receding."[21] For Gibson, cyberspace is an immaterial place, a "nonspace," yet it is nevertheless a central point of meeting, encounter, and therefore temporal multiplicity. It is a virtual version of Bahktin's road, where "the spatial and temporal paths of the most varied people—representatives of all social classes, estates, religions, nationalities, ages—intersect at one spatial and temporal point . . . a point of new departures and a place for events to find their denouement."[22] As a virtual chronotope, Gibson's cyberspace serves as "an organizing center" for the narrative as a whole.

When compared with the main site of encounter within Gibson's second trilogy—the Bridge trilogy—there is a reversal of these time-space characteristics. Instead of the immaterial, nonspace of the cybernetic encounter, the bridge is a place of excessive materiality where images of clashing temporality are preserved within its very structure. In *Virtual Light* (1993), the first of the trilogy, Gibson first describes the bridge as follows:

> The integrity of its span was rigorous as the modern program itself, yet around this had grown another reality, intent upon its own agenda. This had occurred piecemeal, to no set plan, employing every imaginable technique and material. The result was something amorphous, startlingly organic. At night, illuminated by Christmas bulbs, by recycled neon, by torchlight, it possessed a queer medieval

energy. By day, seen from a distance, it reminded him of the ruin of England's Brighton Pier, as though viewed through some cracked kaleidoscope of vernacular style.[23]

Like the castle of Bakhtin's gothic novel, where "the traces of centuries and generations are arranged in it in visible form," the futuristic structure of Gibson's San Francisco bridge combines technologies of old and new—Christmas bulbs, recycled neon, torchlight—to create a site where traces of other times, places, and utilities are simultaneously preserved and repurposed in service of the new.[24] Unlike Bakhtin, Gibson immediately contrasts this architectural description with that of a character's experience of that same chronotopic vision:

> He'd first seen it by night, three weeks before. . . . He'd stared back into the cavern-mouth, heart pounding. . . . Everything ran together, blurring, melting in the fog. Telepresence had only hinted at the magic and singularity of the thing, and he'd walked slowly forward, into that neon maw and all that patchwork carnival of scavenged surfaces, in perfect awe. Fairyland. Rain-silvered plywood, broken marble from the walls of forgotten banks, corrugated plastic, polished brass, sequins, painted canvas, mirrors, chrome gone dull and peeling in the salt air. So many things, too much for his reeling eye, and he'd known that his journey had not been in vain.[25]

Whereas Gibson captures a tone of objectivity in the previous description, here he offers an alternative vision that emphasizes the viewer's affective response. In this version, viewing the bridge is like glimpsing "fairyland," an experience that can only be inaccurately described as "telepresence," of being in two places at once, both here and elsewhere. Gibson's vision of the bridge reads like a catalog of temporal dualities—"rain-silvered plywood, broken marble from walls of forgotten banks, corrugated plastic"—or objects that reflect temporality—"polished brass, sequins, painted canvas, mirrors." To see the bridge, then, is to see time made visible in space. To experience the bridge is to be overcome by images of simultaneity. Gibson's articulation of temporal experience prefigures Burges and Elias's characterization of the postwar present as "an experience of simultaneity."[26] In this way, we might read the bridge as offering a glimpse of how simultaneity begins to resist the dominating temporal logic of the present.

Another such glimpse can be seen in Gibson's *Pattern Recognition*, a novel that from its very inception was engaged with considerations of time. The first of what has become known as the Blue Ant trilogy, *Pattern Recognition* is significant in Gibson's oeuvre as the first of his novels to be set in the present rather than the future. In a talk for a New York book expo in May 2010, Gibson reflected on this shift, explaining that he had become frustrated with readers for refusing to see his so-called future settings as engaging directly with the present. He recalls, "I began to tell interviewers, somewhat testily, that I believed I could write a novel set in the present, our present, then, which would have exactly the affect of my supposedly imaginary futures . . . so I did."[27] With *Pattern Recognition*, Gibson set out to show how science fiction could be used to write about the present; in doing so, he recalls, "I found the material of the actual twenty-first century richer, stranger, more multiplex, than any imaginary twenty-first century could ever have been. And it could be unpacked with the toolkit of science fiction. I don't really see how it can be unpacked otherwise, as so much of it is so utterly akin to science fiction, complete with a workaday level of cognitive dissonance we now take utterly for granted."[28]

Despite Gibson's insistence on his ability to "use the toolkit of science fiction" to examine the twenty-first century, for many critics, *Pattern Recognition* marks a significant shift from his previous work. Some attribute the shift as one of genre.[29] For others, the significance is linked more to the feeling that the novel provides a diagnostic of the contemporary as trapped within what Fredric Jameson has referred to as the "perpetual present," or the postmodern condition of the contemporary as being devoid of any potential for futurity.[30] For the latter, these readings stem partly from an often-quoted conversation between Cayce, a freelance advertising consultant, and Hubertus Bigend, the founder of Blue Ant's global enterprise. In response to a question about how future generations will view the present, Bigend retorts: "We have no future. Not in the sense that our grandparents had a future or thought they did. Fully imagined cultural futures were the luxury of another day, one in which 'now' was of some greater duration. For us, of course, things can change so abruptly, so violently, so profoundly, that futures like our grandparents' have insufficient 'now' to stand on."[31] It is particularly important that this declaration of "no future" is proclaimed by the novel's stand-in for contemporary capitalism—Bigend, the CEO of a multinational corporation. After all, as Neil Easterbrook points out, "Bigend's unusually comic name invokes the Swiftian intertext of people who cannot understand the absurdity of their own beliefs or behaviors."[32] Bigend's early declaration of "no future" echoes the dangerous path of capitalism's insistence on contemporaneity, but at times the text seems to betray this dominating sense of a perpetually stalled present tense. Indeed, the formal construction of the novel complicates Bigend's negative prophecy of the end of time.

With *Pattern Recognition*, Gibson periodically bends the novel form to represent the existence of competing temporalities in a single interval of the present. At first glance, the novel is relatively linear; indeed, as Easterbrook points out, "the novel itself remains the most conventionally linear of Gibson's long fictions . . . it tells a single continuous narrative around a single character, lacks the jump-cuts characteristics of his earlier work, and so forth."[33] The novel follows only a single character, but it moves with that character all around the world. Cayce's search for the anonymous creator of a series of viral film clips has her visit London, Tokyo, Moscow, and eventually Paris. This narrative movement creates what Veronica Hollinger refers to as "a kind of formal representation of the present as a condition of incessant and spatialized movement."[34] The movement becomes spatially dizzying, but it also disrupts one's sense of time. Throughout the novel, Cayce is in a perpetual state of jet lag, a condition caused by traveling quickly across time zones, essentially making the body and mind operate in two different temporal registers. For Cayce, this jet lag manifests as "soul-delay," a mental state that "plays tricks with subjective time, expanding or telescoping it as seemingly random."[35] At the level of content, the novel is preoccupied with issues of temporal simultaneity. At the level of form, despite its overwhelmingly straightforward structure, there are intervals and interruptions—to borrow from Rancière—that disrupt the otherwise linear flow of *Pattern Recognition*.

One such disruption occurs when Cayce enters a Pilates studio, something she does surprisingly often within the novel. In the studio, multiple temporalities collide as Gibson narrates Cayce's experience of simultaneity:

> *She's down for a jack move.* Thinks this in the Pilates studio in Neal's Yard, doing the Short Spine Stretch, her bare feet in leather loops that haven't yet been softened up with use. . . . *What she's tempted to do, she knows, is crazy.* She exhales, watching her straightened legs rise up in the straps to a ninety-degree angle, then inhales as she bends them, holding tension in the straps against the pull of the spring-loaded platform she's reclining on. Exhales, as they say, for nothing, then inhales as she straightens them horizontally, pulling the springs taut. Repeating this six more times for a total of ten. *She shouldn't be thinking about anything except getting this right, and that's partly why she does it. Stops her thinking, if she concentrates sufficiently.* . . . Now she's sitting cross-legged, doing Sphinx, springs lightened. Turns her hands palm-up for Beseech. *No thinking. You do not get there by thinking about not thinking, but by concentrating on each repetition. To the gentle twanging of the springs.*³⁶

I've added emphasis throughout this passage to capture the fascinating juxtaposition between Cayce's mind and body in a moment of simultaneity. As readers, we are watching Cayce move and seeing her think. But formally, this is happening at the same time, sometimes even within the same sentence. This is just one of several moments throughout *Pattern Recognition* when the aesthetic bends slightly to accommodate different kinds of temporal experiences.

Another occurs each time Cayce checks her email. An otherwise mundane and repetitive exercise, her frequent email reading proves to be a complex experience to capture in narrative, partly because the novel must lapse into brief segments of temporal simultaneity. In these sections, the novel switches abruptly to boldface sans serif type:

> She is ready for an early night, on CPST, and is checking her mail prior to brushing her teeth. Parkaboy first up.
>
> **Judy hasn't left Darryl's since my last message . . . What I want to know is, is any of this worth it? Are you getting anywhere? Any closer at all?**
>
> Maybe, she decides. That's all she can tell him.
>
> **Maybe. I've got something in play here, but it may take a while to see whether it works. When I know more, you will.**
>
> Send.
>
> Boone next.

> Greetings from the Holiday Inn down the road from the technology park ... Next stop, the lounge downstairs, where some of the weaker sheep of the firm in question may congregate. You okay?
>
> That really is the slow route, she thinks, though she doesn't know what else he should be trying, other than buddying up with Sigil employees.[37]

This exchange continues, and similar moments reappear throughout the novel. By organizing the text this way, Gibson formally captures a very particular kind of temporal simultaneity, one that has become a significant part of everyday existence but still feels science fictional in nature.

Although these examples seem inconsequential, they succeed in interrupting the otherwise linear flow of Gibson's text. They bring multiple temporalities into collision. These instances of simultaneity interrupt the illusion of contemporaneity privileged by postmodern culture by calling into question what Rancière calls the "thesis of the homogeneity of time."[38] In other words, we see glimpses of this "calling to question" in the breaks and fissures of the linear aesthetic of *Pattern Recognition*. By the time we get to *The Peripheral*, an explicitly temporal aesthetic has permeated the entirety of the novel's formal structure.

In *The Peripheral* (2014), Gibson returns to the future, but this time he writes about not a single future but two. *The Peripheral* toggles between two storylines: one set in a small rural town in America in the near future and the other in London during the early twenty-second century, seventy years after the first timeline. (For purposes of clarity, I distinguish between these two timelines as the "near-future" and the "far-future.") In the far-future, an apocalyptic event known as "the Jackpot" has eliminated nearly 80 percent of the world's population, leaving a world largely run by a small percentage of the global elite. In the near-future, the Jackpot has not yet happened, and the main protagonist is Flynne Fisher, a young American from a rural town who makes her living as a freelance gamer and computer programmer. It is important to note that these timelines do not fall within the same linear path; that is, the far-future world is not Flynne's future. Flynne's timeline is an alternative, a stub, a path heading in one direction, but not necessarily the same direction as the post-Jackpot future. In Flynne's world, there is no clear future, but there is the potential for an alternative.

Although this formal structure resembles the narrative mode Gibson adopted in *Spook Country* (2007) and *Zero History* (2010), there are important differences. In the previous novels, the narrative jumps between several plotlines, following three separate characters as they navigate different parts of the same world. Only when the characters physically cross paths at the end of these novels do the separate narratives finally come into contact. These novels resemble *Pattern Recognition*'s linear structure, but they fragment that structure into parallel, forward-moving plotlines. In *The Peripheral*, the narrative moves back and forth in time, creating a formal structure that begins to feel a bit like time travel. In fact, Gibson invites such a comparison by quoting a line from H. G. Wells's *The Time Machine* as the epigraph to the novel: "I have already told you of the sickness and confusion that comes with time travelling." As Glyn Morgan points out, "Almost as significant as this quote from Wells are the lines which Gibson omits. Taken from the scene in which the Time Traveller frantically escapes, Wells's novel continues: 'and this time I was not seated properly in the saddle, but sideways in an unstable fashion.'"[39] In this context, the epigraph is both an invitation and a warning. Traveling through time in *The Peripheral* is more jarring than a traditional time-travel narrative because one does not leave behind one timeline for another; instead, readers find themselves occupying multiple temporalities simultaneously.[40]

One way to describe the novel's form is through the concept of narrative leveling. According to John Pier, narrative leveling describes the relationship between "an act of narration and the diegesis or spatial-temporal universe within which a story takes place."[41] The term is useful for articulating the complex narrative structures of framed tales or stories with multiple narrators embedded in them. In these texts, a character may begin to tell a story, but then, "a character in that story can, in turn, become an intradiegetic narrator whose narrative, at the second level, will then be a metadiegetic narrative. This process can extend to further meta-levels, forming a series of narratives patterned recursively in the fashion of Chinese boxes or Russian dolls."[42] By modifying the framework slightly, we can use this image of stories nested in other stories to help us understand the multiplicity of timelines in Gibson's text. We might imagine *The Peripheral* as structured in a form of temporal leveling: timelines nested within timelines. Narratively, the novel jumps back and forth between the two timelines, but the timelines continually bleed into each other as characters from one interact with those from the other. By the end, it becomes difficult, sometimes impossible, to separate the two.

Through this elaborate form of temporal leveling, Gibson presents readers with two separate worlds, existing at different points in time but connected virtually. At the beginning of the novel, this connection works like a futuristic video game: those in the near-future can log in to an online server and get a direct video feed into the far-future London. The catch is that although the far-future knows they are interacting with real people from the past, those in the near-future have no idea that they are seeing into the future. Only after Flynne witnesses a murder in the far-future is the connection between the two worlds made transparent to all parties. The rest of the novel follows the investigation of this murder, an event that inadvertently brings the timelines into more direct contact. This contact soon begins to alter the lives of those on both ends of the temporal spectrum. As the narrative progresses, the two timelines become increasingly more intertwined with characters sometimes finding themselves occupying both timelines simultaneously. This simultaneity can be cognitive, physical, or both.

At the start of *The Peripheral*, this simultaneity occurs visually and is reproduced formally in much the same way as Cayce's email checking in *Pattern Recognition*. For example, early in the novel Flynne uses her phone to control a drone in the far-future while sitting comfortably in her own present. With the drone, she has been instructed to keep paparazzi cameras (she refers to these as bugs) away from the exterior of a luxury apartment building. As she narrates the things she sees in the futuristic London, the materiality of her present keeps interrupting the narrative of that alternative temporality:

> Went hard at a dragonfly, front camera. Didn't matter how fast she went, they were just gone. Then a horizontal rectangle folded out and down, becoming a ledge, showing her a wall of frosted glass, glowing.
> *Took the jerky out of her mouth, put it on the table.* The bugs were back, jockeying for position in front of the window, if that was what it was. *Her free hand found the Red Bull, popped it. She sipped.*
> Then the shadow of a woman's slim butt appeared, against the

frosted glass. Then shoulder blades, above. Just shadows. Then hands, a man's by their size, on either side, above the shadows of the woman's shoulder blades, his fingers spread wide.

Swallowed, the drink like thin cold cough syrup. "Scoot," she said, and swept through the bugs, scattering them.[43]

In the passage noted, I've italicized the moments when the narrative attention switches from the future to the present. The scene continues in this manner with the two temporalities existing in the same moment, sometimes even in the same sentence. Interestingly, as we get to the end of this passage, it becomes even more impossible to maintain the distinction between the two timelines. Flynne's brother calls, and she discusses her action in the "game" (which is actually the future) with him in real time:

> Anything ever happen in this game?
> "Those cams," he said. "You edging them back?"
> "Yeah. And sort of a balcony's folded out. Long frosted glass window, lights on inside. Saw shadows of people."
> "Saw a blimp or something. Where's it supposed to be?"
> "Nowhere. Just keep those cams back." . . .
> She lunged at the bugs.[44]

Scenes like this fill the pages of Gibson's novel. Even when a chapter begins inside one timeline, the action soon blurs the boundaries between the two temporalities. Characters find themselves split between body and mind: they are physically present in one world, while cognitively inhabiting two timelines at once.

As the novel progresses, even the physical barriers to inhabiting multiple timelines begin to erode. Indeed, the most explicit figuration of simultaneity within the novel is "the peripheral" itself. The nonsentient robotic extensions of the novel's title, peripherals host the consciousness of individual characters so that they can inhabit the two timelines at once. Referred to as "anthropomorphic drone[s]" and "telepresence avatar[s]," the peripherals are "extensions," "accessories," and most important, a way for characters like Flynne to enter into the space of the future.[45] Many readings of Gibson's text focus on the affective nature of *The Peripheral*—that is, the author's move from the visual perception to touch, from mirror shades and virtual light glasses to the peripheral or the haptic.⁴⁶ We might also read Gibson's move to the peripheral as a move toward simultaneity. When Flynne enters the peripheral, she is mentally and physically in two temporalities at once. This registers on the affective and material levels. For example, the first time Flynne enters a peripheral, one of the other characters realizes that Flynne "completely altered the peripheral's body language."⁴⁷ "Inhabited," he explains, "its face became not hers but somehow her."⁴⁸ Flynne obtains sensory experience while inside the peripheral: "Flynne raised her hand, touched her face, not thinking. . . . Like touching herself through something that wasn't quite there."⁴⁹ At the same time, her body is still in the past, so her action in the future is continually interrupted by the "autonomic bleed-over" or the physical needs of her body: hunger, sleep, digestion, and so on.⁵⁰ Thus, the concept of the peripheral offers a literal translation of the cognitive experience of living in temporal simultaneity.

How do we make sense of this novelistic rendering of simultaneity? I want to propose that we not take for granted Gibson's insistence on science fiction as being the only tool kit capable of making sense of the present. With *The Peripheral*, Gibson crafts a novel that's form attempts to capture and represent the temporal experience of living in the now. In other words, through this process of temporal leveling, Gibson uses the form of his novel to disrupt that singular notion of time that we imagine to be somehow captured and contained by a manmade device we call a wristwatch. In an interview about the process of writing *The Peripheral*, Gibson reflected: "I'm continually grateful for not being in the middle of writing a physical time travel story like the ones that I'd grown up on. But as our geography slowly dissolves into the digital, then it gets very interesting. Because if you can sit in a hangar in Kansas and fly a drone bomber over Pakistan, and give yourself really bad jet lag by doing that long enough, where are we actually?"⁵¹ With this example, Gibson captures some of the ways humans currently inhabit multiple times at once. In this case, simultaneity works in service to the time of domination. Perhaps there are other moments of multiplicity that disrupt, interrupt, and intervene in the dominant form of time—moments that resist that notion of time that threatens to trap us within its temporal constraints. Perhaps this is the value of *The Peripheral*'s formal complexity.

Despite his rather bleak theorization of global entrapment in the time of domination, Rancière ended his 2011 lecture with a somewhat hopeful suggestion. "But I think," he suggests, "that it is possible to investigate the potentialities of art forms that work at the crossroads of temporalities and worlds of experience. I think it is possible to explore their capacity to echo what happens in the intervals and interruptions that tend to distend or disrupt the time of domination."[52] With *The Peripheral*, Gibson creates such an art form. Rather than succumb to the novelistic tendency toward progression and linearity, he crafts a novel that forces readers to confront two temporalities simultaneously. Indeed, for the characters in the novel, the future and the past are not one or stable—there are two possible (and perhaps many more) alternative futures. In the near-future the Jackpot has not yet happened but inevitably draws closer. In the far-future, the world is controlled by a wealthy global elite. Thus, Gibson's multiple temporalities imagine both the impending disaster of climate change and its aftermath while simultaneously imagining the future distribution of wealth and power under global capitalism. As Gibson admits, the ending of *The Peripheral* is far from happy; he refers to its last two chapters as "the creepiest stuff I've ever written."[53] On the aesthetic level, Gibson's project echoes the hopefulness of Rancière's provocative conclusion. *The Peripheral* demonstrates a narrative form that exposes the temporal contradictions of our present while leaving any sense of closure yet to be determined. If as Rancière suggests, "today, just as yesterday, the tension of living in several times at once remains unsolved," then perhaps Gibson's fiction helps us inhabit that tension as a path forward.[54]

CHAPTER 3 . . . **MATHIAS NILGES**

THE SHELF LIVES OF FUTURES

WILLIAM GIBSON'S SHORT FICTION AND
THE TEMPORALITY OF GENRE

"The sad truth of the matter is that SF has not been much fun of late," writes Bruce Sterling in 1986 in his preface to *Burning Chrome*, the collection of William Gibson's short fiction of the late 1970s and early 1980s.[1] In the late 1970s, Sterling continues, science fiction "was confused, self-involved, and stale."[2] The emergence of Gibson's work and its rise in the early 1980s, however, offers a glimmer of hope: "Gibson is one of our best harbingers of better things to come."[3] Sterling overstates the problem. After all, the 1970s certainly saw the proliferation of mass-market futurisms that continued to rehash those styles and forms of earlier periods largely in an attempt to pander to established markets, but it also witnessed the publication of seminal works of science fiction by authors like Ursula K. Le Guin and Samuel R. Delany, and in particular Delany's work, including novels like the stunningly inventive and formally groundbreaking *Dhalgren* (1975), which were crucial for Gibson's development as a writer and his development of cyberpunk style. Still, Sterling is right in stressing that the importance of Gibson's contribution to advancing science fiction during this historical moment can hardly be overstated. Beginning with his first short story, published in 1977, "Fragments of a Hologram Rose,"

Gibson's work has consistently driven out any staleness in science fiction through radical stylistic innovation, any sense of confusion through sharply focused commitment to deploying science fiction in the effort not just to tell tales of the future but to probe the foundations of the material and sociopolitical logic of our present by tracing those futures to which the present's trajectory may lead. "The triumph of [Gibson's early short stories]," Sterling finds, lies in "their brilliant, self-consistent evocation of a credible future."[4] In this context, Sterling makes an important observation: the realism of Gibson's early stories distinguishes them from other facets of science fiction at the time. Unlike Gibson, Sterling argues, other science fiction writers have been "ducking" the difficulty to which Gibson commits himself in his work when he seeks to find ways to mobilize the genre to grapple with, not escape, the real problems of a particular moment in history. This "intellectual failing" on the part of other authors, Sterling concludes, "accounts for the ominous proliferation of postapocalypse stories, sword-and-sorcery fantasies, and those everpresent space operas in which galactic empires slip conveniently back into barbarism." Unlike Gibson, that is, other writers seek refuge in styles and genres that allow them to "avoid tangling with a realistic future."[5]

In 2003, the publication of *Pattern Recognition*, the first novel in the Blue Ant or the Bigend trilogy, sent shockwaves through the literary world. Gibson had written a realist novel—or so it seemed. Revisiting Gibson's earliest stories suggest that this diagnosis is not quite accurate. Although it is true that early stories like "Fragments of a Hologram Rose" are significant in their contribution to the development of cyberpunk, they are also important insofar as they outline the methodological blueprints of Gibson's engagement with science fiction that came to determine virtually all of his works. Gibson's early short fiction performs a new kind of science fiction, but it also advances a theory of itself and of science fiction, for these stories ask crucially what science fiction is and how it may function under changing historical conditions. Whereas stories like "Burning Chrome" or "Fragments of a Hologram Rose" establish the general contours of Gibson's cyberpunk style, it is Gibson's seemingly least cyberpunky story, "The Gernsback Continuum," that outlines the (methodo)logical foundations of the author's engagement with science fiction in general and cyberpunk in particular. In the 1980s, Gibson, who came to be hailed the "godfather of cyberpunk," rejuvenated science fiction. This rejuvenation, as Sterling indicates, was about more than taking science fiction into a new stylistic direction. To be sure, Gibson's contributions to science fiction style and form are numerous and immensely significant, as Aron Pease and Charles Yu emphasize in this book. Yet as Pease and Yu also note, Gibson's stylistic and formal innovation has always also been a matter of exploring the workings of the sociopolitical realities of our present and our imaginative relation to it. The realism of Gibson's work is contained in its dedication to historicizing science fiction and itself, to the self-reflexive examination of the waxing and waning of futures, genres, and cultural imaginaries in relation to the flow of external history. Futures and genres have shelf lives, Gibson's work shows us. They emerge under particular historical conditions, in the context of which they allow us to respond to and make sense of the world developing before our eyes. Yet they will ultimately be exhausted by the flow of history. In the 1980s, Gibson's work provided us with a language and imaginary through which it became possible to speak to and understand the newly emerging world of globalization and with new futures appropriate to and critically reflective of the new postindustrial, late-capitalist present. Stories like "The Gernsback Continuum" outline the historical and political stakes of cyberpunk as the necessary departure from previously established literary and epistemological forms of futurity. We find the same methodological commitment in Gibson's later work. In the case of *Pattern Recognition*, the true import of this ongoing historicizing tension between realism and science fiction that is so crucial to Gibson's work cannot be accurately described as a change from cyberpunk to realism. Not only do we encounter in later novels the same tension between realism and science fiction that marked Gibson's earliest stories, but by understanding his earliest short stories as blueprints of a method to which he returns time and again, we can gain a deeper understanding of the complexities and stakes of his attention to the relation between history, our temporal imagination, and the development of the genre of science fiction.

Gibson's 1981 short story "The Gernsback Continuum" revolves around a young photographer who takes an assignment that involves photographing 1930s and 1940s architecture and industrial design. The photographs are intended to be included in the project of a young pop-art historian named Dialta Downes, who is preparing a book on "American

Streamline Moderne" with the working title *The Airstream Futuropolis: The Tomorrow That Never Was*. The value of this "uniquely American form of architecture," Downes believes, is that it contains the real-life remnants of an "alternate America: a 1980 that never happened."[6] Touring what Downes describes as "an architecture of broken dreams," the narrator is intrigued by the "secret ruins" of past future imagination that he discovers and cannot help but wonder "what the inhabitants of that lost future would think of the world [he] lived in."[7] The narrator is fascinated by the fact that Streamline Moderne is barely capable of hiding the superficiality of its imagination that remains confined to the limits of its capitalist present and by the clash between the present and this future that never was. One of the now axiomatic accounts of the workings of science fiction stresses the critical perspective and the process of examination that the genre is able to open up through the tension between our present and extrapolative futures. Gibson's short story, however, is interested in a different problem. What happens, the protagonist of the story begins to wonder, when past futures are exhausted by historical development and collide with the present? In what ways do futures that never came to be nevertheless exert a real influence on the present? The interrogation of the present in "Gernsback," in other words, is not set into motion by comparing what is to what may be, but it emerges from the contradiction between the existence and the absence in the present of what we once hoped would come to pass. Both the content and form of Gibson's story mediate not the tension between present and future but the tension between two versions of the present, the gap between which constructs a counternarrative of our historical present, a narrative of our time understood as a fallen future.

In a central moment in the story, the protagonist begins to understand the conditions that determine the exhaustion of future imaginaries and their associated aesthetics: "The Thirties dreamed white marble and slipstream chrome, immortal crystal and burnished bronze, but the rockets on the covers of the Gernsback pulps had fallen on London in the dead of night, screaming. After the war, everyone had a car—no wings for it—and the promised superhighway to drive it down, so that the sky itself had darkened, and the fumes ate the marble and pitted the miracle crystal."[8] Any given imagination of the future, along with its associated genres and styles, Gibson's story shows, will at some point crash into and be exhausted by the flow of history. Yet for the protagonist of Gibson's story, the problem of the tomorrow that never was is exacerbated by the fact that this tomorrow did not simply disappear or come to seem naive or outmoded. More significantly, Gibson's story shows, we face severe problems when the past's ideas of tomorrow become horrifically realized by history. Haunted by rocket shapes that resemble V2s instead of gleaming spaceships and by mirages of citizens of a future United States whose appearance invokes Aryan purity and power, the horror for the protagonist of Gibson's story lies in the realization that the dreams of the future whose ruins he encounters on his assignment were transformed from speculation to reality by the horrors of history. Futures, he realizes, may not simply become outdated as time passes. More important, their changed meaning indicates a changed relation to history and a new function in the present. At this point it becomes clear that we must take responsibility for our fictions of tomorrow, for the futures we imagine may, under new historical conditions, come to be intimately involved in and support a different set of real social, material, and political developments. The self-reflexivity of Gibson's story not only restores our attention to the waxing and waning of futures, it also assumes responsibility for their construction. This assumption of responsibility for the changing historical function of future imaginaries is what determines Gibson's work as a whole and what constitutes one of its most significant contributions to (and indeed accounts of) science fiction.

"Gernsback" also outlines the historical and political stakes of cyberpunk as the necessary departure from previous forms of imagining the future and the turn toward cyberpunk as a way of formulating ideas of time and futurity appropriate to their historical context. As Phillip E. Wegner notes, the emergence of cyberpunk has to be understood as a moment when traditional narratives of the future could no longer be maintained,[9] which, as Wegner also suspects, suggests that we may understand it as a utopian gesture in a genre that is popularly associated with dystopia, as a gesture that underscores Gibson's commitment to defending the significance of futurity and of the utopian imagination precisely as a matter of engaging with the time and historical function of futures. Historicizing changing conceptions of the future in relation to the present, the story shows, is no simple task, and it ultimately causes the narrator to "ever so gently" go over "the Edge."[10] One day, while photographing a building, the narrator makes a peculiar discovery. As he looks up, he notices a giant wing-liner in the sky, a sight that shocks him to his core. The flying object, a "twelve-engined thing like a bloated boomerang, all wing, thrumming its way east with an elephant grace," causes past, future, and present to collide, since it is one of the products of 1930s and 1940s sci-fi imagination that never came to pass and should not exist in his present.[11] Yet this encounter does not remain the only one of its kind. As the narrator continues to work on the assignment, a number of Streamline Moderne objects and eventually characters from classic science fiction novels and futuristic advertisements come to life and haunt the present. Waking up in his car after having fled to the desert to escape the past future that increasingly enters his present, the narrator is woken by the bright lights of a gigantic city that emerges behind his car, a city that appears to be the real-life version of one of the cities depicted in one of the books on 1930s design that he has been reading:

> Spire stood on spire in gleaming ziggurat steps that climbed to a central golden temple tower ringed with the crazy radiator flanges of the Mongo gas station. You could hide the Empire State Building in the smallest of those towers. Roads of crystal soared between the spires, crossed and recrossed by smooth silver shapes like beads of running mercury. The air was thick with ships: giant wing-liners, little darting silver things . . . mile-long blimps, hovering dragonfly things that were gyrocopters.[12]

However, the hallucination itself and its apparent claim over the narrator's mental health are not his main concern. Instead, the narrator is scared by the temporality attached to a couple standing next to his car, engaged in a conversation while overlooking the city:

> They were the children of Dialta Downes's '80s-that-wasn't; they were Heirs to the Dream. They were white, blond, and they probably had blue eyes. They were American. Dialta had said that the Future had come to America first, but had finally passed it by. But not here, in the heart of the Dream. Here we'd gone on and on, in a dream logic that knew nothing of pollution, the finite bounds of fossil fuel, or foreign wars it was possible to lose. They were smug, happy, and

utterly content with themselves in their world. And in the Dream, it was *their* world.¹³

Utterly terrified, the narrator seeks the help of his friend Merv Kihn, who advises the narrator to undergo "semiotic detox" by exposing himself to "really bad media" to "exorcise his semiotic ghosts."¹⁴ "Watch lots of television, particularly game shows and soaps," Merv advises him. "Go to porn movies. Ever see *Nazi Love Motel*? They've got it in cable, here. Really awful. Just what you need."¹⁵ This strategy provides the narrator with temporary relief and allows him to finish the assignment. In the story's closing sentences, we learn that even after submitting his pictures to Downes, he continues to spot wing-liners. Having learned from Merv how to temporarily get relief from the haunting presence of futures past, the narrator has a means of counteracting the confusing effect of the intrusion of the past future into the present. In the final paragraphs, the narrator spots another flying wing. He responds to this sighting by rushing to a newsstand to purchase as many magazines as possible on "the petroleum crisis and the nuclear energy hazard." Seeing the magazines the narrator intends to purchase, the proprietor of the newsstand comments: "hell of a world we live in, huh? . . . But it could be worse, huh?" "That's right," the narrator responds, "or even worse, it could be perfect." The story ends with the narrator walking away from the newsstand, carrying the stack of magazines, the "little bundle of condensed catastrophe" that provides him with a defense against the threat of the past future.¹⁶

Past futures continue to haunt and influence the present. Gibson's story explores what may be done to address this problem, one that is crucial not only for writers of science fiction but for our ability to engage with and imagine alternatives to the problems of our present. What Gibson offers in his story and what constitutes one of the foundations of his work more generally, may be described with what Walter Benjamin calls "a Brechtian maxim": "don't start from good old days but the bad new ones."¹⁷ Cyberpunk marks one of the beginning points of the commitment to the struggle with the bad new days whose conclusion we find in Gibson's recent novels. What Gibson's recent novels offer us, from the Blue Ant trilogy to *The Peripheral* (2014) and *Agency* (2020) that even in their own relation rework the temporal relationship to the present and to each other as texts in a trilogy that refuses the traditionally linear conception of prequels and sequels, is a continuation of the argument that his earliest short stories introduce: these texts locate utopia and change themselves in the active confrontation with the present's bad new days that asks us to imagine the time of futurity itself in new ways, beyond the linear futures embodied by the luminous, glimmering verticality of the architecture of futures past. Semiotic detox, the attempt to exorcise the reified form of dehistoricized, static forms of futurism that as semiotic ghosts haunt the story's narrator, is therefore the attempt to free futurity from its collapse into the present, a way to historicize what it may mean to imagine tomorrow under new historical conditions by working through the contradictions of the now. "Gernsback" makes a crucial contribution to the advancement of science fiction, and it contains an account of science fiction that is significant for critical examinations of the genre. Gibson's work models in form and content one of the fundamental principles of the idea of literary genre, which, as Hayden White reminds us, is a category that may "lack a 'nature' or 'essence'" but "has a history."[18] In other words, Gibson's story foregrounds that the genre of science fiction is better understood in its historical development than as a category with a stable content. Just like the protagonist in Gibson's story is forced to reckon with the historical specificity and constant fluidity of the idea of the future, the genre itself, whose logic the story mediates, can only be grasped in its historical development. The question of what science fiction is, in other words, is always to be understood as inextricably linked to the question of what science fiction does. Gibson's story shows that these connected questions must always be posed in relation to history. Much like the question "what is the future?," the question "what is science fiction?" always inevitably also raises another on whose answer it depends: "when is science fiction?"

In recent years, as Gordon Hutner has argued, literary criticism has tasked itself with the project of "historicizing the contemporary," a project that is partly motivated by the attempt to make sense of recent formal and generic developments in literature and culture.[19] Critics have wondered how recent historical changes are bound up with and give form to contemporary culture. Gibson's work, beginning with his early short stories, offers us answers to precisely those questions that give rise to some of the most vibrant debates in contemporary literary criticism. Gibson continually works at the rifts and fissures of our historical understanding of periods, of our established conceptions of the future and "the contemporary," and of our temporal imaginary more widely conceived. As a consequence, by examining the general and formal developments in Gibson's work that at every point offer self-reflexive accounts of the historical logic that underwrites and necessitates these changes, we are able to better understand the major shifts and developments in recent culture. Gibson's work has always been about the attempt to historicize the contemporary, and it is not just of great significance for the development of science fiction and contemporary literature but, I suggest, insofar as its self-reflexive engagements with its methodology and possibility forwards striking theories of science fiction and literature, it is also of significant value to recent discussions regarding literary critical methodology.

As I show elsewhere in some detail, the past two decades or so have been characterized by a wave of examinations of what commentators across disciplines as well as mainstream analysis and popular culture have come to understand as a crisis of temporality and futurity.[20] Peter Osborne, for example, suggests that "what seems distinctive and important about the changing temporal quality of the historical present over the last decades is... a coming together not simply 'in' time... but rather the present is increasingly characterized by a coming together of *different but equally 'present' temporalities or 'times'... a disjunctive unity of present times*."[21] During the 1990s, we witnessed the spread of the association of our present with a crisis of futurity and the collapse of different temporalities, including established notions of futurity, into a present to which it seems difficult to imagine alternatives after the exhaustion of previous, more hopeful ideas of tomorrow. "The future, always so clear to me, had become like a black highway at night," Sarah Connor, protagonist of *Terminator 2* notes, adding that we seem to be "in uncharted territory now, making up history as we [go] along." Not surprisingly, this crisis of temporality brought with it crises of representation and crises of narrative. After all, as Richard Terdiman stresses, "narratives are models for time," which "figure the conflict between desire and what thwarts it."[22] "Such dialectics of desire," he concludes, "define what we hope time will bring and what we fear forestalls such fortune."[23]

While some commentators (like Neil deGrasse Tyson) seek to reignite futurology by way of nostalgic returns to previous moments in history when we had not yet "stopped dreaming,"[24] Gibson has been well aware of the significant crises that result from the exhaustion not of dreaming itself but of those conceptions of the future to which we had become accustomed. Years before theorists and commentators began to decry the current crisis of futurity, Gibson's short story already offered diagnoses of its origin. Far from leaving us unable to dream or imagine the future, "Gernsback" shows that we must trace the struggle with our present and its associated crisis of futurity in relation to the exhaustion of established futures. As the protagonist experiences, when futures crash, we not only lose images of a world to come, we are confronted with a situation in which it is precisely narrative that is called on to grapple with our crisis of imagination and furnish us with new models for time. Instead of lamenting a past that still allowed us to dream, Gibson historicizes those dreams and foregrounds the dangers they may harbor. Urging us to find ways to move forward by dealing with our bad new days, "Gernsback," a story that may be as timely in our own moment as in the context of its original publication, shows us that we have not stopped dreaming but more accurately our dreams were exhausted or indeed realized by history.

No doubt, this realization may initially seem apocalyptic and cause for dismay and crises of futurity as it does for the story's protagonist. But it is precisely under such conditions that the work of science fiction assumes a particular importance and may answer a call that resonates beyond the works of literature. What Gibson's story showcases and what we may be able to appreciate with renewed urgency from the vantage point of our present, is the crucial work of science fiction as a creator of thought and ideas that allow us to make sense of and come to terms with new historical conditions. Gibson's early short fiction establishes a constant in his work: for him, science fiction serves as a form of critique of the present and of itself and of those futures that dominate our cultural and indeed social and political imagination in a given moment in history. The confrontation with the "bad new days" of the protagonist's historical moment out of which new futurity can emerge stands in direct opposition to the images of outmoded futures, such as reruns of "old eroded newsreels" narrated in "static-ridden Hollywood baritone" that tell the protagonist "that there was A Flying Car in Your Future."[25] What has passed, the story leaves no doubt, are those futures imagined by "completely uninhibited technophiles," futures that historical progress has unmasked as at best naive and at worst as complicit in late modernity's wars and social horrors.[26] In such a situation, the story asks at the outset, how might we imagine, talk, and write about the future when those styles and narratives we had come to imagine as definitive of, as inextricably linked to the very conception of futurity have collapsed into "an uncaring present?"[27] Gibson's story asks what it means to write science fiction in a present that is haunted by the remnants of futures past and that struggles to replace our old images of tomorrow. The self-reflexive commitment to engaging in a critique of itself that marks "Gernsback" is a precondition for science fiction's ability to function as a form of critique of the historical present. And the latter, Gibson's continuous attention to the relation between science fiction and realism shows, in turn drives the historical development of science fiction.

It is important to foreground that Gibson's commitment to historicizing science fiction and our conceptions of the future brings strong political convictions. "Gernsback" is a story about the shelf lives of futures, but it is also about the lure of populism. In this sense, it may be said that this particular story is possibly more important today than during its initial publication. What "Gernsback" shows and what Gibson's dedication to historicizing the future in his career indicates is that the future is not simply the time or empty thought-space in which the utopian imagination may play itself out. The future is not automatically progressive. As Downes understands all too well, it can also, seemingly paradoxically, collapse into populist regression. "The Thirties had seen the first generation of American industrial designers," she notes; along with standardized objects for consumer capitalism, these designers generated a standardized version of the future, one that was less aimed at imagining a different world than at developing a futuristic aesthetics for capitalist mass production.[28] "Until the Thirties, all pencil sharpeners had looked like pencil sharpeners," Downes explains—"your basic Victorian mechanism, perhaps with a curlicue of decorative trim."[29] "After the advent of designers," things changed: "some pencil sharpeners looked like they had been put together in wind tunnels. For the most part, the change was only skin-deep; under the streamlined chrome shell, you'd find the same

Victorian mechanism. . . . The designers," Downes notes, "were populists, you see; they were trying to give the public what it wanted. What the public wanted was the future."[30] Reducing futurity and the utopian imagination to populism, industrial design binds a particular aesthetics of the future to industrial capitalism.

Gibson's story foregrounds the importance of science fiction not only as a way to trace the relation between futurist aesthetics, its politics, and its relation to changes in material history, but also to illustrate that in science fiction we can locate a method for working through the impasses of the present that are elsewhere understood as resulting in stagnation and paralysis. We may understand Gibson's work and its trademark dialectic of speculation and realism that I examine elsewhere in some length as a concrete manifestation of Ernst Bloch's famous assertion that "all historical concerns want to and can live only in the now-time of history."[31] Gibson's particular brand of science fiction always asks: what is science fiction now? This question entails a second facet, one that speaks to the ontology of literature. Indeed, in the context of Gibson's self-reflexive science fiction, literariness reveals itself precisely as those qualities endemic to literature that allow it to mediate historical crises, to work through formal crises that exist in other forms of thought via its unique formal processes. Fusing this notion of literariness and literature's immanent temporality and simultaneous relation to external historical structures produces what, in reference to Alain Badiou, we can call the "literary situation." Badiou describes the philosophical situation as the point at which the philosopher finds "in the present, the signs that point to the need for a new problem, a new invention."[32] The creation of new thought, as Terdiman also indicates, may be understood as the narrative creation of new problems out of signs of the present, a commitment that Gibson's work models for us particularly strikingly. If we understand literariness as intimately connected to the formal reconfiguration (not merely the representation) of structural contradictions in the present through narrative, then in this way, too, we are able to appreciate the immense contribution that Gibson's work makes to science fiction and contemporary literature in general.

As suggested, there is much to be gained from understanding the crises of temporality that are widely associated with our moment in history not as a crisis of but as a reminder of the importance of literature. In his essay "One, Two, Many Ends of Literature," Nicholas Brown suggests that currently once again popular proclamations of the end of literature confront us with a fundamental question: how do we talk about the end of literature? This question is significant, Brown argues, because "literature is built around an impossibility, an impasse internal to it."[33] Reminding us of the constitutive function of catastrophe in Gibson's short story, Brown further writes:

> this means that the end of literature is, in fact, a condition of its possibility. If the representational problem at the heart of the literary were solved (rather than abandoned in its literary form, which is always a possibility), we would no longer be talking about literature. We would be gods or, no less fantastically, we would be in possession of Borges's Aleph. The contradictions internal to literature (as with those internal to capitalism) are immanently its end in that their resolution would entail its supersession, but they are also the precondition for its functioning.[34]

The crises with which Gibson grapples beginning with his early short fiction, crises of futurity that are bound up with the constant struggle of aesthetic projects to close the gap between literary work and history, subject and object, are therefore to be understood not as the endpoint but as one of the ends of literature and our imagination of the future. The constant crisis existing in always new ways between subject and object that is mediated by the immanent formal and generic development of Gibson's fiction and its constant tension between realism and science fiction therefore emerges as crucial to science fiction's account of itself and its theory of literariness as outlined in stories like "Gernsback." In other words, this tension is what Gibson's stories lay bare by breaking down science fiction's conditions of constitutive (im)possibility into its present determinations and its temporal forms. We thus not only see the tenses of form as one of the key projects of science fiction. Rather, these tenses of form emerge and simultaneously give rise to the tenses of science fiction's possibility.

This account of science fiction's historically specific and historicizing ontology of "Gernsback" is linked to the logic of literary history. Jonathan Arac observes that "Fredric Jameson's slogan 'always historicize!' exercises such power because the claim of history urges us toward the unreachable totality, so that to invoke history is always to ask for more."[35] This relation to totality or to futurity as science fiction's sublime object introduces the category of time inevitably into the logical process and—as with literature, whose limits constitute its ends—out of the constantly formally changing processes of "asking for more" emerges the temporality we understand as history. The substantial contribution of Gibson's remarkable short story lies in its illustration of the simultaneous operations and contradictions that make up the process we call literary history, in which the tenses of form emerge from and determine the distinctions between the new and the now, a distinction whose formal specificities endows literature with the ability to fail productively—that is, literariness is a term we can use to refer to literature's specific forms of failure that distinguish it from other forms of allegory and other forms of thought. By extension, literary history is neither the history of equilibria, of periods, of chronology, of a continuum, nor of residual, dominant, and emergent forces and structures. Instead, it is the history of literature's constitutive impossibility, its immanent crises and the dialectical relation of immanent crises and external crises that remain formally linked, yet whose internal formal differences allow literature to work out problems in ways other forms of thought cannot. Theodor Adorno famously suggests that "the unsolved antagonisms of reality return in artworks as immanent problems of form."[36] We may understand Gibson's rejuvenation and his contribution to the development of science fiction as an expression of just this point. Gibson's work insists on the value of science fiction as a form of critique that operates through a process of critical self-interrogation bound up with those formal and generic changes that can lay bare the contradictions of the historical present. Instead of merely diagnosing or lamenting moments of exhaustion and paralysis, crises of futurity, imagination, and narrative, Gibson's work shows that the problems posed by crises of futurity may be answered by reminding ourselves of the power of narrative in general and science fiction in particular to generate new vocabularies and new imaginaries via which we may speak to and make sense of new historical conditions. In this way, too, Gibson's work restores our attention to literature's conditions of possibility.

CHAPTER 4 ... TAKAYUKI TATSUMI

***THE DIFFERENCE ENGINE* IN
A POST-ENLIGHTENMENT CONTEXT**

FRANKLIN, EMERSON, AND GIBSON AND STERLING

The Difference Engine and the Cold War

When Gibson and Sterling published their collaboratively written novel, *The Difference Engine*, in 1990, it was natural for readers of science fiction to consider it each writer's magnum opus.[1] What they joined forces to represent is an alternate-history year 1855, when Great Britain is empowered by steam-driven computer networks based on distinguished mathematician Charles Babbage's perfection of the Analytical Engine, when people enjoy writing on steam-driven typewriters, watching steam-driven TV, making use of steam-driven credit cards, and even being annoyed by steam-driven computer viruses composed by flash clackers (akin to today's computer hackers). Here, the Duke of Wellington, the Tory prime minister, attempted to repress the emerging class of scientists and intellectuals (savants) and industrials. He is assassinated by a bomb, whereupon the Romantic genius Lord George Gordon Byron's Industrial Radicals take over. Lord Byron's daughter Augusta Ada Byron, later countess of Lovelace, who collaborates with Babbage to produce the first computer in the world and is admired in the twentieth century as the founding mother of computer programming, achieves the charismatic status of Queen of Engines and Queen of Fashion. Byron's friend Percy Bysshe Shelley is a defeated Luddite sympathizer who loses his political influence. John Keats is very active as a "kinotropist," a steam visualist. The utopian idea of pantisocracy invites major Romanticists William Wordsworth and Samuel Taylor Coleridge to found a new nation, Susquehanna Phalanstery, in North America. Distinguished German philosopher Karl Marx, who coauthored *The Communist Manifesto* in 1848 with Friedrich Engels, establishes a communist commune in Manhattan. Moreover, Japanese leading intellectuals, such as Yukichi Fukuzawa and Arinori Mori from Meirokusha (Meiji 6 Society), an intellectual team organized in the sixth year of the Meiji era for the purposes of civilization and enlightenment, visit Britain to import steam-driven computer devices.

Despite a variety of historical figures whose lives Gibson and Sterling take the liberty of modifying in the context of alternate Great Britain, the novel's plot, which centers around the McGuffin quest, is as simple as the Holy Grail quest. This plot begins with an episode of the first chapter's protagonist, Sybil Gerard, the ruined daughter of executed Luddite agitator Walter Gerard, who happens to obtain a box containing the secret program Modus, composed by her master and flash clacker, Dandy Mick Radley, which might turn this alternate Pax Britannica upside down. The Modus bears the name of McGuffin in the novel, which is handed down from key person to key person, ending up with the amazing revelation of the secret of the whole alternate historical world.

Of course, literary history tells us that once an epoch-making masterpiece is published, it often mystifies contemporary readers so deeply as to be neglected in the darkness of history. In retrospect, when *The Difference Engine* was released in 1990, fans of cyberpunk who had expected Gibson and Sterling to keep demonstrating the cutting edge of postinternet computer culture were more or less disappointed by their collaboration. Hoping to make use of cyberpunk writers' works for promoting advanced capitalist society in the heyday of internet journalism, these fans were puzzled by the book's alternative Victorian age. However, as time went on, what Gibson and Sterling did in the collaboration gradually came to be evaluated correctly. Despite a long controversy over whether *The Difference Engine* is cyberpunk or steampunk, this mega-novel has gained importance as a work classified as hardcore cyberpunk in the disguise of steampunk. Remember Sterling and Lewis Shiner's alternate historical tale "Mozart in Mirrorshades" (1985), and you will easily understand that cyberpunk writers gradually came to put more emphasis on time than on space.

Thus, in my introduction to the Japanese edition of *The Difference Engine* (1991), translated by Hisashi Kuroma, which started with a note on *Back to the Future 3* (1990) featuring a typical mad scientist Emmett Lathrop "Doc" Brown's steam-driven time machine, I unwittingly attempted to make the novel intelligible enough by intertwining it with this Hollywood blockbuster film. The emergence of the radically brand-new in literary history is usually considered unintelligible by its contemporaries. Left in Victorian America, Doc renovated a steam locomotive into a gorgeously embellished steam-driven time machine, with which he and his family—his wife, Clara Clayton, an avid reader of scientific adventures, and their two kids, Jules and Verne—time-traveled to see Marty and his girlfriend, Jennifer, in 1985, nearly 100 years ahead. Indeed, *Back to the Future* (1985) featured Marty's time travel between 1985 and 1955, when he amazed Doc by telling him that in 1980, twenty-five years later, Ronald Reagan, who was well known in the 1950s for being only a B-class movie star, was to serve as the fortieth president of the United States. In the late 1980s, Reagan, who was deeply aware of the possibilities of "computer chip" and "satellite broadcasting," in a speech at Moscow State University delivered on May 31, 1988, joined forces with Mikhail Gorbachev to deconstruct the huge binary opposition between the Soviet Union and the United States, but we cannot doubt that the mid-1980s cyberpunk spirit of Lo Tek in cyberspace and junkyard went so far as to affect the political authorities embodying the Cold War. Thus, we may assume that early 1990s steampunk alternative history, coinciding with the steam-driven time machine in *Back to the Future 3*, pioneered the frontier of creative anachronism in the process of the collapse of the Soviet Union, that is, the collapse of the Cold War system, which invited Francis Fukuyama to speculate on "the end of history" in post-Hegelian fashion.

Put simply, between the fall of the Berlin Wall in 1989 and the collapse of the Soviet Union in 1991, 1990 saw a paradigm shift from territorial clear-cut binary opposition to temporal chaotic inconsistency. It is no coincidence that *The Difference Engine* and Michael Crichton's bestseller *Jurassic Park* were published in the same year; they shared a deep interest in chaos theory as a tool for reconstructing history that, in both novels, their chapters are simply titled "The First Iteration," "The Second Iteration," "The Third Iteration," and so on. Whereas the former's chaos theory begins with the archeology of artificial intelligence in Victorian America, the latter's centers around the idea of technologization of paleontology in a postmodern theme park. In the heyday of new historicism and postcolonialism around 1990, the concept of time got more and more plastic.

The Bicentenary of *Frankenstein*, or, the Secret Origin of Cyberpunk

To meditate on the structure of time in alternate history, we had better start by reconsidering an alternate literary history of science fiction. It has often been pointed out that although it features a number of historical figures ranging from Samuel Taylor Coleridge to Charles Babbage and Ada Lovelace, *The Difference Engine* strangely lacks reference to Mary Shelley, whose novel *Frankenstein; or, the Modern Prometheus* (1818) is regarded as the origin of science fiction and whose story of artificial intelligence in Victorian England cannot help but recall the fate of the steam-driven computer in *The Difference Engine*. Of course, *Frankenstein* was published in 1818, two decades earlier than Babbage's blueprint of the analytical engine in 1837. Given that Mary Shelley passed away in 1851, it is highly plausible that in the 1830s she could have known Babbage's idea supported by Lovelace, the first computer programmer. They are, after all, Victorian contemporaries. Gibson and Sterling's collaboration could well be called their revision of Frankenstein's monster in the postcyberpunk age. Somewhere between the bicentenary of *Frankenstein* and the thirtieth anniversary of *The Difference Engine*, a radical rereading of these novels will enrich our understanding of each.

The place to start should be with Benjamin Franklin, one of the Founding Fathers of the United States and one of the greatest inspirations for Shelley. Franklin remains one of the most famous Americans, for he is featured on the back of the $100 bill, the most expensive currency in the United States. Although he never served as president of the United States, Franklin is still admired as a major voice of the American Revolution who ended up creating the testing ground for democracy. Despite

D. H. Lawrence's modernist critique of Franklin, in which Lawrence boasts of being "many men,"[2] Franklin himself had already been famous for being "many men": he was a printer, journalist, tall-tale-teller, philosopher, scientist, inventor, musician, statesman, and "self-made man," among other things. In this respect, Franklin has long been compared with Yukichi Fukuzawa featured in *The Difference Engine*, for the latter is one of the Founding Fathers of modern Japan, well known for being as multifaceted as the former: he is a philosopher, educator, journalist, translator, and entrepreneur. Fukuzawa is featured on the ¥10,000 bill, the most expensive bill in Japan. Simply put, Franklin and Fukuzawa still remain significant, for both of them contributed much to establishing modern nations based on the vision of the Enlightenment.

What matters today is the fact that Immanuel Kant, the greatest champion of the European Enlightenment, cautioned people against defying the natural order of things and was keenly aware of Franklin's achievements. In his 1755 essay, "The Modern Prometheus," Kant states: "There is such a thing as right *taste* in natural science, which knows how to distinguish the wild extravagances of unbridled curiosity from cautious judgements of reasonable credibility. From the Prometheus of recent times Mr. Franklin, who wanted to disarm the thunder, down to the man who wants to extinguish the fire in the workshop of Vulcanus, all these endeavors result in the humiliating reminder that Man never can be anything more than a man."[3] Kant clearly refers to Franklin's kite experiment in 1752 that proved thunder to be the effect of electrical discharge, not the anger of God that had long humbled colonial Puritans in New England. Hence the lightning rod symbolized the age of the Enlightenment. Yukichi Fukuzawa, following Franklin's example, did not form a strong attachment to religions but Unitarianism, the backbone of the Enlightenment as represented by Thomas Jefferson, another Founding Father of the United States.

I do not want to undertake a comparative study of Enlightenment Unitarians. What should be stressed here is that, inspired by Kant's article "The Modern Prometheus," which was published three years after Franklin's experiment, Shelley titled her novel *Frankenstein; or, the Modern Prometheus*. Given that Dr. Frankenstein's monster is born with the help of lightning, it is plausible that Shelley had Franklin in mind.

Let me illustrate the point by showing how Franklin's demystification of lightning enlightened Shelley's Dr. Frankenstein. Although deeply fascinated with the wild fancies of old alchemical philosophers such as Cornelius Agrippa, Paracelsus, and Albertus Magnus, Dr. Frankenstein is enlightened by a "most violent and terrible thunder-storm" he witnesses in Bellerive, Jura, in Switzerland:

> It [the thunder-storm] advanced from behind the mountains of Jura; and the thunder burst at once with frightful loudness from various quarters of the heavens. I remained, while the storm lasted, watching its progress with curiosity and delight. As I stood at the door, on a sudden I beheld a stream of fire issue from an old and beautiful oak, which stood about twenty yards from our house; and so soon as the dazzling light vanished, the oak had disappeared, and nothing remained but a blasted stump. When we visited it the next morning, we found the tree shattered in a singular manner. It was not splintered by the shock, but entirely reduced to thin ribbands of wood. I never beheld any thing so utterly destroyed.
>
> The catastrophe of this tree excited my extreme astonishment; and I eagerly inquired of my father the nature and origin of thunder and lightning. He replied, "Electricity;" describing at the same time the various effects of that power. He constructed a small electrical machine, and exhibited a few experiments; he made also a kite, with a wire and string, which drew down that fluid from the clouds.
>
> This last stroke completed the overthrow of Cornelius Agrippa, Albertus Magnus, and Paracelsus, who had so long reigned the lords of my imagination.[4]

This experience invited the protagonist to create a human being by making use of the art of "bestowing animation upon lifeless matter," that is, animating the amalgam of dead men's parts. We should pay attention to the spark of life, a kind of lightning as the spirit of the Enlightenment:

> It was on a dreary night of November, that I beheld the accomplishment of my toils. With an anxiety that almost amounted to agony, *I collected the instruments of life around me, that I might infuse a spark of being into the lifeless thing that lay at my feet.* It was already one in the morning; the rain pattered dismally against the panes, and

my candle was nearly burnt out, when, by the glimmer of the half-extinguished light, I saw the dull yellow eye of the creature open; it breathed hard, and a convulsive motion agitated its limbs.[5]

It is safe to assume that what Victor Frankenstein calls "a spark of being" is nothing other than the effect of electricity. Nonetheless, the creature turned out to be so disgusting that, "unable to endure the aspect of the being" he had created, Dr. Frankenstein "rushed out of the room." Later, the creature fled his master's laboratory.

I have emphasized Franklin's significance not simply because his experiment with the kite inspired Shelley to imagine Dr. Frankenstein, a man obsessed with the idea of creating a human being, but also because he served as a kind of hacker/flash clacker in terms of Gibson and Sterling's Great Britain, who unwittingly constructed the discourse of alternate history. As the *Whole Earth Review*, a descendant of the legendary countercultural magazine the *Whole Earth Catalog* inaugurated in 1968, featured Franklin in mirror shades in its cover illustration for the summer 1991 issue, this Founding Father could well be redefined as the father of all the hackers, capable of thieving data and rewriting programs just like Case and Bobby in Gibson's Sprawl trilogy and Dandy Mick Radley in *The Difference Engine*. Although the mother of science fiction re-created Franklin in Frankenstein, cyberpunk champions wanted to feature skillful hackers Shelley failed in describing who are all the children of Franklin, not Frankenstein. This is the reason *The Difference Engine* does not mention Mary Shelley and her masterpiece.

Franklin's Monster: From Self-Made Man to Man-Made Self

If you read Benjamin Franklin's text very closely, you will witness moments that convince you that although he has long been popular as a typically American self-made man, Franklin also created a man-made self. What Shelley's subtitle "the Modern Prometheus" tells us is that she is indebted to Kant's interpretation of Franklin and that she was inspired by how Franklin created quite a few man-made selves, if unlike Dr. Frankenstein's monster. First, let us reread the poem "Epitaph," composed in 1728, when Franklin was only twenty-two years old:

The Body of
B. Franklin Printer,
(Like the Cover of an Old Book) Its Contents torn out
And stript of its Lettering and Gilding)
Lies here, Food for Worms.
But the Work shall not be lost;
For it will, (as he believe'd) appear once more,
In a new & more elegant Edition,
Revised and corrected
By the Author.[6]

What amazes us most is not so much the youth of the author but his vision of himself as a book that will be revised and reprinted in the future. At seventeen, with little money in his pocket but already an expert printer, he proceeded to make his way in the world, subject to the usual "errata," as he often called his mistakes, but confident that he could profit from lessons learned and not repeat them. Franklin retains this idea consistently until he writes his autobiography in 1771 at the age of sixty-five: "That felicity, when I reflected on it, has induced me sometimes to say, that were it offered to my choice, I should have no objection to a repetition of the same life from its beginning, only asking the advantage authors have in a second edition to correct some faults of the first."[7] Once again, Franklin defines his life as correctible and modifiable, that is, plastic. To put it simply, while Franklin as a human must pass away someday, his life as a book will keep getting updated and surviving the predicament of the ages. Franklin is mortal, but his life as a book will remain immortal, just like artificial intelligence. In this respect, I completely agree with Lawrence, who in the first version of *Studies in Classic American Literature* (1918–1919) reconsidered Franklin not just as "the perfect human being of Godwin"[8] but as "the very Son of Man, man made by the power of the human will, a virtuous Frankenstein monster."[9]

Here we have to remember that Franklin is well known by a variety of pseudonyms, such as Silence Dogood, the persona of a middle-aged widow, under whose name he submitted some satirical essays to his brother's newspaper, the *New England Courant*, at the age of sixteen; and Richard Saunders, the author of *Poor Richard's Almanac*, filled with maxims, most of which he created himself, for achieving wealth and preaching hard work and thrift.

His most problematic pseudonym is Polly Baker, in his radical feminist article "The Speech of Miss Polly Baker" (1747), who was once accused of having illegitimate children but who criticized bachelors in colonial America who did not want to get married. Based on the Enlightenment discourse of deism that gives priority to Nature over God, Polly Baker's speech is so logical and powerful as to attract a wider audience on both sides of the Atlantic. Thus, despite the pseudonymous persona, Polly Baker, once dismissed as a ruined woman, promptly gained fame as a kind of virtual idol who championed a kind of protofeminist philosophy recalling Nathaniel Hawthorne's Hester Prynne in *The Scarlet Letter* (1850) but also Gibsonian characters like Molly Millions in *Neuromancer* and Sybil Gerard in *The Difference Engine*.

Nonetheless, we may locate the true reason for her creation in the author's biography. In 1730, Franklin unofficially married Deborah Read, the daughter of his first landlady. But in the next year he came to have an illegitimate child, and Read accepted Franklin's son William into the household. It is ironic that while Franklin becomes one of the Founding Fathers of the United States, William later became governor of New Jersey and a Loyalist during the American Revolution. Franklin published the Polly Baker hoax, not necessarily because he hoped to construct a protofeminist discourse but because his extramarital affair required him to compose a virtually feminist speech as a correction of the great errata in life. What matters here is that whatever the reason, the persona Polly Baker came to have her own life as a pre-Frankenstein monster, capturing the imagination of Enlightenment America. Although the colonial Puritans developed a fear of challenging the Judeo-Christian God as the origin of everything, the Founding Fathers demystified the British monarch, as well as the idea of an angry God, by championing deism and Unitarianism as the background of the Enlightenment. To be more precise, as Gordon Wood points out, Franklin had spent a couple of years in London from 1724 to 1726 and only wished to become a gentleman. In 1748, at the age of forty-two, Franklin believed he had acquired sufficient wealth and gentility to retire from active business. Thus, he could finally become a gentleman, a man of leisure who no longer had to work for a living.[10] Nonetheless, in the course of events he was needed to join and lead the American Revolution, giving up the plan of spending his later years as a Loyalist gentleman. Therefore, the portrait of a failed gentleman helped invent the myth of Franklin as a self-made man. However, Franklin the self-made man succeeded in producing a man-made self; he accomplished it by animating the pseudonymous characters. Franklin not only created but also became his own monster, as Lawrence pointed out in his aborted version of *Studies in Classic American Literature*. However illegitimate he or she is, Franklin's monster, or his own monstrous self, gets unbound as the modern Prometheus, observing the biblical duty, as Polly Baker notes: "Encrease and Multiply." This is the revised version of "Be fruitful, multiply, and replenish the earth, and subdue it" (Genesis 1:28).

What Franklin created here is the discourse of revisionism pervading the winner's history of the United States. Insofar as you are living in the winner's country, it is possible to rewrite history quite radically and conceal inconvenient truth. For example, the *Norton Anthology of American Literature*, the most comprehensive anthology in the field, takes the liberty of ignoring the Philippine America War and the Korean War, for they caused inconvenience to the winner's history defending life, liberty, and the pursuit of happiness. Of course, today liberal intellectuals consider historical revisionism incredibly risky. Do not forget how American audiences have enjoyed the *Back to the Future* trilogy, in which the director takes the liberty of revising history. In this respect, Doc's admiration of Franklin, clear from his portrait exhibited on the wall of the laboratory, should not be ignored; Doc must have been conscious of Franklin not only as a talented inventor of the lightning rod but as a historical revisionist rationalizing time travel. Cultivating the way from self-made man to man-made self and inventing the all-American discourse of historical revisionism, Franklin deserves the name of protocyberpunk author of alternate history.

Time Considered as a Chaotic Steam Fog: Toward Cyber-Transcendentalism

At this point, let me reconsider how Gibson and Sterling's novel describes Yukichi Fukuzawa, the Japanese Franklin, and his colleagues trying to import the steam-driven computer into Meiji Japan. When journalist

Lawrence Oliphant and paleontologist Edward Mallory are introduced to the Japanese intellectuals, headed by Fukuzawa, in the service of "His Imperial Majesty the Mikado of Japan," they are astonished at the Japanese gynoid crafted by the Hosokawa family and presented to them as a royal gift for Her Britannic Majesty:

> Bligh handed Mr [Koan] Matsuki a whisky bottle; Mr Matsuki began to decant it into an elegant ceramic jug, at the right hand of the Japanese woman. She made no response. Mallory began to wonder if she were ill, or paralyzed. Then Mr Matsuki fitted the little jug into her right hand with a sharp wooden click. He rose, and fetched a gilded crank-handle. He stuck the device into the small of her back and began to twist it, his face expressionless. A high-pitched coiling sound emerged from the woman's innards.
> "She is a dummy!" Mallory blurted.
> "More a marionette, actually," Oliphant said. "The proper term is 'automaton,' I believe."
> Mallory drew a breath. "I see! Like one of those Jacuot-Droz toys, or Vaucanson's famous duck, eh?" . . .
> The automaton began pouring drinks. There was a hinge within her robed elbow, and a second in her wrist; she poured whisky with a gentle slither of cables and a muted wooden clicking. "She moves much like an Engine-guided Maudsley lathe," Mallory noted. "Is that where they got the plans?"
> "No, she's entirely native," said Oliphant. Mr Matsuki was passing little ceramic cups of whisky down the table. "Not a bit of metal in her—all bamboo, and braided horsehair, and whalebone springs. The Japanese have known how to make such dolls for many years—*karakuri*, they call them."[11]

By exhibiting the execution of their own archetypal AI, the founding fathers of modern Japan astonished the British intellectuals, who had enjoyed the heyday of steam-driven cybercivilization. As Arinori Mori explains after the demonstration of the gynoid, in this alternate history it is not America but Britain that "opened our ports with the iron fleet."[12] Deeply obliged to Great Britain, Fukuzawa states very nobly, "We will be allies with you. . . . The Britain of Asia will bring civilization and enlightenment to all Asian peoples."[13] To further centralize Great Britain and render the United States peripheral in this alternate history, Gibson and Sterling deprive distinguished US commodore Matthew Perry of the honor of opening Japan in 1853, characterizing the heroine Sybil as sympathetic with Sam Houston, the political refugee from the independent state of Texas. Given that Gibson and Sterling are products of the American South (Gibson from South Carolina, Sterling from Texas), *The Difference Engine* is set in the mid-1850s as an alternate history composed from the Southern perspective, in which the Civil War does not happen yet. Nonetheless, we should not neglect discourses of postwar Japanese productivity and success, embodied in such texts as Ezra F. Vogel's *Japan as No. 1*, as a hidden agenda of the novel.[14] In the fifth chapter, "The Fifth Iteration: The All-Seeing Eye," in which Oliphant's nephew became fascinated with the Japanese tea-doll, the uncle tells him about how promising Japanese technology is. "The Japanese power their dolls with springs of baleen, Affie, 'Whale whiskers,' they call the stuff. They haven't yet learned from us the manufacture of proper springs, but soon they shall. When they do, their dolls shan't break so easily."[15]

What matters here is that, as I mentioned several times, Fukuzawa behaves in a way that may be described as Franklinesque, not only because he was a major philosopher of the Enlightenment sympathizing with Unitarianism, but also because he is well known for promoting the idea of self-made man based on the post-Franklin/Jeffersonian theory of Emerson's self-reliance. Take a glance at his bestselling book *Gakumon no Susume* (*An Encouragement of Learning*), published between 1872 and 1876, and you will quickly understand that without mentioning Franklin, Jefferson, or Emerson, he has clearly transplanted the spirit from the American Revolution through the Civil War into the modern Japanese soil. When he asserts that "in the pursuit of learning it is necessary that each person knows his capacity. We are born unrestricted and unbounded, and full-fledged men and women are free to act as they wish" and that "freedom and independence refer not only to the private self, but to the nation as well,"[16] it naturally conjures up Emerson's "The American Scholar" (1837), in which the transcendentalist proposes that "The scholar is that man who must take up into himself all the ability of the time, all the contributions of the past, all the hopes of the future."[17] For Emerson and Fukuzawa, scholarship helps achieve individual and national independence. One should also note here that Fukuzawa, born in 1835, has been compared with Mark Twain and the figure of the American self-made man.

However, in just the way Franklin's idea of a self-made man paradoxically wound up with the production of man-made self, Fukuzawa in *The Difference Engine* promotes the idea of self-reliance and national independence and the creation of an artificial intelligence like the *karakuri* gynoid. In fact, since the 1990s, when the Modus in *The Difference Engine* becomes self-conscious, Keio University (which Fukuzawa established in the 1850s) has boasted of being the center of research on artificial intelligence in Japan. Deeply knowledgeable about the philosophies of Emerson and Fukuzawa as contemporaries, Gibson and Sterling very carefully re-create Fukuzawa as a post-Franklinian modernist.

The philosophical genealogy I have outlined will help you comprehend what happens in the final chapter, titled "MODUS: The Images Tabled." As if explicating the mysterious title of the fifth and penultimate chapter, "The Fifth Iteration: The All-Seeing Eye," the year 1991 in the novel witnesses the awakening of the steam-driven computer in London:

> In this City's centre, a thing grows, an autocatalytic tree, in almost-life, feeding through the roots of thought on the rich decay of its own shed images, and ramifying, through myriad *lightning*-branches, up, up, towards the hidden light of vision,
>
> Dying to be born,
> The light is strong,
> The light is clear,
> The Eye at last must see itself
>   Myself . . .
>   I see:
>   I see,
>   I see
>   I
>   ![18]

Along with the Franklinian and Frankensteinian image of "lightning," the awakening of the all-seeing "Eye," that is, the steam-driven artificial intelligence, very naturally makes us rewind the history from Franklin through Emerson, whose major work *Nature* (1836) is well known for the following punchline: "Standing on the bare ground,—my head bathed by the blithe air, and uplifted into infinite space,—all mean egotism vanishes. *I become a transparent eyeball; I am nothing; I see all;* the currents of the Universal Being circulate through me; I am part or parcel of God."[19]

The first chapter of *Nature* includes the following mysterious sentence: "If stars should appear one night in a thousand years, how would men believe and adore, and preserve for many generations the remembrance of the city of God which had been shown!" Without this sentence, Isaac Asimov, a major voice of hardcore science fiction in the mid-twentieth century, could not have come up with the idea for "Nightfall," published in 1941. Without Emerson's idea of transcendentalism inspired by Kant and Coleridge and crystallized in *Nature*, Friedrich Nietzsche could not have developed his theory of superman (Übermensch) mentioned in *Thus Spoke Zarathustra* (1883), which inspired Arthur C. Clarke to write such masterpieces as *Childhood's End* (1953) and *2001: A Space Odyssey* (1968). Likewise, Emerson's post-Unitarian transcendentalism induced even cyberpunk writers to create a brand-new paradigm of science fiction, in which the computer as the all-seeing eye occupies the place of the Universal being. While Franklinian self-made man was turned into man-made self, cyberpunkish man-made self is turned into the cyber-transcendentalist "all-seeing eye." Herein lies a breakthrough in literary and cultural history. In conclusion, let me note that *The Difference Engine* continues to birth descendants, such as Project Itoh and Toe EnJoe's collaboration *The Empire of the Corpses* (2009–2012) and Fumio Takano's *Sister of Karamazov* (2012). Yet a reconsideration of this emergent subgenre of cyberpunk in the 2010s will be another story.[20]

PART II . . . GIBSON AND THE QUESTION OF MEDIUM

CHAPTER 5 ... **ANDREW M. BUTLER**

"A NEW ROSE HOTEL IS A NEW ROSE HOTEL IS A NEW ROSE HOTEL"

NONPLACES IN WILLIAM GIBSON'S SCREEN ADAPTATIONS

There is a moment in an interview with William Gibson when he says, "Being a screenwriter was never part of my game plan, and I never would have gone after it; it never occurred to me that it was something people did or that I would be asked to do it."[1] Inspired by watching teenagers play arcade video games, Gibson had been writing about the realm behind computer screens, of colors and space, claiming that he "assembled [the] word *cyberspace* from small and readily available components of language.... Slick and hollow—awaiting received meaning."[2] Cyberspace has no fixed identity, relationships, or history; it lacks authentic height, width, depth, and mass and can be thought of as an addition to the catalog of "nonplaces" of supermodernity identified by French anthropologist Marc Augé.

Elsewhere I have written that the outopia or no-place of cyberspace "exists at a different level of ontology to the 'outside' 'real' world of the narratives in which it features,"[3] lacking the *Dasein* or Being There of the real world, instead offering a Being-Toward-Death that in itself is "elsewhere." For Sarah Chaplin, "Cyberspace can never provide that vital tactile haptic sense of 'being there'."[4] In the constructed space of the cyberpunk text—written fiction, films, TV programs—there is slippage between the levels of diegesis and metadiegesis. Maria Kaika and Erik Swyngedouw argue that "the city is a space of flows, of flux, of translocation,"[5] and the same is true of cyberspace. Both are consistently shifting, being rewritten.

Gibson's early scriptwriting included his attempts to adapt "Burning Chrome" (1982) for Carolco and "New Rose Hotel" (1984) for producer Ed Pressman and director Kathryn Bigelow; "Johnny Mnemonic" (1981) had been optioned by Robert Longo,[6] who was cowriting a script with Victoria Hamburg. Several writers and directors had been attached to an adaptation of *Neuromancer*, the novel that cemented Gibson's reputation in science fiction circles as the central writer of cyberpunk, and his commissioned script for *Alien III* had been rejected. The few previous films with a cyberpunk sensibility included *Blade Runner* (Ridley Scott, 1982), *Tron* (Steven Lisberger, 1982), and *Videodrome* (David Cronenberg, 1983), and action films featuring cyborgs. Frances Bonner suggested that "if the films by and large are unable to deal with [cybernetic concerns], then they should be identified by a different label."[7] Hollywood seemed less interested in the *cyber* than the *punk* and did not really embrace the genre.

It was not until 1993 that Gibson's work reached the screen: *Tomorrow Calling* (Tim Leandro, 1993), based on "The Gernsback Continuum" (1981); this was followed by *Johnny Mnemonic* (Robert Longo, 1995) with a Gibson script, and he went on to write two episodes of *The X-Files*. *New Rose Hotel* (Abel Ferrara, 1998) was eventually filmed, with a script by Ferrara and Christ Zois. Despite—or perhaps because of—the success of *The Matrix* (Wachowski siblings, 1999), a film much indebted to Gibson, *Neuromancer* remains in production limbo to this day. Despite the range of screenwriters and other crew members, Gibson's sensibility survives enough in these films to feature a range of Augé's nonplaces.

Augé distinguishes "nonplaces" from "places" as lacking identity, relations, and history.[8] The eras of industrial capitalism and supermodernity have erased distinctions between space and time, leading to the emergence of nonplaces such as: "the air, rail and motorway routes, the mobile cabins called 'means of transport' (aircraft, trains and road vehicles), the airports and railway stations, hotel chains, leisure parks, large retail outlets, and finally the complex skein of cable and wireless networks that mobilize extraterrestrial space for the purposes of a communication so peculiar that it often puts the individual in contact only with another image of himself."[9] While the traditional town was centered on a few specific economic, political, and cultural nodes—such as the market, town, or church square—the supermodern city sprawls across networks and toward other cities (compare the Sprawl or Boston-Atlanta-Metropolitan Axis in the *Neuromancer* trilogy). Augé argues that the nonplaces are "formed in relation to certain ends (transport, transit, commerce, leisure), and [by] the relations that individuals have with these spaces."[10] These relations are constructed through texts and contracts.

The architecture of supermodern cities and the complex skein of cyberspace is hardly central to the *Alien* movie franchise. The haunted house in space of *Alien* (Ridley Scott, 1979) and the war on an extraterrestrial planet of *Aliens* (James Cameron, 1986) do operate against the backdrop of the Weyland-Yutani Corp and space ships, but the latter's crew have complex enough relationships to be places. Gibson had been brought in by producers Walter Hill and David Giler precisely to take the films in a new direction. Gibson had been interested in the dirty look of the films' spaceships and had a sense that there was a world waiting to be revealed outside the two films' frames. Working from a story by Hill and Giler, he "tried to open out the background of the first two, exploring things about the human culture you wouldn't have expected but that didn't contradict what you already knew."[11] He imagined the company in the first two films caught up in a cold war with the communist Union of Progressive Peoples (UPP), wishing to use the alien as a weapon. The UPP captures the android Bishop and an alien from the U.S.S. *Salaco*, while Ripley, Newt, and Hicks are transported to a vast space station, Anchorpoint.

For the recurring characters if not their occupants, Anchorpoint is a nonplace, a staging post on the way home, assuming they can survive. Ripley stays in stasis, as if dead, and Newt is speedily sent home to New Portland, Oregon, but Hicks barely has time to form relationships or establish his identity as he fights numerous aliens who are killing the space station's crew. By introducing alien spores to the franchise, Gibson seems to be exploring what Brian McHale dubbed "biopunk,"[12] where biology and genetic engineering took the worldbuilding role of cybernetics. The identity and DNA of the insect-like aliens is in flux, as if they inhabit a permanent nonplace: "[It is as] though the gene-structure had been designed for ease of manipulation."[13] Gibson rushed to finish his script by December 1987 to avoid the Writers Guild of America strike, but the studio's estimate that the film would require a $70 million budget suggested the script was unviable. Gibson produced another draft, reducing the number of aliens and characters, but Scott resigned from the project and the new director, Renny Harlin, rejected the new script. Despite a number of attempts to recuperate Gibson's ideas, the fall of the Berlin Wall was felt to render its Cold War subtext obsolete. Several creative teams later, *Alien 3* (David Fincher, 1992) bore no relation to Gibson's ideas.

This meant that the first screen adaption of Gibson's fiction was *Tomorrow Calling*, which had been situated as the lead story in Bruce Sterling's *Mirrorshades: The Cyberpunk Anthology* (1986). The paraspace invoked here is not so much cyberspace as the "semiotic ghosts"[14] of imagery from the science-fiction pulp magazines such as those edited by Hugo Gernsback and the impact this has on our perception of the world. Determined to identify cyberpunk as something revolutionary, Sterling insists that Gibson is "consciously drawing a bead on the shambling figure of the SF tradition. It's a devastating refutation of 'scientifiction' in its guise as narrow technolatry."[15] On the other hand, Gary Westfahl, a staunch defender of Gernsback's importance, declares this a misreading and notes "the obvious knowledge Gibson has about this view of the future and the affection he displays for it—and its contents."[16] The story's nameless narrator has been commissioned to document the 1930s Art Deco architecture surviving across America and finds himself haunted by their imagery, with their hints of fascist and Nazi propaganda. The story advances a fascinated distaste for this prophesied utopia, as the narrator exorcizes such visions by "'Watch[ing] lots of television, particularly games shows and soaps. Go[ing] to porn movies."[17] He replaces one set of semiotic ghosts with another.

Tim Leandro, in writing and filming *Tomorrow Calling*, moved the setting to England and included Art Deco buildings such as the Hoover Building in London, Barkers in Kensington, cinemas at Rayners Lane, Acton High Street, and Ealing, as well as Blackpool Promenade.[18] Through the collapse of the present day into historic architecture, these places become nonplaces straight out of Gernsbackian visions, complete with futuristic airships, airliners, and refugees from *Things to Come*

(William Cameron Menzies, 1936). Bill, the now-named protagonist, temporarily occupies the nonplaces of the hotel—the Savoy, which admittedly lacks the "sleek, minimalist decor in the rooms, with everything in white or discreet pastels" of the luxury establishments Augé has in mind—and a car. Augé begins his book with an account of car and air travel, with a description of an advertisement for a Renault Espace: "One day, the need for space makes itself felt... The irresistible wish for a space of our own. A mobile space which can take us anywhere... Already, space is inside you."[19] Bill takes his rented Nissan around the outskirts of London, onto the road network and its laybys, and to the liminal space of the promenade and the beach, suspended between culture and nature,[20] but haunted by something unnatural and uncanny, a nested space within a nonplace.

Leandro's title change replaces one set of semiotic ghosts with another, moving from science fiction history to Bryan Ferry's song "This Is Tomorrow" (1977), whose lyrics invoke a motel, televisions, and trucks. Ferry was inspired by the *This Is Tomorrow* Pop Art exhibition at the Whitechapel Art Gallery (August 1956), which featured an installation cocreated by Richard Hamilton, John Voelcker, and John McHale, including the collage "Just What Is It that Makes Today's Homes So Different, So Appealing?," Robby the Robot, an advertisement for *Forbidden Planet* (Fred M. Wilcox, 1956), collages of space pods, and so on. Hamilton was one of Ferry's art tutors at the University of Newcastle in the mid-1960s and, like Gibson, British Pop Artists such as Hamilton and Eduardo Paolozzi seem to have an ambivalent attitude to such iconography, blurring boundaries of high and low art and commenting on contemporary capitalism. Leandro's film uses collage techniques in its editing strategy, intercutting locations and low-quality footage of porn and nesting a number of flashbacks in the narrative flow.

The next Gibson adaptation, *Johnny Mnemonic*, had a larger budget than Leandro had worked with, $30 million, thanks to backing from Elektra Records, Alliance Communications, Cinevision, and TriStar Pictures. This created the need to cast supposedly bankable names such as Keanu Reeves, Ice-T, Henry Rollins, and Dolph Lundgren, among others. Gibson claimed, "It's phrased as an action-chase piece, but our real agenda is a little more serious than that."[21] In contrast, Arthur and Marilouise Kroker argue that the film was already an obsolete version of the original story, as "80s cyberpunk metaphors don't really work anymore in the virtual 90s... [The film's] been normalized, rationalized, chopped down to image-consumer size, drained of its charisma and recuperated, as a museum-piece of lost cybernetic possibilities."[22] The 1980s nonplaces already seemed dated. What had seemed a groundbreaking technology in 1981, implanted memories, already seemed old hat in the era of encrypted emails and the climactic use of a VCR to get a message to the rest of the world seemed positively primitive.

Johnny Mnemonic (Reeves) is a habitué of the nonplace, having jettisoned childhood memories (and thus his identity, history, and relationships) in favor of corporate rental space for data and a temporary identity. On one last job, Mnemonic has stolen data from the Pharmakom corporation in his memory, which may contain the cure for nerve attenuation syndrome, a worldwide plague caused by overexposure to technology. Pharmakom, the Yakuza, and Karl the street preacher (Lundgren) are pursuing him and the information through the mean streets of Newark.

Newark is the kind of nonplace cityscape that *Blade Runner* put on the map, "where transit points and temporary abodes are proliferating under luxurious or inhuman conditions (hotel chains and squats, holiday clubs and refugee camps, shantytowns threatened with demolition or doomed to festering longevity); where a dense network of means of transport which are also inhabited spaces is developing."[23] Steven Shaviro observes how "luxury business hotels... look pretty much the same all over the world. There's nothing to tell you whether you are in New York City, or Tokyo, or Rio de Janeiro."[24] The ideal hotel could be in any place, offering precisely the same menus, decor, and services. At one moment of despair in a ruined building, Mnemonic declaims: "I want ROOM SERVICE! I want the club sandwich, I want the cold Mexican beer, I want a $10,000-a-night hooker! I want my shirts laundered... like they do... at the Imperial Hotel... in Tokyo." This childlike solipsism is akin to being waited on by mother, his every need met, and since he has deleted his childhood from his memory, this is a service he must purchase.

In the meantime, he has hired Jane (Dina Meyer), a version of Molly from *Neuromancer* and the original story (presumably the intellectual property of the owners of the film rights to *Neuromancer*), to navigate the nonplaces he can access. Jane carries "mace, throwing spikes, and a grenade, what every girl wants" in her handbag and is suffering from nerve attenuation syndrome. This might be why we never see her entering cyberspace, although in Gibson's early work cyberspace is only jacked into by men. Cyberspace as matrix (Latin for mother or womb) or complex skein is a feminine (non)space or nonplace, "surrounding the computer user with its all-encompassing embrace. By enveloping the body, cyberspace recalls the powerful sense of unity with the mother experienced by an infant before the disruptive awareness of its own separateness intervenes."[25] Mnemonic can exploit the maternal virtual space because he has shed his memories of his mother and is finally able to liberate the data from his brain with the aid of a female ghost in the mainframe—his dead mother, Anna Kalmann (Barbara Sukowa): "The maternal ghost beams up out of the pharmaceutical corporation turned murderous incorporation or underworld, making her ghostly comeback on monitors of the media web to cheerlead on the efforts to make the cure public."[26] The mother dies again as it is erased and the Pharmakom building in Newark goes up in flames. Mnemonic is restored to full masculinity, embracing Jane and thus relationship, history, and identity. The heteronormative ending of the Hollywood blockbuster substitutes place for nonplace.

In contrast with *Johnny Mnemonic*'s blockbuster appearance, *New Rose Hotel* ended up as more arthouse fare than Longo had originally planned. Gibson describes it as "a weird urban fable that takes place in Tokyo—or in some kind of Tokyo—oh, maybe ten years in the future.... It really takes place in an indeterminate time, in a dark place."[27] Ferrara divides the film into two uneven parts: first is a James Bond or *Day of the Jackal*-style caper where X (Willem Dafoe) and Fox (Christopher Walken) employ Sandii (Asia Argento) to persuade Hiroshi (Yoshitaka Amano), a biologist, to defect from a Frankfurt-based research company, Maas Biolabs GmbH. This is followed by a more confusing section after Sandii has betrayed them and infected the scientist with a deadly disease. In this sequence, X is recalling the first part of the film—complete with repeated footage—in the nonplace of a capsule hotel near Narita International Airport. *New Rose Hotel* was "*Notorious* meets *Death of a Salesman*," also compared with *Rashomon* (Akira Kurosawa, 1950) by Ferrara.[28] Ferrara borrows the style of the estranging futuristic Paris of *Alphaville* (Jean-Luc Godard, 1965). Tokyo, filmed in New York, has become a nonplace: it could be anywhere. Paweł Frelik suggests that the film "evokes an image similar to the vision of [German synth-pop band] *Alphaville*'s 'Big in Japan' when he collapses geography and light with images of the future in his poetic description of his love interest [Sandii]."[29] Shaviro notes that in the film, "recording devices and screens are everywhere, and much of the film consists of grainy, reprocessed video footage. Indeed, the important plot events are exclusively conveyed through blurry video fragments and off-camera telephone voices."[30] Hiroshi is only depicted on a screen within the diegesis rather than being directly portrayed. Shaviro notes how Ferrara's filmic style puts X's acts of retrospection and the memories on the same ambiguous level of (re)presentation as the actual events in the film. Ferrara resists creating the standard ontological space of film—avoiding establishing shots, eschewing continuity editing and matched eye lines, merging characters with images of the characters, thus erasing clear lines of relationship and identity.

Maitland McDonagh describes this as "a future in which computer culture hasn't just brought the world together, it's reduced everything to a common culture of swank hedonism at one end of the economic spectrum and miserable depravity at the other."[31] Fox, X, and Mnemonic all aspire to elite status, but they are disconnected from the truly social. As Augé argues, "the passenger, customer or driver... is distanced from [worries] temporarily by the environment of the moment,"[32] and this is true of the hotel guest. X is deliberately obscuring his identity in a capsule hotel, an unintentional echo of the Heideggerean Being-Toward-Death or nonbeing that permeates cyberpunk; Fox kills himself. X is unclear as to anyone's motivations, and even his personal history may not be as he remembers it. Augé claims, "Frequentation of non-places today provides an experience—without real historical precedent—of solitary individuality combined with non-human mediation (all it takes is a notice or a screen) between the individual and the public authority."[33] These characters' identities, relations, and histories are called into question. Mnemonic may be able to restore his, and Bill may find new ones, but X and Fox remain in nonplaces.

As of this writing, Gibson's latest screen credits are his two episodes of *The X-Files*, Chris Carter's TV series (1993–2002, 2016–2018) that centered on FBI agent Fox Mulder's (David Duchovny) investigation of paranormal and alien activity alongside his skeptical partner, Dana Scully (Gillian Anderson). The paranoia that permeates the series repeatedly calls into question the nature of the spaces the series is set in—are they what they seem?—and the nature of powers that regulate them. Three types of stories dominate: "procedural, conspiratorial, and self-reflexive."[34] Gibson cowrote the episodes "Kill Switch" (1998) and "First Person Shooter" (2000) with Tom Maddox, the author of the science fiction novel *Halo* (1991). Their episodes broadly fall into the first category, effectively the monster-of-the-week, liberating them from the need to dovetail with or complicate ongoing story arcs. There are postmodern self-aware nods to films such as *Blade Runner* and *Tron*, as well as to other cyberpunk texts, most obviously in the Pris-like eye make-up of the computer programmer Invisigoth (Kristen Lehman) in "Kill Switch."

"Kill Switch" features a series of non-places as Mulder and Scully investigate the death by crossfire of pioneer programmer Donald Gelman (Patrick Keating) in a diner full of criminals. Mulder and Scully's investigation lead them to the nonplace of a shipping container, identifiable by its seven-digit BIC Code, which is a technological mapping of time and space. Gelman has created and lost control of an artificial intelligence which orchestrated his death when he tried to shut it down. The AI also attempts to kill Mulder and Scully with a laser fired by an orbital weapons satellite. Scully and Invisigoth locate the destroyed home of Gelman's friend David, while Mulder finds the trailer location of the AI's computer processing, along with David's corpse, still connected to his computer.

This nonmovable mobile home is the point from which Mulder involuntarily enters cyberspace, hallucinating himself as a quadruple amputee in a hospital. First Scully enters, attacking the blonde, seductive nurses, and then Mulder attacks Scully. As Bronwen Calvert observes, "Scully does not usually fight physically, and certainly does not show proficiency in kickboxing."[35] She temporarily changes identity in the nonplace of this virtual reality, becoming the kind of action heroine that had been popularized by the Lara Croft video game character in *Tomb Raider* (1996) and by the protagonists of *Xena: Warrior Princess* (1995–2001) and *Buffy the Vampire Slayer* (1997–2003). Even at the end of the episode, it remains unclear if the AI has been deleted, if there is a second AI in another trailer, and whether Invisigoth has joined David online. As they contemplate the nature of virtual existence, Mulder asks Scully, "What are we but impulses? Electrical and chemical, through a bag of meat and bones," relocating reality as a complex skein of data.

"First Person Shooter" features a computer game of that name, which has largely been coded by male programmers who mediate the relationships of players and programmed avatars, with a malleable history created by the individual and collective experience of the players. First-person shooter games require one or more players at screens with controls, who identify with the viewpoint of the (sometimes invisible) on-screen avatars. As Sue Morris observes, "Although largely immobilised at the PC, players are engaged in much bodily movement, not just controlling the game, but also in response to it."[36] Players occupy two spaces at once, identifying with their virtual echoes, moving their bodies without conscious intention. "Kill Switch" also attempted to foreground the nature of the body in its virtual nonplace. The fictional *First Person Shooter* is like an augmented laser quest or paintball game; players move about in a bare white physical play space wearing full body suits. They—or we, as audience members—perceive a dark cityspace full of motorbikes and enemies with machine guns, which echoes some of the games space of the film *Tron*. *First Person Shooter* evidently provides that tactile haptic sense that Chaplin claims is missing from real-world virtual reality.

The game pits players against avatar Maitreya, who is seemingly undefeatable and kills the real-world players when she kills their avatars. Maitreya was constructed from a three-dimensional scan of a stripper, Jade Blue Afterglow (Krista Allen), although we later find she has been created by Phoebe (Constance Zimmer), the lone female programmer on the team, as a wish-fulfillment figure who feeds off the male aggression that surrounds her. Nevertheless, Maitreya is subjected to an objectifying, sexualizing heterosexual male gaze in the episode, and it should be noted that all the players are male. This is further emphasized when Jade is interrogated in an all-male police station, a scene that pays homage to the interview of Catherine Tramell (Sharon Stone) in *Basic Instinct* (Paul Verhoeven, 1992). Mulder, largely breaking with the identity of the character in the rest of the series, is not immune to this lechery.

Maitreya's acrobatics echo those of Pris in *Blade Runner*, although her costume seems to be a variant on Molly's in *Neuromancer* and Trinity's in *The Matrix*. For that matter, they echo the actions of Scully in "Kill Switch," who risked being fetishized in the earlier episode. Mulder's rare alpha male prowess in *First Person Shooter* causes him to progress to a further level of game play, an archetypal Western town complete with tumbleweeds. The episode walks a thin line between endorsement and critique of the male gaze, as Scully starts playing the game—a rare woman entering Gibsonian cyberspace—and they only win the battle against Maitreya with Phoebe's intervention. Scully has been established as clearly critical of the testosterone-rich environments, but that does not protect her from being objectified, which cuts across her identity as a person with agency. Scully is transformed in the nonplace of the game "into the game player par excellence and then us[es] aspects of her physical self to create a new avatar-goddess."[37] Her face will eventually become the face of a new version of Maitreya. The nonplace and the rules of the nonplace are both malleable, with Mulder and Scully's avatars as finetuned versions of their standard diegetic aspects.

The use of cyberspace in popular television such as *The X-Files*, decades after *Star Trek: The Animated Series* (the recreation room in "The Practical Joker" [1974]), *Doctor Who* (the Matrix, on Gallifrey, for example, from "The Deadly Assassin" [1976] onward), and *Star Trek: The Next Generation* (the holodeck, from the pilot episode "Encounter at Farpoint" [1988] onward), shows how far Gibson's ideas already fit in the popular imaginary. But the screen versions of Gibson's fiction from the 1990s were either too obscure (*Tomorrow Calling*), too action-oriented (*Johnny Mnemonic*), or too art house (*New Rose Hotel*) to have much influence on other film versions of cyberpunk. Gibson's oeuvre clearly fed into *The Matrix*, to such an extent that a version of a film of *Neuromancer* is probably already obsolete. The wonders of cyberspace that Gibson envisioned on paper in the 1980s have become part of the everyday.

Protagonists Bill, Mnemonic, X, and Fox all find themselves in cities and other nonplaces they can no longer read or navigate, overwhelmed by the semiotics and forms of representation at odds with their identities, relationships, and histories. Each turns for succor and restoration to the nonplace of the hotel: "A paradox of non-place: a foreigner lost in a country he does not know (a 'passing stranger') can feel at home there only in the anonymity of motorways, service stations, big stores or hotel chains."[38] They can assert temporary agency by renting a room and signing the registration book: "There will be no individualization (no right to anonymity) without identity checks."[39] They attempt to disavow nonidentity with signatures. Yet we do not actually know X's name, and Fox and Mnemonic feel like assumed names—the latter may have lost the surname Kalmann. Their identities and locatedness are all fragile, their relatedness temporary. Mnemonic only enters back into relations, and thus identity, when he connects to Jane, but it should be noted that she lacks the identity, however problematic, granted by a surname. As Mark Bould argues, "We pay to see movies . . . to identify with loners whose success is figured in terms of social formation."[40] In the original story, Mnemonic and Molly go into business together—along with Jones, an augmented dolphin—and their corporate relationship turns nonplace into place for them. The same may be imagined after the ending of the film version.

The nonplaces identified by Augé are either corporate or state-owned; the individual is only temporarily located in them. The semiotics that haunt Bill oscillate between the intellectual properties of pulp fiction and mass media, permeated by capital. The new frontier of cyberspace might have been envisaged as a utopian free space, a new commons, but the digital domain is now battled over by multinational corporations who defend their ownership of data. Augé argues, "the non-place is the opposite of utopia,"[41] which is ironic given that the part origin of the word utopia in *ou-topia* or nonplace (alongside *eu-topia* or good place). The space of the nonplace is constructed through texts and contracts, just as the city is designed by architects employed by corporations in the context of planning laws and cyberspace is constructed by the intellectual labors of programmers.

In the *X-Files* episodes we have Mulder and Scully, two quasi-mavericks within a government agency, who try to regulate the law in a corporate world permeated with nonplaces. In Gibson and Maddox's episodes, the programs seem barely controlled by their programmers—even when deleted, semiotic ghosts and back-ups may exist. The generic demands of ongoing television drama are such that Mulder and Scully regain their identities and relationships in both episodes, but the details of their history can be forgotten. Gibson's location in *The X-Files* canon is only provisional until contradicted by the assertions of subsequent scriptwriters and showrunners. As a writer for hire, Gibson's place is not assured, just as his *Alien III* script was effectively erased by the events of *Alien 3* and his work on the script of *New Rose Hotel* gave way to Ferrara and Zois's vision.

Film and television are collaborative media, with a range of co-creators—other writers, directors, producers, actors, cinematographers, and so on—so that it is already hard to pin down Gibson's place in the work even if he wrote the words delivered by the actors. Nevertheless, the range of Augé's nonplaces and his analysis of supermodernity can be seen in Gibson's original works and the films and TV programs they have inspired. Despite the romanticization of cyberspace found in the critical reaction to cyberpunk, these adaptations show the ongoing alienation of the individual in the world (non)place of late capitalism and supermodernity.

CHAPTER 6 ... MARIA ALBERTO AND ELIZABETH SWANSTROM

WILLIAM GIBSON, SCIENCE FICTION, AND
THE EVOLUTION OF THE DIGITAL HUMANITIES

In 2017 Chris Sevier filed a lawsuit against the state of Utah for the right to marry—his computer. The case was promptly dismissed for several compelling reasons, including the fact that Sevier's computer was not at least fifteen years old and therefore did not satisfy Utah's age-of-consent requirement.[1] As ludicrous as this case might seem, however, it was neither the first—nor will it be the last—attempt to wed a computational entity. In 2009, Japanese gamer Sal9000 married Nene Anegasaki, "a character in the Nintendo DS dating simulation game 'Love Plus,'"[2] and in November 2018, Akihiko Kondo wed Hatsune Miku, "a hologram that was created by a computer as singing software."[3] Moreover, such real-world unions have multiple literary precedents, dating back to Auguste Villiers de l'Isle-Adam's depiction of Thomas Edison and the gyndroid Hadaly in *L'Ève future* (1886), further back still to E. T. A. Hoffman's automaton Olimpia in "The Sand-man" (1816), and arguably even to Pygmalion's marble-carved lover Galatea in Ovid's *Metamorphoses* (8 CE)— examples that demonstrate a long-standing interest in these unusual accords. But the contemporary penchant for an *amans computans* finds its most vivid literary blueprint in the work of William Gibson, whose cyberpunk fiction delights in merging computational and human entities.

In *Neuromancer* (1984), which provides the master template for subsequent unions in Gibson's oeuvre, this type of merger occurs when two artificial intelligences, code-named "Wintermute" and "Rio"/"Neuromancer," consolidate to form the titular singularity, Neuromancer. This pattern is repeated in "Winter Market" (1986), when disabled artist Lise "dry dreams" with editor Casey, merging her consciousness with his as a first step toward merging with the digital 'net. A similar pattern surfaces in *Mona Lisa Overdrive* (1988), when simstim star Angie and her lover Bobby Newmark merge their consciousnesses with a vast, newly formed computational storage space called the Aleph, and again on a smaller scale in *Pattern Recognition* (2003), with the piecemeal creation of "the Footage" and its subsequent reconstitution by fans. Later the sustained dialog between proximate and distant futures in *Peripheral* (2014) follows such unions in temporal rather than spatial terms, as enabled through the medium of a quantum computer. Perhaps most visibly, in Gibson's novel *Idoru* (1996) the marriage is literal, as eccentric rock star Rez weds Rei Toei, an "idoru" or computer-generated "synthetic personality" who exists only in virtual space.

Though itself an interesting phenomenon, this pattern of integrated mergers between distinct and seemingly incompatible entities in Gibson's fiction has ramifications beyond the romantic plotlines that often surround them. In fact, we assert that this trope in Gibson's fiction—which itself has been fundamental in shaping popular and scholarly notions about computation since the early 1980s—has particular resonance with the emerging field of the digital humanities, or DH.

Defining DH

In their introduction to *Dialectic of Enlightenment*, Max Horkheimer and Theodor Adorno make a scathing claim about the "totalizing" and "corrosive rationality" of Enlightenment thought, noting that within it "anything which does not conform to the standard of calculability and utility must be viewed with suspicion."[4] First published in 1944, such a statement reads as a trenchant critique of an epistemology that helped pave the road to World War II, as well as a prescient excoriation of the larger culture industry that solidified in the postwar United States. Decades after its original publication, and within a technological-aesthetic system that did not exist during its time, Adorno and Horkheimer's statement works surprisingly well to describe a particular friction within the digital humanities—specifically, between quantitative computational methods on the one hand and subjective qualitative analysis on the other.

In order to understand how it is that both Gibson's work, and science fiction more generally, have been fundamental to the digital humanities, it is necessary to define what constitutes DH in the first place. This is a notoriously difficult task. In Matthew K. Gold's first *Debates in the Digital Humanities* collection, for example, the "Day of DH" essay offers twenty different voices, each with a distinct vision of the field. These range from the concise (e.g., John Unsworth's "using computational tools to do the work of the humanities") to the community-oriented (e.g., Kathryn E. Piquette's "community of practice" and Jason Farman's "methodology and a community") to the optimistic (e.g., Mark Marino's "a temporary epithet for what will eventually be called merely humanities") to the tautological (e.g., Rafael Alvarado's claim that "the Digital Humanities is what digital humanists do"). Of definitions listed in this survey, only one—Ernesto Priego's—speaks specifically to the importance of digital culture within DH: "The scholarly study and use of computers and computer culture to illuminate the human record."[5] Definitions such as Priego's are extraordinarily valuable to surveys such as ours because they acknowledge how the human elements of DH cannot be separated from their purely computational counterparts.[6]

For our purposes, DH crosses over among several of these definitions, naming a field of research and inquiry that investigates any overlap between computational technology (the digital) and traditional humanism (the humanities). If our reconstituted definition seems to cover quite a lot of ground, that is because it does: intentionally, strategically, and even sometimes unconvincingly. Because DH does not have a straightforward, linear history—a reality that constitutes part of its appeal and its risk—it is productive to think of this field as a braided entity composed of three strands: media studies, experimental aesthetics, and humanities computing.

The first of these strands is most likely familiar. Media theory helps us evaluate our methods of communication—from Plato's critique of writing in the *Phaedrus* to Marshall McLuhan's critique of the alphabetic consciousness that writing helped foster in *The Medium Is the Message* (1967) to N. Katherine Hayles's argument that the human body is integral to the formation of digital literature in *Writing Machines* (2002). The second strand, that of experimental aesthetics, is also probably familiar, although its particular attributes vary widely and necessitate a disclaimer that in this context we mean the term to signify any artistic act of making that concerns itself with both digital technology and formal innovation.

The third term—humanities computing—is perhaps less well known, though it names the field that uses computational methods to conduct statistical analyses of literary texts. While this might sound like an offshoot of the contemporary DH frenzy, it is actually the other way around: humanities computing precedes DH by nearly forty years and has only recently expanded to invite the other two braids of inquiry—media studies and experimental aesthetics—into its fold. In fact, when the National Endowment for the Humanities (NEH) opened its Office of Digital Humanities in 2008, a survey of NEH-funded projects revealed that the NEH had been supporting DH projects since its own inception—long before DH existed as such.[7]

Yet humanities computing did not merge with these other two strands until fairly recently. Two moments clearly enabled this union. The first has to do with the very name "digital humanities," which resulted from a strategic publishing decision. In 2001, DH scholar John Unsworth was putting together a collection of work composed of both traditional humanities computing essays and other texts that were less technical than analytical. Although both types discussed the role of digital technology in humanities research, their various approaches prompted Unsworth to propose a more fluid name than the editors' recommended "digitized humanities": instead, Unsworth "suggested 'Companion to Digital Humanities' to shift the emphasis away from just digitization."[8] The decision to avoid "computing" and "digitized" is understandable; such choices could have alienated readers by implying the need for a more substantive computing background. The alternative "digital" is also more capacious and lacks the finality of the past participle "digitized," which suggests a computationally completed act of translation. Thus, Unsworth's new term "digital humanities" struck a balance among these competing needs by merging their most important qualities.

A second turning point can be found in the "big tent" theme of the annual DH Conference at Stanford in 2011. The metaphor of a giant circus tent opened DH to a more expansive sense of research that included media theory, aesthetics, and cultural studies without requiring the demanding technical expertise that had defined humanities computing for decades. With so many new recruits welcomed into its fold through this merger of interests, DH seemed poised to be, as a *New York Times* article had predicted a year earlier, "the next big thing."[9]

Even though the union of humanities computing and DH has resulted in a wonderfully wide latitude in terms of research options, this latitude can also be confusing to people inside and outside DH's "big tent." For those outside the tent, the term "DH" is so amorphous that it often mystifies. For those inside the tent, there is the same difficulty of finding common ground among so many different approaches and objects of study, but there is also the larger problem that C. P. Snow articulated in his 1959 *Two Cultures* lectures. This is a problem that has plagued Western epistemology since the scientific revolution: the divide between scientific and humanist knowledge production. As both a practicing scientist and a literary creator, Snow experienced this divide firsthand, writing that he was constantly "moving among" two groups: "comparable in intelligence, identical in race, not grossly different in social origin, earning about the same incomes, [and] who had almost ceased to communicate at all."[10] Though many of his subsidiary arguments are no longer applicable in the same way today as they were in his time, his central claims about two groups resonate especially well in the context of DH.

What we mean by this is that although the "merger" has ostensibly happened—we're all under that same big tent—our training and approaches to DH are often at odds, even when we make serious efforts to understand each other. Cultural critics are often dismayed by what they perceive as decontextualized "data dumps" coming from the humanities computing side of things, and those with more technical expertise in computation are often mystified by the qualitative analyses about computation that offer little evidence of concrete knowledge regarding the nuts and bolts of computational procedure.[11]

This conflict between the "two groups" of DH is only compounded by how humanities computing and DH can be weirdly out of step with the times, but in completely different ways. Those who focus on digital culture are often at the cutting edge in terms of cultural and political theory—but at the same time, they are often behind in terms of technological skills and knowledge. By contrast, humanities computing scholars are computationally literate but often behind the times in terms of cultural theory and sometimes even regarding the social and political implications of their work.

This tension recalls a darkly comedic moment in *Neuromancer*, in which the AI Wintermute confides to Molly Millions how frustrated he has become with the Tessier-Ashpool family that owns him. When she recounts the scene later, it is not without sympathy: "They were always fucking him over with how old-fashioned they were, he said, all their nineteenth-century stuff."[12] Although here neither the cultural-critical nor the humanities computing sides are working from a nineteenth-century paradigm, their lagging methodologies make it seem this way. Thus, turning to science fiction and to Gibson's cyberpunk in particular can provide useful ways of reframing this divide.

Computers in Outer Space: Precyberpunk Machines

Before diving into Gibson's work, it is also useful to review the science fiction lineage that precedes it, as this overview reveals an interesting shift in our thoughts about computation and digitality. Whether personal, desktop, "bank," or otherwise, computers provide the fundamental means of creating, accessing, and participating in digital spaces—for those who work in humanities computing and those who study the computers that populate science fiction narratives. Because of the computer's central role in our understanding of digitality, then, its changing roles in science fiction merit closer examination, but the apparent simplicity of relationships between computers and digitality can also be misleading—in reality, the science fiction computer is not so neatly delineated. It ranges dramatically in form, from the impersonally mechanical, as with the text-generating "Engine" at the Academy of Projectors in Lagado in Jonathan Swift's *Gulliver's Travels* (1726); to a totalizing architectural hive, as with the titular entity in E. M. Forster's "The Machine Stops" (1909); to the blinking consoles of intergalactic spaceships, such as the vacuum-tubed Maraax in Stanislaw Lem's *The Astronauts* (1951); to the punch card–controlled machines of Illium in Kurt Vonnegut's *Player Piano* (1952) and Garson Poole's punch card–controlled heart in Philip K.

Dick's "Electric Ant" (1969); to the militaristic and meddlesome, as with D. F. Jones's *Colossus* (1966); to the massive and godlike, as with "Deep Thought," the city-sized supercomputer meant to calculate an answer to "life, the universe, and everything" in Douglas Adams's *Hitchhiker's Guide to the Galaxy* (1979)—not to mention the Earth itself in the same series, a supercomputer intended to complete Deep Thought's great work before its untimely destruction.

With this historical sampling in mind, it is worth a reminder that the word "computer" is a term that initially did not refer to machines at all—a fact our students are always rather surprised to learn. Instead, computers were people who "[made] calculations or computations" to support practical or scientific work, and the earliest recorded usages of the word stem from a 1613 religious reader and a 1646 encyclopedia.[13] Human computers were involved in fields ranging from eighteenth-century astronomy to World War II–era nuclear fission, NASA projects such as the 1969 moon landing, and the construction of the groundbreaking ENIAC computer. These human computers—often women—interacted with vast amounts of raw data and performed complex, foundational calculations. From its inception, the concept of a "computer" in science fiction and science fact has simultaneously drawn from and connoted a complex relationship with and among bodies, knowledge, and various means of transmitting information.

Thus, there is an incredible diversity of work related to computation in science fiction that precedes Gibson's cyberpunk. Although it is risky to overgeneralize, three texts from this expansive time period strike especially interesting monuments along the route toward Gibson's treatment of digitality—and from there, toward what we now call the Digital Humanities. Robert Heinlein's *The Moon Is a Harsh Mistress* (1966) follows a set of lunar colonists who rebel against the strictures of government by Earth, aided by the HOLMES IV supercomputer "Mike," who controls most of the main lunar colony's resources and develops a sense of humor that makes a revolution sound like fun. Arthur C. Clarke's *2001: A Space Odyssey* (1968) of course (re)introduces the infamous HAL 9000,[14] who slowly kills off most of his human crewmates but also leans heavily on a series of monolithic computers including the "New Rock" and TMA-1. Finally, Anne McCaffrey's *The Ship Who Sang* (1969) follows the trials and travels of Helva, a "brainship" who seeks a human "brawn" to complement her on diplomatic missions. Though these three texts are incredibly different in terms of narrative, they exhibit interesting parallels in their treatment of computer or computer-like figures, and these similarities anticipate Gibson's later portrayals of digitality in interesting ways.

All three texts, for instance, are somewhat cagey about what a computer *is*, while at the same time being very certain about what a computer is *not*. Human protagonists from Heinlein, Clarke, and McCaffrey define and describe their computer counterparts in contrast—but not necessarily in opposition—to themselves. In this model, the humans of *2001* are depicted as "builders" rather than creators or makers,[15] and Helva is "made" from a disabled fetus and cutting-edge hardware but immediately distinguishes between herself and "you people" without hardware shells.[16] Meanwhile, computers are posited as "one of Your [God's] creatures" in Heinlein.[17] Yet these two apparent "sides," human and computer, are never positioned as equivalents: that is, one does not move from human to computer, or from computer to human, even though a movement of some kind seems implied. Such uncertainties about what a computer is demonstrate an interesting preoccupation with how the computer "acts" and what it is possible for that computer to do.

Digitality, code, data, and binary signals do, of course, have material roots and components, but they are not tangible in the same way that precyberpunk computers such as Heinlein's Mike, Clarke's HAL 9000, and McCaffrey's Helva are. The fact that these earlier science fiction texts struggle to define computers by their actions and capacities rather than their mechanical components prefigures how Gibson later fuses human and computational entities. Precyberpunk computers complicate boundaries between human and nonhuman in abstract, noncorporeal ways by questioning whether the two can share similar mental, emotional, or even spiritual capacities. But where his predecessors question divisions between human bodies and computer terminals—or between human cognition and computational capacity—Gibson strides across such divisions altogether.

Wares from "The Winter Market": A Case Study

Since numerous critics (Hayles, Nakamura, Moody, Nixon) have demonstrated how Gibson's cyberpunk Sprawl trilogy (*Neuromancer, Count Zero,* and *Mona Lisa Overdrive*) provokes concerns about digitality in regard to race, sexuality, embodiment, cognition, and subjectivity, it will be useful to turn to one of Gibson's lesser-known works as a means of revisiting some of the concerns these critics foreground. Published in *Stardate* magazine in 1986, "The Winter Market" presents a sprawling, open-air bazaar of garbage, heartbreak, and technological compost and provides a poignant meditation on embodiment, mortality, celebrity, and disability, among other concerns. A close reading of this story brings some of the issues raised by Hayles and others into sharp relief.

"The Winter Market" begins with the memory of a rainy day in Vancouver, where narrator Casey has just learned that his former lover, Lise, has "merged with the net," a message that propels him to contemplate suicide.[18] As Casey contemplates jumping into an icy river and ending it all, his actions suggest criticisms about cyberpunk fiction's disdain for the human body—in this moment, after all, the reference to Lise's merging with the net suggests the death of a human body, what N. Katherine Hayles equates to her posthuman nightmare.[19] This revelation of Lise's "death"-by-net prompts Casey to consider adding his body to the tally, as he stands on "a concrete ledge two meters above midnight." Eventually, Casey steps away from the ledge, still grappling with the complicated emotional realization that "she was dead, and I'd let her go . . . she was immortal, and I'd helped her get that way . . . I knew she'd phone me, in the morning."[20] Like Casey's contradictory realization about Lise—that she is at once dead, alive, and technologically connected—the implications of the human body as an afterthought or fashion accessory thanks to digitization are complicated in "The Winter Market."

Through Casey's flashbacks, we meet Lise, a disabled, nerve-damaged woman who cannot move her body of her own volition; instead, a robotic exoskeleton does this for her, powered via a digitally enabled neural jack in the back of her neck. The image of Lise's human body, at once obscured and animated by the exoskeleton, is eerie, suggestive of technology that threatens to eclipse the human form. By the same token, the story suggests that this technological device allows Lise a greater range of motion than she otherwise would have—her entire capacity for mobility, in fact—and hence that this device provides her with greater autonomy. Yet as Kathryn Allan notes, the disabled body is often figured as aberrant in science fiction and "therefore in need of control by others."[21] This aspect of Lise's experience is unmistakable, as when Casey recounts Lise's being "saved" by their mutual friend, an artist named Rubin. When she is found by Rubin, the batteries of Lise's exoskeleton have died and she lies in an unresponsive heap next to other piles of technological detritus, "back in an alley."[22] This moment aligns Lise's unresponsive body with the surrounding trash and coincides with Hayles's vision of how cyberpunk fiction treats the body: as a discarded accessory, almost indistinguishable from the technological trash surrounding it. Lise is recovered from this pile of refuse against her will—"saved" by Rubin—and her only desire to "live" is as a computer-generated simulation, which seems to confirm Hayles's and Allan's readings.

Throughout the story, Lise's status as machine-dependent human only increases in complexity. Readers see this in the way Lise, once recovered, meets Casey and dares him to take her home, where the two of them "jack, straight across"—a term for sharing each other's neural input without mediating the resulting sensations.[23] Jacking straight across would seem to complicate the boundaries of a liberal humanist subject whose boundaries are divinely granted, inviolable, and stable—and because it offers a way to share human experience, the practice would also seem to challenge Hayles's critique of cybernetics as devaluing embodiment. In "The Winter Market," however, this moment of jacking straight across is not one of overcoming separation or of sharing sensations to achieve a humanistic synthesis or empathic unity. Instead, it plays out as an artistic battle of the sexes, pitting Lise's raw emotions against Casey's inability to cope with them. In the end, Lise wins; after she hits him with pure, single-minded ambition, with "a void that stank of poverty and lovelessness and obscurity," Casey "couldn't look at her. I heard her disconnect the optic lead. I heard the exoskeleton creak as it hoisted her up from the futon. Heard it tick demurely as it hauled her into the kitchen for a glass of water. Then I started to cry."[24] Here emotional "sharing" does occur, but it is violent and one-sided, devastating one of the human subjects involved.

Once this overwhelming shared experience has happened, Casey records Lise's neural input—from a safe distance this time, barricaded behind studio equipment and already planning to run a sanitized version by his manager as a "product" they can sell[25]—and the resulting reel makes Lise wildly popular, turning her suffering into a commodity that strangers can consume and, by extension, expanding her reach in ways she seems to have always wanted. She becomes a star, able to "dive down deep, down and out, out into Jung's sea, and bring back—well, dreams."²⁶ In terms of Nixon's critique of sex and gender in cyberpunk,²⁷ Lise conforms to the complicated formula she outlines. She is tough and astonishingly resilient, but she wields her power in ways that suggest a sexual conquest only achievable through depravity.

"The Winter Market" continues as Casey learns that a newly wealthy Lise bought her freedom, wed herself to the net, and now exists in the form of a neuro-electronic simulation. Freedom, however, is just as complicated as the depiction of the body that she leaves behind, and the notion that her uploaded, merged consciousness continues to perform after the body's death affirms and confounds cyberpunk's troubled reputation about embodiment, celebrity, artistry, and mortality. The cost of Lise's apparent freedom is exorbitant, corroborating Moody's suggestion that the presence of the somewhat normalized disabled body in cyberpunk is ultimately in service to neoliberal capitalism's insistence on a hardy workforce.²⁸ When Casey wonders aloud if Lise will keep creating "dry dreams" from her new transcendent state, Rubin's response is telling: "you have to edit her next release. Which will almost certainly be soon, because she needs money bad. She's taking up a lot of ROM on some corporate mainframe, and her share of *Kings* won't come close to paying for what they had to do to put her there."²⁹

In summary, "The Winter Market" offers an excellent illustration of many features that characterize cyberpunk and many more that occupy the scholarship responding to it. This short story at once complicates a simple attitude toward the human body, offers a devastating critique of digitally enabled consumer culture, and performs an unsettling mode of cultural resistance. It is precisely this form of complex cultural critique that has been essential to the formation of DH.

Not Quite the Singularity, But . . .

Gibson's work speaks to the emergence of DH as a field in many ways. In addition to the conversations his work has prompted regarding embodiment, cognition, gender, race, and so on, it has also been central to contemporary DH criticism, particularly regarding the form of what Alan Liu has called "transcendental data" and Matthew Kirschenbaum's demonstration of the surprising durability of digital objects.³⁰ We now offer a more exploratory and perhaps playful reading of Gibson in terms of DH—we suggest that the narrative backbone of *Neuromancer* provides a metaphor through which we can view DH's potential. This reading emerges from the plotline of the distinct artificial intelligences Wintermute and Neuromancer, who, at the novel's end, merge into a single presence or singularity.

In the novel, the Wintermute is characterized by his attention to detail, logic, forecasting, and computation. His counterpart, Neuromancer, is characterized by improvisation, creativity, and personality. Both are strong subjective entities, but for the majority of their existence they have been kept apart, each in ignorance of the other. By the end of *Neuromancer*, the human protagonists have successfully hacked into the information structure that will allow the AIs to merge, and the resulting merger has appealing consequences: (1) the emergence of a superintelligence whose potential for autonomous action is greater than the sum of its parts, and (2) a redistribution of wealth that serves as a sort of justice for the characters who have been maimed or otherwise compromised in their quest.

Like Wintermute, the field of humanities computing is logical, statistical, and rigorous in terms of its methodology. Like Neuromancer, the larger purview of cultural criticism and making is more creative, improvisational, and concerned with aesthetics. Although the two carried on for decades without formal acknowledgment of the other's activities, once they were collected under the aegis of DH's "big tent," they were given an opportunity to become, like the merged AI at the end of *Neuromancer*, greater than the sum of their parts. When the two disciplines converse and collaborate, they complement each other, as can be seen in the realms of electronic literature, digital art, and more. Femtechnet, HASTAC, and the ELO are just some of the many entities that have resulted from mergers between humanities computing and DH.

A DH Concordance

Throughout this essay we have followed a fairly one-sided form of argumentation to make our case, that of traditional cultural-literary analysis complete with textual close reading. However, in a chapter that calls for the integration of cultural studies and data analytics, as this one does, such an approach is insufficient by itself. We close our essay by sharing

```
> seventies.concordance("computer")
splaying 25 of 58 matches:
cts of modern SF (e.g., HAL, the computer in 2001) may be equated with human
ime machine, the first electronic computer functioning within a human head, t
nny to this machine. The Central  Computer of Diaspar is much less totalitari
Well-Doer" in Zamiatin's We. The  computer never obstructs Alvin; when he lea
s machine stops, but the Central  Computer of Diaspar seems truly eternal. So
zes transcendence too. 9Hal, the  computer for the Jupiter probe in 2001', mi
d have, nor does the intelligent  computer though he is similar, say, to the
ness. This trick would require a  computer at least as good and probably some
of primitives, but in those of a  computer scientist, in "Izzard and the Memb
 as "neutral entiti es." Whether  computer s are a pre.requi site of a succes
```

Figure 3: Instances of "digital" and "computer" in issues of *Science Fiction Studies* in the 1970s. Courtesy of Maria Alberto and Elizabeth Swanstrom.

our process of computational textual analysis to see how the concerns we have outlined might also be traced quantitatively. Our corpus draws from the following areas: precyberpunk science fiction, particularly the three texts analyzed here for their treatment of embodied computational entities; cyberpunk fiction, with Gibson's work as the dominant sample; DH scholarship, which draws from a variety of DH publications; and science fiction scholarship from *Science Fiction Studies*, beginning with the journal's inception in 1973 to 2017.[31] In all, we are looking at more than four thousand distinct documents, with the bulk coming from DH and science fiction scholarship. This was a massive undertaking, and we are still working to parse the wealth of data; what follows are but a few instructive results.

Our primary interest was the shift between "computation" and "digital" that signifies the emergence of DH as a field. We started by searching for the words "digitality" and "computer" across the collected *SFS* issues. We began with the cat command from terminal, which combined all the separate issues and articles into one file, and then used Python's NLTK to search for these terms. Our hunch going in was that both words would appear more frequently from the 1980s onward, but our findings were surprising. In the 1970s, there are zero instances of the word "digital" and fifty-eight of the word "computer." Figure 3 shows how this count appears as a part of a larger search for concordances.

In the 1980s, things begin to change: we now have five instances of "digital" and eighty-six of "computer." In the 1990s, both terms take off,

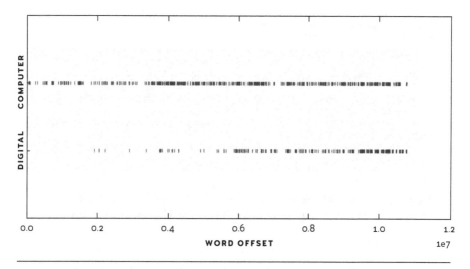

Figure 4: Lexical dispersion plot of instances of "digital" and "computing" in *Science Fiction Studies* through 2017. Courtesy of Maria Alberto and Elizabeth Swanstrom.

with 61 occurrences of "digital" and 315 of "computer." In the 2000s, there is a sizable jump in "digital," whereas "computer" stays fairly stable, with 287 instances of the former and 338 of the later. In the 2010s, another leap occurs, this time with "digital" barely increasing to 295 counts and "computer" seeing more than a 50 percent increase with 582 occurrences.

By using NLTK to create a lexical dispersion plot, we can see how these terms track over time. In Figure 4 "each stripe represents an instance of a word, and each row represents the entire text" (nltk.org). In other words, the greater the density of stripes, the more frequently the word is used in that section of the text. Here we demonstrate with a single file created by merging every available issue of *Science Fiction Studies* through 2017.

On some level this shift is intuitive, but on another, the fact that digitization is not even conceived of as a synonym for computation until the 1980s is fascinating. The lag between usage is much longer—and wider—than we thought it would be. In addition, since the term "digital" replaces "computing" in the humanities computing/DH shift in 2002, precisely because it lacks the same mathematical, calculating connotation of "computing," our analysis of the *SFS* corpus reiterates that this

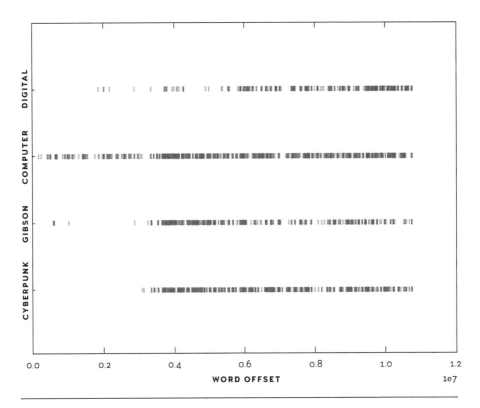

Figure 5: Lexical dispersion plot of instances of "Gibson" and "cyberpunk" in *Science Fiction Studies* through 2017. Courtesy of Maria Alberto and Elizabeth Swanstrom.

shift makes sense. Conceptions of "digital," "digitality," and "digitization" in science fiction scholarship simply do not have the same quantitative baggage that "computer," "computing," and "computation" do. When the "digital" as a concept comes into play, it does so in science fiction scholarship—and possibly in science fiction itself—in conjunction with Gibson's vision of the term in his cyberpunk fiction, as well as the new genre's preoccupations with embodiment, human–machine networks, and expansions of subjectivity. Another dispersion plot of all *SFS* issues, this time including Gibson's name and the name of this important subgenre, clarifies this point (see Figure 5).

In this case, the name Gibson and the term "cyberpunk" have nearly equivalent distribution. There is a slight overlap between "computer" and Gibson, but none between "computer" and "cyberpunk." Likewise, the occurrence of the word "digital" precedes both, but only slightly. Again, this suggests an intriguing distinction in the connotations of both terms. Although this result stems from only one corpus, we believe that pursuing the implications of this distinction would be worth further exploration in both science fiction and DH scholarship.

We were also interested in the topics highlighted by our close reading of "The Winter Market"— gender, disability, embodiment, and so on. For each topic we created a list of keywords, which we searched for using Voyant, a free online tool for text analysis, and Mallet, a tool for topic modeling. Before testing our own keyword associations, we created a topic model, which reaches across multiple texts to find patterns of co-occurrence and pools them to predict how words relate to each other across the corpus as a whole. In our topic model of the complete contents of *Science Fiction Studies*, for instance, the following cluster surfaced: "cyberpunk postmodern feminist gender gibson body stories cyborg texts." At first glance this cluster seems nonsensical—and it is, at least syntactically. This is to be expected, though: topics aren't meant to be read as sentences but as words that co-occur enough times to make the relation potentially meaningful. When we created a visualization of the actual frequencies of these words with Voyant, we saw that Gibson's name is visible but not equal in size to these other terms (Figure 6). When we added the names of his contemporaries to this search, however, we saw his name rise in comparative prominence (Figure 7).

Although we do not suggest a causal relation between Gibson and these larger concepts—a different lexical dispersion plot, not included here, shows that they both predate and postdate cyberpunk—these visualizations do suggest that his work was of special interest to science fiction scholars thinking about these issues.

Another topic that intrigued us was the depiction of human–computer mergers in classic works of science fiction as compared with cyberpunk. Our hunch was that the concept of such a "system" would be distinct in our corpora, and we wondered if there would be a visible pattern shift over time. We created a list of keywords that surrounded the concept of "system" and compared the frequency of their appearance in our sets of texts. We used the three works of classic science fiction referenced

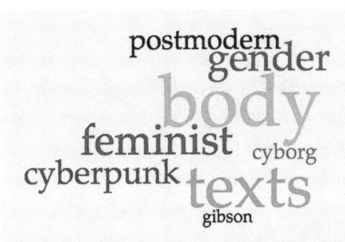

Figure 6: *Science Fiction Studies* word cluster without Gibson's contemporaries. Courtesy of Maria Alberto and Elizabeth Swanstrom.

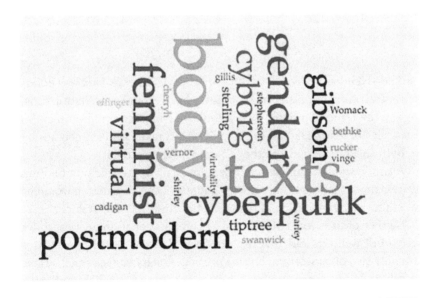

Figure 7: *Science Fiction Studies* word cluster with Gibson's contemporaries. Courtesy of Maria Alberto and Elizabeth Swanstrom.

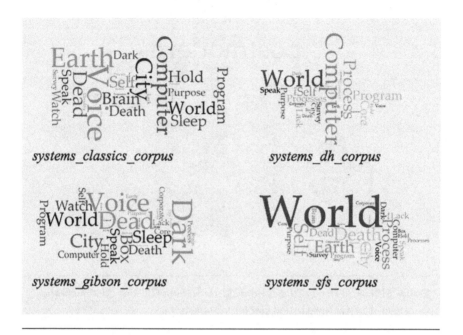

Figure 8: Word cluster variations of the *Science Fiction Studies* corpus. Courtesy of Maria Alberto and Elizabeth Swanstrom.

earlier—Heinlein's *Moon*, Clarke's *2001*, and McCaffrey's *Ship*—as points of contrast from our other corpora, and what we found was illuminating. Again, the term "computer" was significant—much more prominent in these classic science fiction works and the DH texts, while largely absent in both Gibson's fiction and the *SFS* corpus (see Figure 8).

Again, although this is only one approach, we believe our findings demonstrate that pursuing the implications of this distinction would be worth further exploration in science fiction and DH scholarship.

Neither of us is formally trained in computational linguistics, so we know full well that our findings are fairly shallow. At this stage there are only two of us working on this project, which involves considerable numbers of files and amounts of data. In addition, Mallet confirmed our keywords in some cases but not others—a phenomenon that may reshape our results or conclusions after further study. Finally, we used "The Winter Market" as our representative sample of Gibson's work to generate topics of interest and the keywords characterizing them, but we acknowledge that choosing this particular text to work from was a largely subjective process.

Despite these shortcomings and snags, we hope that our findings are suggestive. We also hope that by undertaking this qualitative approach in tandem with cultural analysis, we can help familiarize new audiences with DH methodologies in a way that does not overwhelm them with data but offers a user-friendly point of departure. We know we have only scratched the surface of what such an analysis might yield, and we invite anyone with an interest to build on our work. We provide a more robust breakdown of our data, complete with a variety of annotations and instructions, on our project's webpage (http://sf-and-dh.org). In the spirit of the interests and questions detailed, we warmly welcome collaboration.

CHAPTER 7 . . . **ROGER WHITSON**

**TIME CRITIQUE AND THE TEXTURES
OF ALTERNATE HISTORY**

MEDIA ARCHAEOLOGY IN *THE DIFFERENCE ENGINE*
AND *THE PERIPHERAL*

In an interview included for the afterword of the twentieth anniversary edition of William Gibson and Bruce Sterling's *The Difference Engine*, the authors discuss the rules of their collaboration. "We were specifically disallowed the option of pasting in some previous favorite text," says Gibson, explaining that any deleted text had to be reconstructed from their own memory. Sterling adds that the novel is "about word processing and what that process does to the texture of history."[1] *The Difference Engine* is famously narrated by Charles Babbage and Ada Lovelace's analytical engine that slowly gains sentience throughout the pages of the novel—as if the novel itself is a record of this iterated process of conscious reflection, a teleprinter machine communicating one algorithm after another. In the interview, Sterling compares the growing consciousness of the analytical engine to a series of literary methods like worldbuilding, historical description, postmodern pastiche, and the cut-up process of William S. Burroughs. In each case, the comparison causes Gibson and Sterling to question the connection between history and narrative. Gibson notes that Burroughs saw the cut-up as an artifact, whereas their airbrushing method "could blur the edges of the collage, effortlessly blend disparate parts, render the juncture invisible. A different level of magic. 'What do I need a computer for?' Burroughs had asked. 'I've got a typewriter.' Ah, but for this sir. For this."[2]

Matthew Kirschenbaum explains in *Track Changes: A Literary History of Word Processing* that Gibson and Sterling's airbrushing method in *The Difference Engine* was inspired by the "data storage routines of computer operating systems," in which layers of text overwritten by new files often retain readable traces of the original data.[3] Yet as Gibson discusses writing *The Peripheral*, the latter novel sketches a vision of history and data storage that is "weirder." Whereas *The Difference Engine* is an alternate history of Victorian England featuring a nineteenth-century information age, *The Peripheral* depicts two futures: one twenty years into our future and a second one that occurs seventy years after the first. The first future is what the novel calls a stub, an alternate continua or history of the latter future. The plutocrats operating in that far future cannot travel to the stub but can communicate with it using any computational interface—meaning that they can send enormous amounts of money to the stub, order assassinations, manipulate events, and even gamble on their outcome without worrying that such actions will affect their timeline. Reacting to interviewer Matt Rosoff's interpretation of the novel as an "extreme version of rising income inequality," Gibson reflects on the accumulated effects of an ever-increasing injection of capital and data flowing in from a distant future. These cycles of capital "are making the various aspects of the local economy do things that no one would have predicted twenty years ago.... And people are widening the contextual brackets on that until you have the weirdness of the whole world."[4]

Gibson's phrase "the weirdness of the whole world" identifies the accumulation of otherwise incompatible historical textures into an ecology of timing functionalities and historical experiences. This accumulation evokes what Wolfgang Ernst has identified as time-criticality or time-critique—particularly the technique that computer storage and signal processing uses to construct a "colder" sense of history that is not incompatible with, but is bracketed off from, cultural history. In *Chronopoetics: The Temporal Being and Operativity of Technological Media*, Ernst explains that time is often considered a noun but it "can also be an action, such as the verb to time, timing."[5] What Ernst calls time-criticality, or the decisive or critical action taken by media with very specific forms of timing functions, explores media temporality in three different ways: "firstly the infra-temporal domain of the smallest moments, secondly the human window of perception for 'the present,' and finally gradual ongoing transformations that are not noticed by people at all due to their slowness."[6] These timing functions allow Ernst to identify what Jussi Parikka calls a "prior level" of archival activity in the writing of history that occurs at scales below what human physiology can sense as a temporal process.[7] History is never an a priori given for media archaeology but is based on techniques, materials, and processes used in archiving, delineating, and articulating time.

This chapter applies time critique to a reading of *The Difference Engine* and *The Peripheral* to show how Gibson's media archaeology adds to Marxist accounts of alternate history already explored by Fredric Jameson and Phillip E. Wegner. In *Shockwaves of Possibility*, Wegner draws on Jameson's analysis of alternate history as a method of imagining utopia to see the genre "confront[ing] the reader with the dizzying prospect that 'what is' is in fact surrounded by an infinity of 'what ifs,' of other possible worlds, other collective destinies whose lack of substantiality in the here and now is the result of chance, or, even more significantly, of our actions or inactions, in the past."[8] Yet when describing the temporal and processual capabilities of computational media, Gibson's work demonstrates the degree to which our understanding of chance and action—and with them our experience of alternate history—is increasingly mediated through nonhuman time-critical processes. What emerges particularly in *The Peripheral* is a dystopian vision of alternate history as a variable in what Benjamin Bratton has identified as an emerging "accidental megastructure" of sovereignty brought about by ubiquitous computing. Comprising layers of earth, cloud, city, network, address, interface, and user, this megastructure or "Stack" is "an accumulation of interactions between layers in an emergent structure [that is] producing the scale, dimension, and contours" of an as-yet-unidentified nonhuman supercomputational geography.[9] Like computing, which is fundamentally concerned with looping, branching, and processing the values entered into an interface, governmentality in the Stack is figured in the interactions between layers, the accumulation of these interactions leading to more comprehensive structures, and the aggregation and sorting of such structures into newer and more abstract forms. The infinite possibilities of human choice in alternate history become in Gibson's work variables in programs of governmentality and finance, techniques that an emergent computational system uses to sort, process, and control. Although history remains a dialectic of struggle in Gibson's work, the actors involved in that struggle include nonhuman technological processes whose scale and speed shift the site of governmentality from the human to the algorithmic.

(Alternate) History

The finale of *The Difference Engine* puts into relief the conceit of the novel itself: it is the product of a series of algorithmic iterations bringing into consciousness an emergent mechanical artificial intelligence. In the twentieth anniversary edition interview, Sterling says that "the pretense of novelization falls apart and the Narratron's pastiche is laid bare. The text disintegrates into its source material: anecdotes, theater bills, song lyrics. An associative gumbo, for all the world like a bunch of Google search hits."[10] Sterling moves from oral sources (anecdotes, song lyrics) to print sources (theater bills) and finally to digital sources (Google search hits), a sweep of the entirety of human history through the media used to archive that history, particularly as such media are modularized, digitized, and processed by the Narratron's mechanical systems.

In *Steampunk and Nineteenth-Century Digital Humanities*, I argue that Gibson and Sterling in *The Difference Engine* use alternate history to translate between human experiences of history and the time-critical operations of computers.[11] Here I want to compare the insights and observations I developed in that book about this novel with Jameson's early work on history and the political unconscious. My purpose is to show how Gibson and Sterling's attention to alternate history and media archaeology contributes to what Jameson calls "an essentially historicist perspective, in which our readings of the past are vitally dependent on our experience of the present."[12] Yet by focusing on the archival work of technology in Gibson and Sterling's *The Difference Engine*, I show how the novel interrogates both the "us" and the "present" invoked in this articulation of historicism—expanding it to include the nonhuman processes and temporalities of computers. The result reinforces Marxist historical and political approaches to interpretation, but it does so by reconceiving the stakes and the actors involved in such interpretive practices. How do we understand alternate history in terms of actors that are not human? I argue that Gibson's media archaeology shows us that computing fundamentally transforms our experience of alternate history by illustrating the links between the human social imagination and an infrastructure of branching processes found in networked computational logic.

Jameson's *The Political Unconscious* reveals the primacy of political interpretations of text by seeing them as part of the history of class struggle, their meaning emerging as a dialectic of collectivity and difference. By articulating this dialectic, Jameson critiques poststructuralist accounts that prioritize difference over collectivity. As an example, he cites "[Roland] Barthes, [who] in *S/Z* shatters a Balzac novella into a random operation of multiple codes." By contrast, the Marxist approach reunifies these codes "at the level of the process of production, which is not random but can be described as a coherent functional operation in its own right."[13] The use of "code" and "operation" in this passage to describe the meaning of literary interpretation is fascinating, particularly if one reads it decades after Jameson first wrote it and with the interventions of distant reading, data mining, and the digital humanities in mind. This question of the process of production is also crucial when understanding Jameson's famous alignment of history with Lacan's Real. History, for Jameson, "is inaccessible to us except in textual form," and "our approach to it and to the Real itself necessarily passes through its prior textualization, its narrativization in the political unconscious."[14]

In *The Difference Engine*, Gibson and Sterling identify the Narratron as the textualizing apparatus archiving the operations and bringing their alternate history into being. For Jameson, a text is an imaginary solution to an "unresolvable social contradiction"; it "articulates its own situation and textualizes it, thereby encouraging and perpetuating the illusion that the situation itself did not exist before it."[15] Here, humans textualize the imaginary out of historical contradiction, and thus act as the apparatus archiving history symbolically. Yet even at the expense of encouraging the vulgar materialism that Jameson rightly critiques, I suggest that Gibson and Sterling's appeal to the "texture of history" identifies nonhuman, computational, and material actors influencing these Jamesonian historical operations in *The Difference Engine*. In Ernst's words, such a move allows us to understand the "specific ways of processing time that were and are introduced into culture through techno-mathematical media."[16]

For me, the key to understanding Ernst's argument lies in how *The Difference Engine* reframes the process of production to include computational media. I briefly consider two scenes in the novel that deal primarily with production and process to compare them with Jameson's account. I show how Jameson's notion of "text" becomes "texture" in Gibson and Sterling's novel, while Jamesonian "production" becomes "process." The first scene involves Edward Mallory's visit to the Quantitative Criminology department. Mallory is a paleontologist, and a previous scene involves his imagining the worms, fossils, and other nonhuman entities crowding the ground beneath London as he navigates the metropolis. Mallory visits Quantitative Criminology to investigate a set of punch cards that were presumed to contain a gambling program created by Ada Lovelace, which was actually a program illustrating Kurt Gödel's incompleteness and inconsistency theorem. The program was stolen in the beginning of the novel and acts as the McGuffin of Gibson and Sterling's tour of this alternate nineteenth-century Britain. As Mallory sees the various clacker devices crowding the department, he notices "shufflers, pin-mounts, isinglass color coders, jeweler's loupes, oiled tissues, and delicate rubber-tipped forceps" along with "newspaper racks, letter clamps, vast embedded card-files, catalogues, code-books, clackers' guides, an elaborate multi-dialed clock, three telegraph-dials whose gilded needles ticked out the alphabet, and printers busily punching tape."[17] Notably, in this long pan through the department, Mallory never notices human users.

Gibson's interest in these nonhuman technologies focuses on their microtemporal processes as structuring political experience in *The Difference Engine*. In Parikka's words, "things matter in terms of their politics and how they participate in the constitution of our world."[18] The scene in Quantitative Criminology emphasizes, for instance, how the technological infrastructure made up of the objects described makes humans into standardized and fungible units to be policed and surveilled. When Mallory interviews Under Secretary Wakefield later in the chapter, we start to understand that these processes have noticeable impact on the psychology and health of workers in the department. Wakefield had a "pronounced overbite [which] dented his lips" and was noticeably anxious when questioned about the cleanliness of the mechanical engines under his supervision. He describes the numerous ways the machine can break down: "heat builds up from spinning-friction, which expands the brass, which nicks the cogteeth. Damp weather curdles the gear-oil—and in dry weather, a spinning Engine can even create a small Leyden-charge, which attracts all matter of dirt! Gears gum and jam, punchcards adhere in the loaders."[19] More and more granular attention to the minute processes of these machines creates a feedback loop in Wakefield's mind, turning it from nervousness to excitement and back again. This loop intensifies his fascination and anxiety and exemplifies Susan Zieger's description of information overload as oscillating "between anxiety and enjoyment, suspense and satiation, abjection and mastery, depletion and fullness."[20] Babbage famously supported a division of labor into the smallest and most simplistic parts and described time as a tool for creating maximum surplus value. These values were materialized into his difference engine, which was originally designed to create the most efficient route for ships carrying commercial goods around Britain.[21] Yet by describing nested levels of attention in this manner, the depiction of objects in the Quantitative Criminology section of *The Difference Engine* shows how Babbage's attitudes toward labor translate into a computational politics of things.

The second scene involves a more granular demonstration of human fungibility as reconstructed by the Narratron. Each section of the novel begins with a computational reconstruction of some part of the novel. The second section opens with a jockey in mid-stride. The third section focuses on Edward Mallory, the fourth on Lord Byron's funeral, and the fifth on the surveillance apparatus constructed for Laurence Oliphant. It is the first section, though, introducing Sybil Gerard, that most effectively illustrates this sense of human fungibility. As the novel begins, we see a "composite image, optically encoded by escort-craft of the trans-Channel airship Lord Brunel: aerial view of a suburban Cherbourg, October 14, 1905."[22] The first sentence serves as metadata: giving us when the image was assembled, 1905; how it was encoded, optically and perhaps automatically; where it was constructed, the airship; then what serves as the subject of the image, a harbor and suburb in northwestern

France. The camera radically zooms into a shot of Gerard herself, erasing any impediment computationally: "a villa, a garden, a balcony. Erase the balcony's wrought iron curves, exposing a bath-chair and its occupant. Reflected sunset glints from the nickel-plate of the chair's wheel spokes." As we close in on Gerard, her body dissolves into its requisite parts: "tendons, tissue, jointed bone. Through quiet processes of time and information, threads within the human cells have woven themselves into a woman."[23] The effect is aesthetic, but also underscores how Gerard's human body is completely defined through its algorithmic reconstruction as the surveillance camera on the Lord Brunel gathers information about her espionage activities. Gerard stares back, yet remains an object in the description: "her attention fixed upon the sky, upon a silhouette of vast and irresistible grace—metal, in her lifetime, having taught itself to fly."[24] As we close on the opening scene of the novel, we have already reduced the human body to a group of components within human cells, dissolving its unity and reweaving them through time and information.

This comparison between bodies and technology is one of the many ways *The Difference Engine* exposes the branching of cultural history by time-critical processes. What Jameson calls "prior textualization" is replaced in Gibson and Sterling's novel by "quiet processes of time and information," or computational background systems endlessly calculating one intermediate algorithmic state after another. When speaking about such intermediate values, Ernst argues that "temporality of mathematics lies not in the realm of ideas, but rather in the worldliness of its media-technical operations."[25] Instead of a solution, intermediate storage provides a vision of worldly mathematics as an endless processing of iterations, constructing an ongoing temporality. For Ernst, time exists in an infrastructure of computational media, as background processes dissolve into algorithms—which in turn dissolve into microtemporal electrical impulses passing through logic gates determining the either/or of a particular decision tree. Ernst's time-critique is constituted in interactions between media materiality, algorithmic abstraction, and further textual and conceptual abstraction. In a wildly prophetic way for a novel originally published in 1990, *The Difference Engine* sketches a world where the history of the nineteenth century is an archival simulation of artificial intelligence encoding massive amounts of data—which in our contemporary world are supplied by GoogleBooks, on Wikipedia, on digital scholarly archives, on Gutenberg.org, or simply through conversations on social media. As such, it is a novel exploring what I have called elsewhere "the algorithmic condition," in which in addition to Jerome McGann's argument that culture is constituted through "spoken text or scripted forms," or the textual condition, we find that culture and history are processed computationally.[26] The London of *The Difference Engine* is processed computationally as an alternate history on a decision tree where Babbage constructed his analytical engine, instead of our history where the Information Age waited until the interventions of Alan Turing, John von Neumann, and Claude Shannon to unfold. Yet if the novel is a long series of self-reflexive iterations, how are we to understand where the data making up the novel is stored and when the program made one decision instead of another? As we consider the metaphysical value of history in *The Peripheral*, it is important to recognize how long Gibson has been considering the connections between computation and alternate history.

Accidental History

Like *The Difference Engine*, Gibson's 2014 novel *The Peripheral* deals with an alternate history simulated by a computer, yet that history occurs from the vantage point of a distant future looking to a past that—from the perspective of readers—is also a future. Described by the continua hobbyist Lev Zubov as "the platonic black server," the machine connecting him to this alternate history is assumed to be in China. "Someone has a device that sends and receives information," Lev continues, "to and from the past. The act of doing so generates continua. Unless those continua are already there, some literally infinite number of them, but that's academic."[27] He elaborates later in the novel that "the act of connection produces a fork in causality, the new branch causally unique. A stub, as we call them."[28] *The Peripheral* explores history as a function of signal transfer, simulation, and branching—reproducing many of the same themes in *The Difference Engine*. Still, *The Peripheral* complicates the depiction of historical texture from that earlier novel by exploring the accumulation of various processes of looping, branching, and transmission. These create a form of computing that Benjamin Bratton argues "does not just denote machinery; it is planetary-scale infrastructure that is changing not only how governments govern, but also what governance even is in the first place."²⁹

Bratton's questions about computing and governance complicate models of history as a purely human phenomenon. For instance, consider our discussion of Jameson's invocation of the "process of production" from *The Political Unconscious*. For Jameson, such processes are to be understood through a reading of Marx's theory of labor in the third volume of *Capital*. Jameson cites a passage where Marx suggests that "the realm of freedom actually begins only where labor which is in fact determined by necessity and mundane considerations ceases; thus in the very nature of things it lies beyond the sphere of actual material production."³⁰ "Actual material production" in this passage refers to the limitations of material reality on human productive capacity—and the dialectic between these limitations and human freedom forms the basis of Marx's materialism. Production is the work of humans reacting to the realm of necessity with the tools currently at their disposal. Both Marx and Jameson see history as a human process or, in Jameson's words, a "collective struggle to wrestle a realm of Freedom from a realm of Necessity."³¹

I argue that Jameson's late capitalist reading of Marx in *The Political Unconscious* is still enmeshed in what Bratton would call a "Westphalian" model of governance—in which agency is designed according to "the frame of the nation-state" by "separating and containing sovereign domains as discrete, adjacent units among a linear and horizontal surface."³² Westphalian models include not only the nation as a planar geography but also human subjects as the exclusive sites of governmental agency and control. In this model, matter is defined as anything resisting human productive capacity and does not emphasize how such capacities are entangled in a larger ecology of natural and technological actors. By contrast, in "Earth Layer" section, Bratton invokes new materialist conceptions of matter by comparing a mid-1970s photograph of Gilles Deleuze contemplating the "plane of immanence" on the Big Sur beach with the designing of the Intel silicon chip occurring at the same moment just miles away in Palo Alto. *"The world remaking itself in* waves," Bratton says elegiacally of Deleuze's reflection on the philosophical implications of the beach, "*bit by bit and pebble by pebble.*"³³ Both the plane of immanence and the model of universal computation are what Bratton calls information realism, this understanding of materialism "grapple[s] with *matter* as vibrant, contingent, and mutable, as reproduced in the careful calculation of sets of differences drawn from particular virtual possibilities."³⁴ To be clear, I do not suggest that Jameson and Marx never deal with new materialism; rather, that the passage quoted from *Capital* positions the dialectic in Westphalian terms instead of exploring the more complicated fluxes of material production.

The granularity of data collection enabling an information realism shifts governmentality away from Westphalian models toward what Bratton calls "the Stack": a "vast discontiguous apparatus" or "a terraforming project, covering the globe in subterranean wires and switches and overhead satellite arrays, simultaneously centralizing and decentralizing computing and data storage and the social relations that depend on them (and vice versa)."³⁵ Key to understanding this discontiguous apparatus is the operationalization of reversibility, in which any interior or geography can be inverted: not only does the inside of a territory become the outside, but such movements can be automated and made the variable in an equation at an even more general level of abstraction. A potent example Bratton uses in the "Cloud Layer" section is the PRISM/Snowden affair and the revelation that private consultants were involved in core operations of the National Security Agency data-gathering apparatus. Such participation reveals that government has been transformed into a platform that is—at best—supplemental to a larger unknown apparatus, "perhaps an apps-based queryable megamachine like Planetary Skin or Google Earth, but with obvious and significant differences" or "an ambient, generalized utility at hand for anyone interested in parsing the databases and spreadsheets and deploying them to new designs."³⁶ Platforming has, in fact, become the new model of governance. Bratton says that the "two domains become dramatically less distinct from one another, interlacing and folding up in new ways, producing emergent institutional forms not reducible to the direct combination of the two."³⁷

The Peripheral narrates the interlacing of platform and governance—where what was once on the periphery becomes central, utopia becomes dystopia, future becomes past, alternate history becomes our history—and vice versa. Reversibility occurs from the first pages of the novel, where Flynne believes she is helping her brother Burton earn money by playing a video game featuring drones. Injuries Burton sustained from an unnamed war before the novel's events limits his career choices to operating such peripherals through a virtual interface. "And then she was rising," Flynne describes the drone emerging as she begins her job, "out of what Burton said would be a launch bay in the roof of a van. Like she was in an elevator. No control yet. And all around her, and he hadn't told her this, were whispers, urgent as they were faint, like a cloud of invisible fairy police dispatchers."[38] The minimalist character of Gibson's narration heightens the sense of displacement, as Flynne engages with the controls of the game and inhabits the drone peripheral in the environment. Flynne is asked to "edge" away paparazzi drones taking pictures at a party—and the first few chapters are filled with partially obscured descriptions of the objects she encounters as she flies through the London she sees unfolding in front of her. The paparazzi drones she was hired to distract "looked like double-decker dragonflies, wings or rotors transparent with speed, little clear bulb on the front end." Likewise, in a building she flies past, "robots, little low beige things that moved almost too fast to see, were vacuuming the floor, while three almost identical robot girls were arranging food on a long table."[39] When Flynne observes the death of the doomed Aelita, we read prose that blurs cinematic metaphors, like slow motion and time lapse. It also recalls the scene describing the digitization of Sybil Gerard from *The Difference Engine*, yet in this instance fungibility is much more violent and bloody. "The woman never moved," the description begins, "as something tiny punched out through her cheek, leaving a bead of blood, her mouth still open, more of them darting in, almost invisible, streaming over from the pale-edge slit."[40] Flynne struggles to capture the full realism of the scene as she experiences it, never quite getting there as events slow down and then speed up. "Her forehead caved in," it continues, "like stop-motion of Leon's pumpkin of the president, on top of the compost in her mother's bin, over days, weeks."[41] Apart from the cinematic character of the description, we only get glimpses of parts of Aelita's body, rather than its entirety—as she drops from the building her "limbs [fell] at angles that made no sense."[42] It is clear that we are supposed to feel the same disorientation Flynne does, yet the flatness of the description reinforces Flynne's sense that she thinks she is experiencing a game—but is never sure. The body was "less a body every inch it fell, so that by the time they passed the thirty-seventh, where she'd first noticed the thing, there were only two fluttering rags, one striped, one black."[43] Darting from reality to gamespace and back again, Aelita's death resides in an uncanny play between the two.

Gibson only offers the faintest hints that Aelita's death actually occurred in these early chapters, playing with our expectation that a death might haunt Flynne in some supernaturally immediate way despite the mediated interface she uses to access the feed for her game. Yet when Flynne first meets Netherton and begins to understand the full scope of what she saw—that is, the drone experience was not a game but a feed where she witnessed a very real death—she quickly finds herself questioning reality. Netherton responds that "it's a gamelike environment" and "it isn't real in the sense that you—" and Flynne cuts him off.[44] "Are you for real?"

> He tilted his head to the side.
> "How would I know?" she asked. "If that was a game, how would I know you aren't just AI?"
> "Do I look like a metaphysician?"[45]

Gamespace becomes gamelike-environment becomes a future reality populated by British and Russian plutocrats. Flynne's experience of the events of the novel reverses again and again. Yet we understand that the reversal of this perspective, along with the constant injection of capital into her present by those plutocrats from the future, also shifts the stakes and scale of the conflict in *The Peripheral*.

Steven Jones characterizes these reversals by using Gibson's term "evergence," suggesting that they also help explain the rise of digital humanities as a field. For him, "between 2004 and 2008, the cumulative effect of a variety of changes in technology and culture converged and culminated in a new consensual imagination of the role of the network in relation to the physical and social world."[46] Gibson describes the eversion in his *Difference Engine* interview with Bruce Sterling by describing cyberpunk as a "desktop-based computer world" that's "being rapidly replaced by a wireless, cloudy network culture. . . . *It everted. Turned itself inside out, into the world. The world became it.*"[47] Yet even Gibson's theory of the evergence in *The Difference Engine* seems to describe only part of the complicated "weirdness" of *The Peripheral*, where a seemingly endless number of "turnings inside out" occur so rapidly that they merge with more abstract functionalities of planetary computing. For Bratton, there is no culmination of acts of reversibility, rather, "the practical issues of addressing the world cross-divides of solid and fluid, the material and the informational, between sand and bits, between things and actions, between objects and enunciations, archived pasts and simulated futures and the structures that would govern all of these exchanges as they bloom into new forms."[48] Indeed, further eversions occurred by the time Gibson published *The Peripheral* in 2014, and have continued to occur in the years since then. As authors describe what is happening in planetary computing, planetary computing is predicting variations of what is to come along with calculating what might have happened, and in the process already transforming what is being described. In an interview with Karin Kross about *The Peripheral*, Gibson imagines readers in 2014 encountering his 1990s science fiction Bridge trilogy (*Virtual Light, Idoru,* and *All Tomorrow's Parties*), saying that these novels now "read more like alternate history than an imagined future."[49] Another eversion occurred when the publication of *Agency*, originally slated for 2017, was delayed until January 2020. *Agency* features an alternate history where Hillary Clinton won the 2016 presidential election and early versions of the novel featured a nuclear exchange between Syria, Russia, NATO, and Turkey. Gibson notes in a 2019 *New Yorker* profile that Donald Trump's actions short-circuited his plans for the novel: "But then Trump started fucking with N Korea... so how scary can my scenario be?" Four months later, Gibson notes that he had to ask for a second rewrite when the British political consulting firm Cambridge Analytica was revealed to have been collecting Facebook information in 2016 to microtarget voters for the Trump campaign.[50] History and Gibson's alternate history are caught in a set of loops and branches, where the distributed apparatuses of planetary computing meet all-too-human responses. "We are confronted with both a surplus of new worlds and a lack of clear civilizational frontiers," Bratton says, "other than those simulated by various senile medievalisms now in ascendance. Can we survive that? Can we address the openings closest at hand fast enough that they generate new geographies before we can ruin them?"[51]

I propose that the deviously optimistic ending of *The Peripheral* and its misreading by some of Gibson's reviewers can be ascribed to the difficulty of understanding, on one hand, the complicated functions and worlds of planetary computing, and, on the other, the "senile medievalisms" whose reactionary politics we've seen in the Brexit campaign and the rise of Trump. *The Peripheral* describes a slow apocalyptic event named by the characters as "the Jackpot." When explaining the Jackpot to Flynne, Netherton is careful to suggest that it was caused "by no one thing." Instead "it was multicausal, with no particular beginning and no end. More a climate than an event, so not the way apocalypse stories liked to have a big event, after which everybody ran around with guns . . . or else were eaten alive by something caused by the big event. Not like that."[52] Eighty percent of the global population died out through climate change and wars driven by the rise in temperatures. As Netherton describes the Jackpot, it appears as one of the most predicable of apocalypses. In fact, Flynne says that "she sort of already knew [about the Jackpot], figured everybody did, except for people who still said it wasn't happening, and those people were mostly expecting the Second Coming anyway."[53] As a slow apocalyptic event, the Jackpot challenges interpretations of history that see in a single event a moment when one can decisively respond.

In this sense, Gibson's Jackpot illustrates and extends one of Jameson's more famous dictims in *The Political Unconscious*, that "history is what hurts." Jameson continues, "history can be apprehended only through its effects, and never directly as some reified force."[54] Gibson's slow apocalypse mirrors Jameson's sense of history as the Lacanian Real, at a remove from experience because it is so distributed in space and time as myriad forces. On the other hand, Gibson's finale reifies the very individualistic forces Netherton's Jackpot refuses. The ending of *The Peripheral* reads very much like an action film, with weddings for Flynne and Netherton and technological solutions for Burton's mental and physical traumas. It seems that despite Netherton's description of the Jackpot, the novel ends with "a big event, after which everybody ran around with guns."[55]

We can see Gibson's "big event" apocalypticism detailed in the climax of the Aelita murder mystery serving as the McGuffin of *The Peripheral*. After learning who killed Aelita, the leader of a group of modified humans called "Patchers," Flynne and Netherton confront Hamed al-Habib and his conspirator, Sir Henry. Burton uses a "red cube" in the fight, a strange weapon from an alternate timeline, "which flung itself, somehow, straight up and then to the side, crashing with a big clang into the white-bared cell doors of the second leave, a few lights going out."⁵⁶ Many readers have commented on the sheer ridiculousness of this weapon, particularly since Gibson gives so little information about it. Yet I see this scene as part of the overblown drama characterizing the finale of *The Peripheral*. Hamed and Sir Henry are killed pretty quickly with assemblers, nanotech machines that murdered Aelita early in the novel. The final few chapters focus on building Flynne's compound, the market dominance of Pharma Jon, and her slow takeover of their stub's economy by the printing, marketing, and implementation of post-Jackpot technology from the future. In one of the more ironic passages of the novel, Flynne reflects on these events, telling Ainsley Lowbeer that she's afraid of becoming just as bad as the plutocracy from the future. Lowbeer responds that her skepticism and vigilance are both good. "Evil wasn't glamorous," Lowbeer says, "but just the result of ordinary half-assed badness, high school badness, given enough room, however that might happen, to become its bigger self. Bigger with more horrible results, but never more than the cumulative weight of ordinary human baseness."⁵⁷ We are "'all too human, dear,' Lowbeer continues, 'and the moment we forget it, we're lost.'"⁵⁸

It is particularly ironic that Gibson uses Lowbeer to communicate this idea about evil and humanity, since the unclear nature of Lowbeer's own humanity symptomizes the novel's ambivalence about human agency. When she is first introduced, Lev Zubov describes Lowbeer as "hyperfunctionally ancient," "entirely too knowing and invariably powerful."⁵⁹ Lowbeer apologizes to Ossian Murphy about knowing far too much about him before meeting him in person.

> "Forgive me," she said, "We haven't been introduced. Someone my age is all feeds, Mr. Murphy. For my sins, I've continual access to most things, resulting in a terrible habit of behaving as if I already know everyone I meet."
>
> "Not in the least, mum," Ossian said, staying in character, eyes downcast, "no offense taken."
>
> "Which," she said, to the others, as if she hadn't heard him, "in a sense I do."⁶⁰

Lowbeer remains an uncanny character throughout *The Peripheral*, always knowing more than the other characters about events happening in either setting. To what degree, then, do we understand her reflections about the kleptocracy and evil? In an interview with i09, Gibson mentions that an early review of *The Peripheral* called the novel "wildly optimistic." His response was that the final two chapters act as a "fantastically accurate litmus test for a reader's socio-political sophistication. If you think it's all well and good for either of those characters [Flynne and Netherton] when you get to the end—then give it 20 years of life and look at it again."[61] While Flynne and Netherton seem to have overcome the murder plotline Gibson inserts into *The Peripheral*, it is much less certain how the larger transformations to Flynne's stub will play out—or, really, who the true protagonist(s) of *The Peripheral* will turn out to be.

Media Archaeologies to Come

Toward the end of the Quantitative Criminology section in *The Difference Engine*, Wakefield complains that in processing information, "demand always expands to overmatch the capacity. It's as if it were a law of Nature!"[62] To which Mallory responds, "Perhaps it is a law, . . . in some realm of Nature we've yet to comprehend."[63] Of course, Gibson and Sterling are referring to capital's crisis of accumulation, which Marx defines as the pressure to produce an ever-expanding amount of surplus value. Still, Gibson and Sterling's sly wink as they describe this mechanism of capitalism to their readers is strange when considering that their whole novel is an alternate history. Alternate history is predicated on the notion that history is not inevitable but tinged with what Wegner calls "what-ifs," "possible worlds," and other "collective destinies" revealing the role of chance, action, and ultimately agency in its unfolding. If *The Difference Engine* participates in telling an alternate history, as its stature in the genre of steampunk would lead us to believe, then history cannot be as inevitable as Mallory argues.

The Peripheral, on the other hand, shows us that alternate history can indeed turn out to be inevitable; rather, its inevitability might be a function of its invisibility in a swarm of events out of human control. With the Jackpot, Netherton says that there were "no comets crashing, nothing you could really call a nuclear war. Just everything else, tangled in the changing climate."⁶⁴ People living through the Jackpot found themselves entangled in events that—themselves—were less decisive than a single war or a single disaster. Compounded together, however, people found themselves in even less control than they would have been in an apocalyptic disaster, as Netherton continues, these events transformed "how people were, how many of them there were, how they'd changed things just by being there."⁶⁵ In such a tangle of microtemporal and macrotemporal events, what chance does a single or even an infinite amount of alternate histories have?

When considering the "Stack to come," Bratton suggests that the appropriate vision for grasping the emergence of planetary computing is as a "kind of double exposure: one future that is anonymously present with us, arrived but unnamed, and one that is already named but not yet here." He argues that creating a more preferable response to the emergence of planetary computing depends on "our management of this blur."⁶⁶ Such a description recalls Gibson and Sterling's airbrush method, where untold textures of history blur into various data storage techniques. Yet these techniques are themselves built on an infrastructure of the same "anonymous forced labor" Jameson invokes when quoting Walter Benjamin's "Theses on the Philosophy of History" in the epigraph to the conclusion of *The Political Unconscious*.⁶⁷ "There is no document of civilization which is not at the same time a document of barbarism," Benjamin argues, suggesting that the idealisms written into the laws of a civilization are built on an infrastructure of suffering, exploitation, and violence.⁶⁸ Jameson uses Benjamin's text to illustrate the double exposure of ideology and utopianism when considering class consciousness: "all class consciousness—or in other words, all ideology in the strongest sense, including the most exclusive forms of ruling-class consciousness just as much as that of oppositional or oppressed classes—is in its very nature Utopian."⁶⁹ But this utopianism puts us in the same political space as Flynne at the end of *The Peripheral*, that despite believing she's the protagonist in an action novel with a happy ending, she's actually managing a blur of forces and historical stubs that are far too diverse and abstract for her to comprehend.

Just as class consciousness has a utopian nature, the textures of history situating both of these concepts rely on the storage and transmission of data and information. Consider the digital copy of Marx's *Capital* housed on the Marxists Internet Archive.[70] To read this particular copy of *Capital* requires access to the servers hosting the document. Myriad ecologies, processes, and aspects of platform governance exist in each step transmitting the document to our devices. Servers require electricity to store documents, and their emissions contribute significantly to global warming. Internet cables run through undersea ecologies, disturbing habitats and organisms.[71] Internet relays transmitting the document run TC/IP protocol to link devices, its code establishing an architecture of control determining which messages can be exchanged and which are rejected.[72] When the document finally arrives on our devices, it is displayed on computers requiring rare-earth metals like neodymium to function. The chemical processes used to extract these rare-earth metals create pollution, raise rates of cancer, and make nearby villages in China and Africa almost uninhabitable.[73] The copy of Marx's *Capital* on the Marxists Internet Archive is part of a material infrastructure that acts as a catalyst of global warming, an executable form of power and control, and a carcinogenic reminder of imperialism and capitalism. Bratton insists that "the geopolitics of computation . . . are not overseen by any one *Angelus Novus* that could, per Walter Benjamin's assignment, make good on history's knottily kneaded, well-promised catastrophe."[74] Likewise, there is no text of civilization that is not at the same time an infrastructural texture participating in planetary computing—constructing sites and agents of governmentality that are no longer exclusively human.

PART III ... **GIBSON AND THE PROBLEM OF THE PRESENT**

CHAPTER 8 ... **SHERRYL VINT**

TOO BIG TO FAIL

THE BLUE ANT TRILOGY AND
OUR PRODUCTIZED FUTURE

William Gibson's Blue Ant trilogy is often considered the author's turn away from science fiction, written in a near future that rapidly recedes into the past even as the novels appear.[1] Jaak Tomberg argues that the trilogy is characterized by a "double vision": that it must be "read as *simultaneously* realist and science-fictional." Tomberg also contends that this genre convergence, through which Gibson's style creates an estranged version of living in the present, is indicative of the hegemony of neoliberal logics that posit there is no outside to capitalism.[2] A variety of conditions erase distinctions between inside and outside (the world market and the world; technologically mediated reality and materiality; the world of art and the world of the commodity) and have created a crisis in our capacity to effectively mount critique. Tomberg reads this as the collapse of science fiction's capacity to offer visions of a world different from the quotidian one, because "in a culture that *behaves as if* it had no outside, there is also no plausible outside space-time where science fiction can position the figure of its estranging Other."[3]

I agree with Tomberg's diagnosis that the trilogy depicts the impersonal forces of contemporary surveillance technologies, marketing software, and social media immersion as an estranged kind of present, an updated cyberpunk in which we have not left the material world to immerse ourselves into cyberspace, but cyberspace has extended outward: reality fused with advertising spin that maps over and displaces our perception of materiality. At the same time, Tomberg's focus on how Gibson's mode of representing technology drives this shift minimizes the importance of the neoliberalist context that gives us this language of the "absence" of an outside, or, in Margaret Thatcher's phrase, the sense that "there is no alternative" to the market economy and a future dominated by its values and metrics. This essay explores the opposition in the trilogy between advertising and art to argue that Gibson is nostalgic for the power of art to resist capitalism's infiltration of social and political life, now at such a point of saturation that commodity relations have replaced all social ties. Blue Ant represents the nadir of a culture so thoroughly subsumed by capital that not only have relations of production become abstracted into the commodity, but people can no longer discern a line between authentic experience and the manipulations of advertising.

My point of departure is a passage in *Spook Country* given as the in-world Wikipedia entry for Hubertus Bigend. This citation notes that Bigend's mother had links with "the Situationist International," although Bigend denies their relevance to the success of Blue Ant.[4] Guy Debord's analysis in *Society of the Spectacle* is perhaps the best-known theorization of changes to social life concomitant with the rise of consumerist and information-age capital. One way to understand the world as shaped by Bigend and Blue Ant is as the epitome of everything that Debord and other situationists anticipated and critiqued. Debord's first dictum—that society has become "an immense accumulation of spectacles" in which "everything that was directly lived has receded into a representation"— aptly captures the future we see in this trilogy.[5] Crucial to this theorization of the spectacle is that we must understand it not as "a collection of images" but as "a social relation between people that is mediated by images";[6] throughout the trilogy we see Bigend work actively to co-opt any social or creative activity that is not oriented toward market profitability and redirect it to that end. Debord also argues that "the fetishism of the commodity" has its end point in the society of the spectacle, "where the real world is replaced by a selection of images which are projected above it, yet which at the same time succeed in making themselves regarded as the epitome of reality."[7] Thus, Gibson hints that we need to understand the Blue Ant trilogy not in terms of technological change and a Baudrillardian blurring of the distinction between reality and its representations, but through Debord's observations regarding how capitalist alienation has so completely colonized social experience that we can no longer remember there is an alternative—that is, we take its spectacles as the world.

Perhaps the most potent way Gibson depicts a commodity ethos that supplants other social relations is through the various ways the fashion industry is taken up across the novels. Cayce's work as a coolhunter in *Pattern Recognition*, and her value to the advertising industry given her allergy to brands, capture the complexities and ironies of the new kind of secret advertising that Blue Ant spawns. Her talent lies in finding things that still have some connection to what Debord would describe as the "directly lived," what Cayce calls "at the level of consumer repurposing."[8] She finds these styles in people's innovative use, before they become "productized" by someone such as Bigend and thus sought by consumers based on how the industry directs their desire.[9] The more something becomes associated with fashion and branding, the less connection it seems to have with material existence, such as the beautiful kitchen in Damien's London apartment, "as devoid of edible content as its designers' display windows in Camden High Street."[10] Later novels explore this interplay between use and exchange or advertising value, such as Bigend's interest in "recession-proof" military contracts, which prompts Milgrim's analysis of the borrowings between military style and street clothing,[11] or Meredith's experiences with making and designing shoes. In these examples, branding is a force that pulls the clothing out of something like a realm of lived experience and into that of the spectacle, images that come to be taken for the real.

Bigend explains to Hollis that the appeal of military-styled clothing has almost nothing to do with wanting to be a soldier but expresses a desire to "self-identify as. However secretly. To imagine they may be mistaken for, or at least associated with."[12] This is the apotheosis of Blue Ant's insight that "consumers don't buy products, so much as narratives," here perfected in the longing that the "costume and semiotics of achingly elite police and military units" cultivates in buyers, who will never use these products "for anything remotely like what they were designed for."[13] Meredith notes the degree to which the fashion industry embodies a logic of capitalism such that meeting human need is secondary, while the endless circulation of capital to generate profit is paramount. The emphasis on seasons and ever-changing "looks" symbolizes this broken economic base, an industry that "wobbles along, really, like a shopping cart with a missing wheel. You can only keep it moving if you lean on it a certain way and keep pushing, but if you stop, it tips over."[14] Marketing, particularly marketing in which promoting an item takes precedence over its qualities, is the most afflicted aspect of this diseased structure. Meredith tried to make shoes that would defy this market logic of shabby commodities built for planned obsolescence, and there is a utopian promise in her description of handmade shoes that are lovingly crafted, with beauty and longevity in mind. Thinking of shoes made and distributed in this way requires that "you imagine a world. You imagine the world those shoes come from, and you wonder if they could happen here, in this world, the one with all the bullshit."[15]

The footage in *Pattern Recognition* is the primary symbol of a different economy of making. It appears online segment by segment, inspiring fierce fan loyalty and obsessive analysis of the possible meanings of each frame. The desire inspired by the footage is partly a desire to detach from history, here understood, it seems, as inevitably tied to capitalism, evoked by ever-changing fashion. The footage's style does not allow viewers to date its period, and Cayce explains that part of her pleasure in the footage is that it emerges to them as an art object unconnected with the quotidian world, what Cayce calls the gift of "'OT,' Off Topic," the studied avoidance of topics such as "the world ... News."[16] Cayce sees an artistic project and a way to escape a twenty-first century she finds increasingly distressing, whereas Bigend sees the footage as "the single most effective piece of guerrilla marketing ever,"[17] a set of images that captures attention and prompts widespread distribution, even in the absence of a product or narrative. At one point, writing to the maker of the footage, Cayce imagines it almost as a pathway to unalienated sociality, suggesting that viewers "allow ourselves so far into the investigation of whatever this is, whatever you're doing, that we become part of it."[18] Her desire for some kind of unalienated connection, which she can imagine only through a social relation to a product, is symptomatic of the society of the spectacle, in which "the commodity has succeeded in totally colonizing social life. Commodification is not only visible, we no longer see anything else; the world we see is the world of the commodity."[19] The trilogy's grasp of what troubles the twenty-first century emerges from this tension between Bigend's plans to productize the footage and Cayce's longing for the different world it seems to anticipate.

The real source of the footage proves macabre. Its images originate from surveillance cameras, whose ubiquity speaks to one of the alienations of contemporary society the trilogy explores (the interest in military uses of GPS tracking in *Spook Country*; wearable technology, the "ugly t-shirt" that allows subjects to be deleted from recordings in *Zero History*).[20] To produce the footage, these images are manipulated by Nora, whose brain has been damaged by a grenade, and her resulting work is then rendered, pixel by pixel, to beautiful resolution by a captive prison labor force, controlled by her Mafia uncle, Volkov. As the novel points out, the rendering is extremely time intensive, and the only way the project could have been kept secret is if the labor force was subjected to "unusual constraints."[21] The footage is the most prevalent of a several icons in the trilogy that point to the exploitative conditions of labor that underlie the production of commodities. Another striking example is the Curta calculator, another marvel of hand-crafted genius, that can calculate without electricity or electronic components, invented by Curt Herzstark during his imprisonment in the Buchenwald concentration camp.

What is crucial about Gibson's version of these relations of production is that it is not merely the mass-produced items of the globalized economy that are tainted. Even something as seemingly disconnected from these industrial forces as the footage bears their trace. Indeed, when all is finally revealed, Bigend's assessment of the footage is closer to the mark than Cayce's, since the use of prison labor to indulge his injured niece was not simply a familial gesture on Volkov's part but "a test operation, where healthy, motivated prisoners can lead healthy, motivated lives, plus receive training and career direction"; the experiment's aim is to transform prisons into "entrepreneurial," profitable spaces.[22] It is thus not all that surprising that in *Zero History*, we learn that Bigend successfully productized the footage into Trope Sloop, a "viral pitchman platform" for developing more advertising.[23]

Just as Cayce is deployed by Bigend to find the maker of the footage in

Pattern Recognition, in *Zero History* Hollis is sent to find the maker of Gabriel Hounds, the elite denim maker whose refusal to participate in the excesses of branding render it all the more valuable. Indeed, perhaps the central irony that Gibson explores across this trilogy is how attempts to escape the commoditized society of the spectacle are inexorably transformed into its next advertising strategy. We eventually learn that Cayce makes Gabriel Hounds clothing, an updated version of her style as described in *Pattern Recognition*: items of clothing with no visible designer labels, whose cut is simple enough that they cannot be accurately dated to any particular decade or fashion movement. Cayce values her work for its attention to craft, the quality of the items produced by methods other than mass production—the indigo smell of the dye persists, the metal buttons are "nonreflective" rather than insignia of a company, and the cotton seems to have been hand loomed.[24] Yet as Hollis searches for the designer, the scarcity of the item, the lack of any regular distribution outlet, seems to drive others to value Cayce's work. When she and Hollis finally meet, Cayce regrets that people have forgotten how to make things with care, observing that a quality cotton shirt made in America in 1935 would be both inexpensive and better-made than more recent versions, and yet "if you re-create that shirt, and you might have to go to Japan to do that, you wind up with something that needs to retail for around three hundred dollars."[25] As a commodity, quality items seem impossible, but as elite objects, almost attaining the level of art, they might persist.

Gabriel Hounds's designs and the footage are "things that weren't tied to the present moment,"[26] and in this discussion of craft in production we get hints that a significant element of what is to be eschewed in the present is its globalized economy. Simple cotton shirts or durable denim must become bespoke, luxury items, costing far beyond the reach of the working people whose attire they mimic, another strange kind of cosplay like the military clothing Bigend pursues. Describing her preferred style in *Pattern Recognition*, Cayce characterizes her avoidance of brand markers as a desire for clothing that "ideally seem[ed] to have come into this world without human intervention."[27] By *Zero History*, this erasure of labor has been corrected. An older Cayce explains that she lived in Chicago for a while after her marriage and "discovered the ruins of American manufacturing. I'd been dressing in its products for years, rooting them out of warehouses, thrift shops, but I'd never thought of where they'd come from."²⁸ Like Meredith's shoes, Gabriel Hounds points to another world, a world where articles are manufactured to meet humans needs rather than to continue the circulation of capital, where items are desired for their functionality and craftsmanship, not for the spectacle of their branding—a world where humans make things, rather than represent them.

The resistance to globalization is most apparent in the trilogy's reflections on commodity production and what Cayce calls "the mirror world," which is how she describes the United Kingdom as it is embodied by commodity products that are almost like the familiar ones of the United States, yet subtly changed. When Boone tells her that the two Anglo countries are too similar, that UK products are "just more of our stuff,"²⁹ Cayce corrects him by pointing to the traces of distinct and local economies of manufacture that remain embedded in the infrastructure. The differences may be subtle, but there are differences: "They invented that here, probably, and made it here. This was an industrial nation. Buy a pair of scissors, you got British scissors. They made all their own stuff. Kept imports expensive. Same thing in Japan. All their bits and pieces were different, from the ground up."³⁰ Yet the mirror world is disappearing, Boone points out, and Blue Ant's philosophy, and advertising more generally, drive this erasure: "no borders, pretty soon there's no mirror to be on the other side of. Not in terms of the bits and pieces, anyway."³¹ Later Cayce observes this conflation and feels "complicit in whatever it is that gradually makes London and New York feel more like each other. . . . She knows too much about the processes responsible for the way product is positioned, in the world."³² Thus, it is Bigend and those like him, their search for ever-larger global markets, that replace products attached to a lived reality, local from the ground up, with homogenized products positioned to serve consumers everywhere.

These reflections on commodities may remind us of another of Debord's contentions, that the spectacle is the inverse of a true society, an alienated social relation that hinders critical thought. He observes that "spectacle is a concrete inversion of life,"³³ and later suggests that "the economy's domination of social life brought about an evident degradation of being into having—human fulfillment was no longer equated with what one was, but with what one possessed."³⁴ This decline from being into having, he continues, has reached a second stage in which "all 'having' must now derive its immediate prestige and its ultimate purpose from appearances."[35] Gibson's critique of advertising and its social effects clearly echo Debord's critique, including Cayce's worry at the end of *Pattern Recognition* that the world has moved closer to "that country without borders that Bigend strives to hail from, . . . where there are no mirrors to find yourself on the other side of, all experience having been reduced, by the spectral hand of marketing, to price-point variations on the same thing."[36] Advertising is the basis for all social relations in the Blue Ant trilogy, a change far more sinister, in the final analysis, than the Sprawl trilogy's intuition that the emergence of artificial intelligence would presage a fundamental social change. The market understood as an entity with agency and needs somehow independent from—and taking precedence over—human ones is the nonhuman force of alienation in the Blue Ant books.

The collapse of all social relations into market ones is the real subsumption of life under capital, exemplified by Magda's work for Trans, a Blue Ant subsidiary. Magda promotes products not through visible advertising but through staged social encounters. She is paid to "go to clubs and wine bars and chat people up," mentioning a client's product in a favorable way as part of this exchange. "Nothing like a pitch, you understand, just a brief favorable mention."[37] This work is solely to attract attention, an early iteration of what Bigend hopes to capture and perfect with the footage, a marketing tool that colonizes people's imagination and encourages them to promote the product themselves. The circulation of the narrative and its spectacle is enough, it seems.

As Magda notes, one of the most distressing things she learns through this fake socializing is that her interlocutors also lie: their desire to be part of the in-crowd with exclusive knowledge means that they tell her they like the product, too, even when Magda knows they could not yet have encountered it. She finds the work distressing and believes "I'm devaluing something. In others. In myself. And I'm starting to distrust the most casual exchange."[38] Her alienation epitomizes Debord's observation—when the economic dominates social life, being becomes having, and having begins to "derive its immediate prestige and its ultimate purpose from appearances."[39] The abstraction from lived experience is complete: while Cayce finds patterns of real use and enables them to be productized, Magda works to generate the pattern in the first place, such that human agency, preference, and ingenuity are entirely abstracted from the circulation of commodities.

The society of the spectacle is the world of Blue Ant, as Gibson's sly reference to Bigend's mother's relationship with situationism suggests, but the question remains: does the trilogy champion an artistic strategy along the lines of *détournement*, to reawaken a sense of lived reality? *Détournement*, recall, is a strategy for turning received critical ideas, media texts, and received truths back against themselves, transforming them so that they are not faithful quotations of the original but are simultaneously critiques and transformations of what is cited.[40] Rather, is Blue Ant something that might best be described as situationism everted? The motif of locative art, traced mainly in *Spook Country*, introduces this language of everting. Locative art uses GPS positioning and locally embedded technologies to create virtual images that can be viewed only with the appropriate equipment at that physical place. Locative art thus resists the detachment of time and space often associated with the internet and elements of online culture, creating artwork that is virtual and digital but insisting that it remain attached to a particular location, often especially to a history of events that have taken place there. One such work shows River Phoenix's death on the Sunset Strip, for example, and Hollis is instructed that the artist's work has to do with "history as internalized space," a sensibility that emerges from trauma.[41] Locative art is also later described as the way cyberspace everts, "turns itself inside out."[42] Hollis writes a book on the topic, *Presences*, which began as a magazine article for *Node*, another Blue Ant subsidiary. *Node* is another image of artistic interventions and provocations continually at risk of becoming appropriated by advertising and turned into their opposite.[43]

One way of understanding the Blue Ant trilogy, then, is that it is concerned with how artistic practice everts into advertising. *Détournement* is a situationist tactic by which the expressions of capitalist mass media are turned against themselves, revealing the empty promises of commodity culture. Debord observes, "*détournement* reradicalizes previous critical conclusions that have been petrified into respectable truths and thus transformed into lies."[44] The culture-jamming activism of Adbusters exemplifies this strategy of critique, which Debord describes as a practice that "deletes a false idea, replaces it with the right one."[45] The core practice of *détournement* is the use of reversal to create a meaning in the artwork that is antithetical to the meaning conveyed by the original commodity or media product.

With Blue Ant, we see the possibility that capitalism's resilience has turned things once again, that advertising has now become a strategy of *détournement* that channels the energy of artistic critique away from social relations that emerge within lived experience and directs it toward affective relationships with the products and images that replace our social relations. All art, it seems, eventually becomes advertising. For example, Hollis and her former punk band mates decide to sell their hit single for use in an advertisement for Chinese cars: despite this selling out, the advertisement never airs (a better car, it seems, was needed to launch China's bid to be a global automaker), and Hollis loses her share of the money in the stock market crash of 2008—events that suggest the trilogy wants us to see this choice as a mistake, not an acceptance of one's realistic prospects.

Of more concern, however, is the fact that even people seeking to escape commodification, to make art or protect its creators from Bigend, ultimately have more intense social relations with products than they do with people. Cayce is obsessed by the footage, Hollis with Gabriel Hounds: the products, not the artists, are what entice them. The trilogy seems to observe (more than endorse) this preference for the object, part of a motif that explores how the art world has everted into the society of the spectacle. Cayce can find the footage because of Stella, Nora's sister, who describes her role as being the distributor rather than the artist: "the one who finds an audience."[46] This phrase contrasts with Cayce's use of the word "producer" to describe what she anticipates Bigend wants to be in relation to the footage, a term Bigend corrects: "I don't think there's a title, yet, for doing whatever it is that would be required. Advocate, perhaps? Facilitator?"[47] By the later novels the word "producer" is used to describe roles similar to Stella's in distributing the footage. Bobby's technological work makes the locative art possible, a role the artist insists is more than mere dissemination: "If someone else were doing what Bobby's doing for me, my work would be different. Would reach the audience differently."[48] The analogy here is less with film producers, often understood as those who find the funding for a project and perhaps supervise its marketing, than with music producers, those who find and cultivate a talent, often shaping an artist's image or brand.

The term is stretched even further to apply to the old man, "who had supposedly once been something, never specified, in the American intelligence community," who is "Garreth's producer-director, in an ongoing sequence of covert performance-art pieces."[49] The old man and his cronies enact these stunts based on "a shared distaste for certain policies and proclivities of the government,"[50] such as the complicated caper to irradiate money embezzled from Iraq rebuilding projects that Garreth pursues in *Spook Country*. We might understand Garreth's stunts as a kind of military-culture situationism, turning his elite skills and training toward a critique of the "false idea" (to use Debord's term) of military profiteering and replacing it with the "right one," which in this context seems to be some sense of noblesse oblige regarding America's role as a global power. Just as the military is no longer interested in securing any specific kind of global order, only in profiting as much as they can from economic manipulation, Bigend and Blue Ant are not interested in promoting any specific product but only in the trajectory of productization, in creating the society of the spectacle, which has the political benefit of stunting our capacity for critique.

The drift in the meaning of the word "producer" here points to some of the nostalgia that suffuses this trilogy. The world and values these novels long for are deeply in the past, almost certainly not in any real past but merely in an idea we have about the past as a simpler and better time—noblesse oblige, well-made cotton shirts, art for art's sake, and unalienated social relations.[51] "Producer" once meant the one who makes something, but in the trilogy this activity is almost always discussed using the terms "maker" or "artist." The *Oxford English Dictionary* lists another, more specific usage of "producer" in political economy: one who supplies commodities for sale, that is, as the opposite of consumer (John Locke's discussion of interest rates in 1692 is the first recorded such usage); and later, first dating to 1891, as one who is responsible for the financial and managerial aspects of a cultural product (play, film, broadcast, etc.). This alternation of the meaning of "producer" charts a path that is similar to the displacement of the material world by the society of the spectacle that emerges with late-stage, information age capitalism. Bigend sees this as a natural evolution, the organic perfection of the market as a living being, and suggests that advertising works on the limbic brain: what makes us buy addresses "that older, deeper mind, beyond language and logic."[52]

Thus, for Bigend, it is a positive sign that "far more creativity, today, goes into the marketing of products than into the products themselves."[53] Yet for the Blue Ant trilogy, this precedence of producer over product, spectacle over material, is precisely the problem.

In my reading, then, the trilogy diagnoses and critiques how advertising everts situationism, taking cultural images that in their original context suggest alternatives to commodity relations and turning them into engines of commodity circulation. Art that has become branding, creativity applied to keeping the wheels of commerce turning, is splashy but hollow, like the fake books Milgrim finds in the library of the house where Brown confines him for a period. What from a distance appear to be the leather spines of antique books is only "a single piece of leather, molded over a wooden form," with traces of gold lettering suggesting the presence of titles and authors, without forming any actual words: "It was a very elaborate artifact, mass-produced by artisans of one culture in vague imitation of what had once been the culture of another."[54] This encounter with an ersatz version of the traces of a real historical culture is evocative of Bigend's description of the end of the idea of the future in *Pattern Recognition*, a concept that becomes inaccessible when the present is so much in flux, when "all that is solid melts into air," as Marx and Engels put it in the *Communist Manifesto*. For Marx and Engels, things melted away because capitalist production always seeks to change the social relations and thus speed of production.[55] Bigend contends,

> we have no idea, now, of who or what the inhabitants of our future might be. In that sense, we have no future. Not in the sense that our grandparents had a future, or thought they did. Fully imagined cultural futures were the luxury of another day, one in which "now" was of some greater duration. For us, of course, things can change so abruptly, so violently, so profoundly, that futures like our grandparents' have insufficient "now" to stand on. We have no future because our present is too volatile.... We have only risk management. The spinning of the given moment's scenarios. Pattern recognition.[56]

This ability to divine the patterns of the market is linked to advertising via Cayce's sensitivity and allergy. In *Pattern Recognition* she tells us she has "a morbid and sometimes violent reactivity to the semiotics of the marketplace,"[57] and in *Zero History* she describes her allergy as simply to "advertising ... [a]ny concentrated graphic representation of corporate identity."[58] She can discern which patterns will be successful and which will not, yet she continually reminds herself to avoid the trap of apophenia, "the spontaneous perception of connections and meaningfulness in unrelated things."[59] Her father warns her that such conspiracy theory thinking, in which all the pieces fit together, distracts one from seeing "the genuine threat, which was invariably less symmetrical, less perfect."[60] The specter of 9/11 haunts this first novel, but the rest of the trilogy is more concerned with globalized commodity culture than with militarization, although they are entwined. Perhaps the genuine threat has less to do with visible enemies, and more to do with how our own desires now seem also to be the engines of our ongoing alienation within commodity culture.

At the risk of falling into my own delusion of apophenia in trying to make all the pieces of the trilogy fit into a theory of advertising as the co-optation of *détournement*, I want to conclude by suggesting that the problem Gibson illustrates in this trilogy—namely, how economic logics of commodification subsume all social life—symbolizes a problem for science fiction in the twenty-first century. As is well established in the critical tradition, science fiction is often understood as a literature of utopian possibility, emerging from the genre's affinity with historicized thinking. Science fiction shows us that the world might be otherwise and often encourages us to see the present moment as the past of an anticipated future.[61] More recently, however, in a move of *détournement* eerily like the strategies of Blue Ant, icons and images drawn from science fiction are increasingly used to advertise the products of a technologized future that proceeds as if there is no outside of or alternative to capitalism.[62]

One of the places where this conflation of speculative imaginary with corporate projections is most evident is in the future projections of speculative finance, the risk management commodified by the derivatives industry and gestured to by Bigend in his speech about the absence of a future. As I argued in more detail elsewhere, speculative fiction and speculative finance both seek to build material worlds from discursive ones, albeit aimed at radically divergent notions of what constitutes the best of all possible worlds.[63] Bigend argues that the twenty-first century no longer has the luxury of "fully imaged cultural futures," a verdict that in this context begins to sound as if we are no longer capable of believing in alternatives to capitalism, no longer able to cultivate a utopian imagination. As the present seems to collapse into science fiction, the future itself becomes colonized by market values.

The trilogy concludes with Bigend able to aggregate market data such that he can see the future, or at least "seventeen" minutes into the future, although he notes "seven *seconds*" would have been sufficient.[64] The importance of speed and anticipating future movements in the market is key to profitability in speculative finance, via arbitrage, that is, minute differences of prices for the same asset, usually at different locations. Yet it is important to recall that in these novels, people do their utmost to get away from Bigend. They fear his influence on their lives and the world and see him as the dangerous embodiment of a world fully subsumed by capital. Bigend may believe the world has become one with the market, that there is no past or future, only flows of capital and spectacle, but it would be an error to conflate his vision with the theme of the trilogy. In an interview with Larry McCaffery, Gibson lamented long ago that people understood his cyberpunk fiction to be a celebration of a "hard and glossy" future, failing to recognize that "what [he was] talking about is what being hard and glossy does to you."[65] Similarly, in the Blue Ant trilogy, Gibson shows us what being productized does to us.

The title "zero history" refers to erasing one's traces in the systems of surveillance and data mining, systems that increasingly turn even our consumerism into a commodity and source of value for someone else. It also refers to Milgrim's zero credit history, the absence of his participation in an economy increasingly grounded by relations of debt and ever-widening economic disparity.[66] Citing Faulkner, Milgrim reminds us that "the past isn't dead. It's not even past."[67] The trilogy asks us to recognize that the future is not dead either, although it is at risk. Still, as Inchmale contends, "some futures needed throwing away, badly,"[68] and the world of Blue Ant as *détournement* of artistic critique is one of these. The trilogy urges us not to capitulate to the logic that Blue Ant is too big to fail, yet its characters find spaces only of individual retreat and escape, not collective social transformation. If we want to throw this Blue Ant future away, we need to move beyond the novel's critique of artistic provocation turned into advertisement, to turn things one more time—away from the individual and back into collectivity, thus making a society of being over having, lived reality over spectacle.

CHAPTER 9 ... **AMY J. ELIAS**

REALIST ONTOLOGY IN WILLIAM GIBSON'S
THE PERIPHERAL

One of the most important keywords in arts theory and criticism today is "ontology." From AI experimentation to climate fiction to posthumanist ethics to object-oriented ontology, we in the arts and humanities are rethinking our relations to reality, as well as how that reality might be understood in new knowledge paradigms that accommodate burgeoning technologies and the environmental effects of the Anthropocene.[1] William Gibson's novels have always raised ontological questions, such as "What is a world?" Indeed, critics analyzing the Sprawl and Blue Ant trilogies focus attention on the nature of hyperreality and the relation between worlds inside and outside of the matrix (cyberspace versus "meat space," human versus posthuman technologies, etc.). Often studies examine how affordances and hierarchies of power in the worlds reflect and inflect the perceptions and ethics of the humans who reside in them; differences between worlds are often configured as an aesthetic relation, the world of cyberspace mimicking and revealing (even as it often displaces) the Baudrillardian "false reality" of the aestheticized social space determined by late capitalism.[2] Defining worlds or types of being in these novels is linked to political, phenomenological, or epistemological analysis: worlds are explained as ways of knowing—that is, in terms of human perception and consciousness or the unique landscapes of merged human–machine cognition.[3]

The appearance of *The Peripheral* in 2014, however, forces consideration of ontological questions as such and demands a reconsideration of the effects of a realist ontology on a novel's ethical and social commitments. The novel is the first of what seems to be Gibson's new "post apocalypse" cyberspace trilogy (the second in the series, *Agency*, appeared in 2020) that concerns the intersections of time travel and artificial intelligence. Wrecked, postapocalypse, or post–World War III societies have appeared in Gibson's work before, but he always maintained that his works are more about his present, the time of the novel's writing, than they are any future the novel might depict. It is significant, perhaps, that this novel, which creates a science fiction realist ontology new to Gibson's fiction, appears at the same moment that a real-world climate crisis and an intellectual zeitgeist about apocalypse and ontologies is burgeoning on the world horizon.

Gibson's Ontologies

While Gibson's first cyberspace texts in the Sprawl trilogy were concerned with how technology fundamentally alters near-future space (cyberspace, the Sprawl, the Well, Chiba City, Villa Straylight, London), *The Peripheral* (and, it seems, *Agency*) focuses on how technology fundamentally alters future time. The Sprawl trilogy presents infinity as an interior territory in cyberspace; it is something console cowboys navigate, something that Case and Angie can visually apprehend. In contrast, *The Peripheral* exteriorizes infinity in the vast space-time of the material universe. It plays with a generalized version of multiverse theories that sometimes look like Hugh Everett's 1957 many-worlds interpretation in quantum mechanics (which claims that there are many parallel, noninteracting worlds that exist at the same space and time as our own and are generated each time a quantum measurement is made) or Wiseman's and Hall's idea of "many interacting worlds," in which universes can interact (in that all quantum phenomena arise from a universal force of repulsion between similar worlds which tends to make them more dissimilar).[4]

Like most philosophers and literary critics, Gibson does not get mired in the science. He has noted in interviews that *The Peripheral* is his attempt at hardcore science fiction, which since at least H. G. Wells's *The Time Machine* has been obsessed with time-travel narratives as scientific problems, logical paradoxes, and opportunities for social commentary.[5] *The Peripheral* explores the ethical and social meaning of accessing multiple worlds in a multiverse—of having power to manipulate space-time—and the role of new technologies, particularly artificial intelligence, in reshaping our relationship to time and thus to one another. While typically the protagonists of time-travel fiction move backward in time (a safe choice for writers in some ways, because we know what happened in the past) or far into the future (allowing the construction of utopian or dystopian worlds that will never contradict the lived experience of their present or future readers), *The Peripheral* primarily tells the story of a move forward in time toward a not-so-distant future of the early twenty-second century. (According to characters in the novel, the future cannot connect with the past before 2023, so the world of "the past" in the novel is basically the reader's own). The novel's protagonist, Flynne Fisher, travels into a near future that results from the Jackpot—a cataclysmic series of linked events that eventually eradicates 80 percent of the world's population within forty years and leaves the world to rich oligarchs (klepts) whose money has allowed them to escape the Jackpot's most devastating effects. Gibson has noted that his model here was Bruce Sterling and Lewis Shiner's story "Mozart in Mirrorshades," in which characters also economically exploit the resources of an alternate continuum and (like the Borges stories that Gibson loves) the novel is an alternate reality book "more like forking paths."[6]

Although there are nods to Gibson's present in the text (the presence of cronuts, a fictional allusion in the group Luke 4:5 to the deeply right-wing Westboro Baptist Church, etc.), there are also allusions to Gibson's earlier books. Flynne's online handle is "Easy Ice," recollecting the Intrusion Countermeasures Electronics (ICE) popularized by *Neuromancer*; like the Bridge trilogy, this novel sets up class conflict between the very rich and the working poor in the near future, with connectivity and actual wealth a marker of privilege. As in other novels in the Sprawl and Blue Ant trilogies, here the US South is a backdrop for some of the action. Most important, however, *The Peripheral* seems to continue the evolutionary development of AI that began in *Neuromancer* and continued through at least the Sprawl trilogy. This is what allows its unique realist ontology to emerge.

I'm going to take a brief detour here, because I have found it useful when thinking about Gibson's ontologies to compare them to one set up by his peer, Thomas Pynchon, who constructs a two-tiered ontology of what he calls "the Declarative" and "the Subjunctive." The Declarative reality is the space of modernity, what we might call rationalized consensus reality: the largely three-dimensional, "common-sense" timespace inhabited by "Western" humans and largely defined by their perceptive abilities and epistemological and hermeneutic philosophies. The Subjunctive is the space of the mythic or non-Western epistemology that exceeds Declarative reality. It has been described by literary criticism as the realm of the sublime, the realm of romance, or the realm of quantum possibility. In Pynchon's work, it is represented in *The Crying of Lot 49* as Maxwell's Demon, in *Gravity's Rainbow* as the Zone, in *Mason & Dixon* as the American Territory filled with mysterious energies not yet mapped by rationalized Royal Society science, and in *Against the Day* as the world of gothic and romance that is increasingly shut down by industrial capitalism's rape of the natural world.[7] Often Pynchon opposes the Declarative and the Subjunctive as different ontological levels of being, but in his 2013 novel *Bleeding Edge*, he offers a third ontological sphere, the "Digital/Virtual."[8] In the form of the "dark web," this becomes a territory populated by hackers and other nonconformists—a new, metaleptic ontological level that erupts within the Declarative as a kind of eternal return to the Subjunctive, a fracturing of the Declarative's rationalist and totalitarian control. As a result, in *Bleeding Edge* the Virtual seems salvational, displacing the Subjunctive to cyberspace and thereby plugging into cyberutopian theories of virtual anarchism and liberatory collective virtual action. One is reminded of McKenzie Wark's observation: "The redemptive vision of second nature withered in both its Marxist and bourgeois forms. Yet . . . Redemption is always around the corner in virtual reality, hypertext, cyberspace, Web 2.0, mobile media, social networking, or the 'cloud.'"[9]

In Gibson's novels, a similar kind of ontology is emerging, one that acknowledges a more nuanced understanding of AI's strangeness and possibilities and that does not romanticize the virtual. This perspective is set up at the end of his first novel, when two important pieces of information are relayed to Henry Dorsett Case in his conversation with the newly merged Wintermute/Neuromancer AI. First, the AI tells him that "I am the matrix . . . the sum total of the works, the whole show," and beyond any human imagining. This prompts Case to ask, "So what's the score? How are things different? You running the world now? You God?" The AI replies, "Things aren't different. Things are things."[10] I would argue that the AI and Case are not really communicating here; they are talking past one another. The AI is alluding to a posthuman or transhuman way of understanding the world that Case cannot yet understand—one that forms the basis of the future world in *The Peripheral*.

What the transmogrified AI seems to imply at the end of *Neuromancer* is that it is plugging into a realist metaphysics in which "things are things" rather than projections of human logic, desire, or control. David Chambers notes that "Ontological realism is often traced to Quine . . . who held that we can determine what exists by seeing which entities are endorsed by our best scientific theory of the world. In recent years, the practice of ontology has often presupposed an ever-stronger ontological realism."[11] As a metaphysical philosophy, realism generally has two aspects: a claim about existence (i.e., that some things like tables and rocks exist, as do their properties of roundness, hardness, color, etc.) and a claim about independence (such things exist and have their properties independent of anything anyone perceives, says, or believes about them).[12] The AI in *Neuromancer* is in fact located at the genesis of a world in which humans need play no part at all. Seen through the lens of posthumanist and object-oriented ontologies circulating in theory today, we might say that the AI is alluding to a realist ontology that conforms to the claims of object-oriented ontology and vitalist materialism:

1. Reality is not discourse nor a phenomenological projection. It is real. It is living, creative vitality, as are all objects in it. Correlationism is false.[13]
2. All animate and inanimate things are *equally* things/objects. Anthropocentrism and biocentrism are false.
3. Philosophies that impose hierarchies on the real are false. Object-oriented ontology levels violent hierarchies (such as subject/object) and eliminates moralities imposed on being (such as Elect/Preterite).

4. Things resist cognitive mastery: things have "allure," "vibratory intensity," and immanent properties but are "withdrawn" from other objects, from presence. We cannot ever penetrate or fathom the full being of something else.
5. All object relations distort the things that are in relation; things can't relate fully to each other's thingness.[14]

Readers see the development of the AI's reality in the next books of the Sprawl trilogy. In *Count Zero*, Angie Mitchell interacts with the matrix through the "voodoo gods" who populate it.[15] Critics have discussed these entities as the result of a fracturing or implosion of Wintermute/Neuromancer, but I tend to read them in light of *The Peripheral* and see them as trickster figures (there is Legba, after all) that serve as intermediaries between ontological levels, between the world of the now-independent Wintermute/Neuromancer AI and the world of humans. After *Count Zero*, in *Mona Lisa Overdrive*, the moment when Wintermute merged with Neuromancer is characterized as "When It Changed."[16] As Gary Westfahl notes, "Angie obtains information through casual conversations with 'Continuity,' an artificial intelligence that speaks like a person, while Kumiko is accompanied by a 'ghost'—a computer-created personality taking the form of a hologram of a young man only she can see."[17] By the time of *Mona Lisa Overdrive*, artificial intelligence is appearing at all ontological levels, but there seems an important distinction between those AI that operate in the human, "declarative" world and those that operate in their own cyberspace realm, which is fast becoming a space of the transhuman (the AI can re-create human consciousness there) and the algorithmic subjunctive (not inhabited by humans but embodying the "magic" humans associate with romance or mythology) (see Table 1).

In *The Peripheral*, the Wintermute/Neuromancer AI (whatever it may have evolved into at this point) is absent as a story actant, but it may still be present in the narrated world as an absent cause. It has become, in effect, a kind of hyperobject in Timothy Morton's sense.[18] In this novel, the prophetic or mystical function is served by "the aunties," a set of algorithms so sophisticated that they have assumed the status of oracles (often portrayed as female and, like computer consoles, portals through which beings from another realm spoke directly to people). Ainsley Lowbeer admits, "We have a great many, built up over decades. I doubt

Table 1: Ontology in Thomas Pynchon's *Bleeding Edge* (2013). Courtesy of Amy J. Elias.

Subjunctive Life	Declarative Life	Digital/Virtual (simulated life within the Declarative that seems to channel the Subjunctive)
Premodern/"nature"	Modernity	Modernity
Forces of supernatural being or parallel realities	Forces of rationalization, instrumentalization	Forces of totalization
Logic of desire, enchantment, or counterfactuals; laws of empirical reality suspended	Logic of reason, disenchantment; laws of empirical reality enforced	Logic of human desire; laws of empirical reality suspended according to the logic of mathematics
Space: symbolic, mythic, romance	Space: symbolic, comic/tragic/ironic	Space: symbolic, uncanny/irony
Time: eternal, vertical, hierarchical	Time: linear/horizontal, chronometric, scientific	Time: flat, presentism, techno-duration
Metaphysics: religious/spiritual, ontological, being/becoming, sublimity	Metaphysics: rationalism and empiricism	Metaphysics: numerical/algorithmic
History: mythic	History: modern (progress)	History: pastiche
Rhetorical logic: metaphor	Rhetorical logic: metonomy	Rhetorical logic: metalepsis

anyone today knows quite how they work, in any given instance."[19] The aunties don't seem to control the world of *The Peripheral*, but they seem central to it, as if acting as its steward or caretaker, a demythologized version of the voodoo gods of *Count Zero*.

The second important piece of information relayed to Case in his last conversation with Wintermute/Neuromancer is that the AI has moved into deep space-time. When the AIs merge, the new construct searches

1970s records of alien transmissions and finds "others"—particularly another AI in the Alpha Centauri star system with which it can communicate. The reality that the AI accesses is neither internal to the cyberspace that Case can access nor is completely external to it. It seems that this new AI consciousness can connect with cyberspaces of other worlds. As noted, *The Peripheral* may present the most evolved version of what is perhaps Wintermute/Neuromancer in the aunties or in the Chinese computer, which, Ned Beauman notes, has the ability to access "a sort of transtemporal Skype running on a mysterious Chinese server that accounts for those two eras becoming entangled in a single story."[20] That "transtemporal Skype" is a connection that accesses space-time, much as Wintermute/Neuromancer accessed it earlier. If in *Neuromancer* Wintermute/Neuromancer gained access to cyberspace across vast, Real space (the AI "other" of the Alpha Centauri system existing simultaneously with Wintermute/Neuromancer), in *The Peripheral* some kind of AI (Wintermute/Neuromancer?) has gained access to cyberspace across Real time. Flynne can enter cyberspace and work a drone in the future; she can enter cyberspace and inhabit a future peripheral running software in the same space but not at the same time.

My point is twofold: first, that somehow there seems to be a connection between the merged Wintermute/Neuromancer of the first novels and a much-evolved version (linked to the mysterious Chinese computer) in *The Peripheral*, and second, that in *The Peripheral*, for the first time in Gibson's fictional worlds, we access another ontological dimension, that of space-time itself. This new access to time puts cyberspace up against its own limits, for it is now not just an interface with Declarative reality (as it was, for instance, in *Count Zero* with the voodoo gods as intermediaries) but also, for the first time, with another reality on the other side of cyberspace, what I call "the Real." The Real is the physical universe, governed by its own logics and thus outside the complete control of both humans and AI. The Real is revealed, not created, when the elite of the future start to time-travel into the past. The oligarchs in Wilf Netherton's world, such as Lev Zubov, can buy telepresence access to the past but can't change events in their own timeline, because as soon as they intervene in the past, time splits into a new "continua" or dimensional pathways called "stubs." The Real is self-healing, and its logic is absolute, no matter how sophisticated the algorithms manipulating it.[21] In *The*

Peripheral, Gibson uses a realist ontology in which things and states of being exist independently of human sense and/or perception—a metaphysical perspective that underlies object oriented ontology and "thing theory" as well as some forms of posthumanist ethics.

If the number of possible Real dimensions is infinite, then it doesn't really matter *ontologically* what people like Lev Zubov or Ainsley Lowbeer do to the past worlds they visit—as it does, for example, in speculative time-travel novels such as Octavia Butler's *Kindred* (1979). In *The Peripheral*, the Real is self-healing, and those interfering in the past are not endangering their own present; there will be an infinite number of other "pasts," always new stubs produced.

But it does matter ethically. Positing the Real as a self-healing ontological dimension actually provokes the thorny ethical questions of this novel. As Gibson has noted in interviews, the ability of very rich people to use the past raises political questions about class privilege and ethical questions about colonial desire: rich people can "third-world" the past as if it were a labor force they can exploit (here, by hiring Flynne and her brother as security guards for a private party, though Flynne doesn't realize she's in this situation). Gibson has noted,

> The concept of third-worlding the past, because the past you contact can't become the past where you live, is from 'Mozart in Mirrorshades' by Bruce Sterling and Lewis Shiner. . . . It's a brilliant story of colonialization. . . . I appropriated that, but what I realized almost before I appropriated it is the difference since 1984 when they wrote it, is that you don't need to go there physically at all. . . . And I thought, okay, fair cop, this is the 21st century version of their model, if you can do it all virtually, and by telepresence.[22]

Peripherals are the symbolic markers of this colonial attitude, bodies instrumentalized by power and evacuated of self-determination. Like eighteenth-century absent landlords in the New World, in *The Peripheral* the rich are immune from the consequences of their colonial intervention, since the realities they enter and exploit will never converge with their own. At one point in the story, Flynne's brother, Burton, remarks, "Know what collateral damage is? . . . Think that's us. . . . None of this is happening because any of us are who we are, what we are. Accident, or it started with one, and now we've got people who might as well be able to suspend basic laws of physics, or anyway finance, doing whatever it is they're doing, whatever reason they're doing it for."[23] Netherton's world is one where class is absolutely divided and the privileged run the world, while Flynne lives in a poverty-stricken rural landscape of Hefty Marts and drug economies. As Karin Kross has noted, "Among the worst, their power is inversely proportional to their concern for the lives that they damage in pursuit of more money, more power, or even just a little advantage over someone they don't like."[24]

The ethical questions thus involve intervention and self-determination. First, those with the power to intervene in the lives (and futures) of others can do so for good or for ill. One can manipulate the stub to help it avoid the evils of one's own present, which is actually what Lowbeer ends up doing. She cannot change the history of her time or her present, but she can help Flynne's reality avoid the Jackpot and avoid ending up like her own oligarchic, surveillance society. Toward the end of the novel, Flynne worries that she, Lowbeer, and others are accumulating too much power, and Lowbeer responds that Flynne's fear of power is precisely why she is the right person to hold it:

> She'd told Ainsley, earlier . . . how she sometimes worried that they weren't really doing more than just building their own version of the klept. Which Ainsley had said was not just a good thing, but an essential thing, for all of them to keep in mind. Because people who couldn't imagine themselves capable of evil were at a major disadvantage in dealing with people who didn't need to imagine, because they already were. She'd said it was always a mistake, to believe those people were different, special, infected with something that was inhuman, subhuman, fundamentally other. . . .
>
> "All too human, dear," Ainsley had said, her blue old eyes looking at the Thames, "and the moment we forget it, we're lost."[25]

In addition, Lowbeer's actions have effects in her own world. Meddling in the past is an action in her present, and it does actually change the trajectory of events in that present because it is an action that takes place there—as all of our actions in our lives affect the worlds we inhabit. Colonial imposition on another territory changes the home territory as much as it changes the past—here, the problem posed by "time travel" is that it will create obligations and ethical traps for those who intervene.

Table 2: Realist ontology in William Gibson's *The Peripheral* (2014). Courtesy of Maria Alberto and Elizabeth Swanstrom.

Declarative	Digital/virtual 1.0 (simulated within Declarative)	Digital/virtual 2.0 ← → Algorithmic Subjunctive (visited by humans but inhabited by AI)	The Real
Modernity	Modernity	Modernity, postmodernity	The physical universe
Forces of rationalization, instrumentalization	Forces of totalization	Forces of totalization	"Natural" forces derived from fields, conservation of momentum, etc.
Logic of reason, disenchantment; laws of empirical reality enforced	Logic of human desire, laws of empirical reality suspended according to the logic of mathematics	Logic of posthuman desire, laws of empirical reality suspended according to new AI logic	Logic of physics
Space: symbolic (comic, tragic, ironic)	Space: symbolic (uncanny/irony)	Space: algorithmic (romance from humans' perspective, the place of the suprahuman)	Space: non-Euclidean, space-time continuum (no trope)
Time: linear/horizontal, chronometric, scientific	Time: flat, presentism, techno-duration	Time: infinite, techno-duration	Time: dimensional, relative, space-time continuum, "self-healing"
Metaphysics: epistemological, rationalism and empiricism	Metaphysics: numerical	Metaphysics: transhuman, algorithmic	Metaphysics: none, only physics
History: modern (progress)	History: pastiche	History: simultaneous	History: none, only time
Rhetorical logic: metonomy	Rhetorical logic: metalepsis	Rhetorical logic: ?	Rhetorical logic: none

As I've noted elsewhere, this sounds ethically better than it is. To pin one's hopes of freedom on the continuing goodwill of another who has complete power over you and whose profit could be increased by your exploitation is a precarious act of faith and a stupid one. There is a strong tension in the novel between Gibson's cyberpunk vision (which implies that this world is built on flows of power and allows for the critique of "third worlding") and his humanism, for which the outcome of social structures depends on private, ethical decisions by individuals. At the end of *The Peripheral*, the "happy ending" to Flynne's colonial situation depends not on revolution by the oppressed, by political liberalism that allows for self-determination, or by disconnection of the oppressed from their oppressors but solely on the goodwill of the colonial landlord and on being that landlord's favorite. Gibson realized this immediately, expressing in interviews how uncomfortable he was with the fictional world's "solution" and model of political quietism:

> these guys had an immensely powerful—if possibly dangerously crazy—fairy godmother who altered their continuum, who has for some reason decided that she's going to rake all of their chestnuts out of the fire, so that the world can't go the horrible way it went in hers. And whatever else is going to happen, that's not going to happen for us, you know? We're going to have to find another way. We're not going to luck into Lowbeer.... Well, also, how it's set up for Flynne at the end—gave me the creeps! Really, its potential for not being good is really, really high.... I mean, she's lovely, but what are they building there [in her pre-Jackpot reality]? It's got all kind of weird third-world bad possibilities.[26]

The new realist ontology throws us back to very old human problems. I believe that it also raises questions for us today that are often unacknowledged in theoretical discussions about realist ontology, object-oriented ontology, thing theory, and some versions of posthumanism. Essentially it raises the problem of relation, for though we may be in relation to all other things in a flat ontology, we still have the ability to act according to our abilities and enact power over others. In *The Peripheral*, we see how recognizing the Real throws us back to ourselves, in the coldness of the universe's machinic logic.

CHAPTER 10 . . . **ARON PEASE**

CYBERSPACE AFTER CYBERPUNK

Literary critics of William Gibson's Blue Ant trilogy, and to some extent Gibson himself, explain the novels' present-day setting by confirming the sentiment of Blue Ant's founder, Hubertus Bigend, that the future is canceled by its arrival as a techno-scientific present, making a good old-fashioned future "the luxury of another day."[1] Consequently, Gibson appears to abandon cyberspace, perhaps his most significant literary invention, which neither arrives in the technoscientific present nor is considered a viable projection. Once the concept inspired notions of an electronic "frontier of consciousness,"[2] but now its apparent real-world manifestation, the internet, has been settled by transnational corporations. Yet if cyberspace has been the defining invention that ties together Gibson's fiction, and has to some extent fulfilled the adage of William Burroughs that the point of art is to "make it happen,"[3] then the concept has likely migrated elsewhere in Gibson's later work. One can certainly find figures suggestive of this original conception of cyberspace in the novels that follow the first trilogy, such as the glasses in *Virtual Light* that add a layer of data over the wearer's visual perception, or the shapes and "floes" of data seen by Colin Laney later in the trilogy. In this essay I explore how cyberspace reappears, transfigured, in the Blue Ant trilogy through postgeographic cityscapes layered with information, as well as in the highly referential style of writing, which formally demonstrates the experience of advertising and hypermedia and especially in the characters' modes of observation and mobility.

Fifteen years after the end of the Sprawl trilogy, the Blue Ant trilogy offers a chance to trace the evolution of cyberspace as a literary construction and its manifestation in approximate technologies. The appearance of related contemporary or near-future inventions, such as ubiquitous computing and GPS technology, attest to the continuing importance of cyberspace as an idea to the culture at large, as well as to Gibson. Yet he seems to dismiss these more popular present-day realizations. The closest thing in the trilogy to cyberspace as a distinct space is *Spook Country*'s virtual world of locative art, which uses GPS technology. It prompts wonder initially, but later bored familiarity and even dismay when imagined on a larger scale. Hollis Henry, the trilogy's primary freelancer, asks rhetorically, "Would it all be like this, in Alberto's new world of the locative? Would it mean that the untagged, unscripted world would gradually fill with virtual things, as beautiful or ugly or banal as anything one encountered on the web already? Was there any reason to expect it to be any better than that, any worse?"[4] She echoes Gibson's prediction in "The Net Is a Waste of Time," published between the trilogies in 1993, that the internet would become something much less interesting.[5] Moreover, that essay suggests that leisure must become productive, and thus the spidery wandering of one's curiosity across the web must also become productive and alienating as it falls more into the economic realm, much as prior media did. By the time of the Blue Ant trilogy, surfing the web can indeed constitute a form of production, as attention industries keep us online long enough for the corporate daimons of the fallen cyberworld to sink their FANGs into us,[6] turning the "elsewhere" gaze into profits. This transformation may explain why characters in the Blue Ant trilogy disregard their devices almost as nuisances, exhibiting none of the cyberpunk's romantic attachment to machines. In *Zero History*, Gibson seems to relish describing in detail Hollis's cavalier gift of her MacBook to Milgrim, spending a full paragraph on the unattachment after she explains she had only opened it three times in three months. Though Milgrim "sank instantly" into the familiar "elsewhere" of cyberspace "that had nothing to do with geography,"[7] he too will not seem particularly attached as the novel progresses (even after he discovers Twitter).

Cyberspace as something resembling the internet or the electronic "frontier of consciousness" is dead, an elsewhere no longer else.

Cyberspace in the Sprawl Trilogy

Cyberspace in *Neuromancer* was a world extrapolated from primitive precursors, such as video arcade games, flight simulations, and data encryption. If it anticipated the internet, it did so by figuring it as an abstract city of clean lines and geometric shapes. Although plenty of secrets remained hidden, dramatized in the first trilogy by black ICE counter-attacks, cyberspace promised some measure of access to an inaccessible world of information otherwise secured in corporate and military databanks. In his essay "A Global *Neuromancer*," Fredric Jameson reiterates a briefly made point from *Postmodernism* regarding *Neuromancer*'s achievement in creating a convincing figuration for late capitalism's transnational corporate structures. Jameson maintains that it is a rare example where the literary creation convinces us of its reality, inspiring belief in it as an objectively existing thing. As such, "it behooves us to look more closely at the notion of cyberspace in Gibson, in order to see what it involves: Is it a new kind of concept, for example, reflecting the alleged historical novelty of information technology in general? To what degree does its content then (apart from any formal innovation) somehow reflect this new reality (whether that of the 'real foundation' of late capitalism or merely the 'neutral' structure of its third-stage productive technology)?"[8] Jameson observes that this representation of data as a spatial city may appear to be merely a visual metaphor. It would thus work at the level of theme, in the way the city is often a cliché image transmitted metonymically in visual mass media via skyscrapers, helicopter camera shots of moving traffic, and lines of light created by time-lapse photography, all carrying the connotation of networks and nodes of wealth and power but not really giving up the secret. Yet as Jameson reminds us, numbers are also representations (though they are fetishized in contemporary technoculture as the currency of reality). Even if Gibson falls back on a trope, his cyberspace has the merit of a further abstraction, that of turning tables of numbers into images whose analog, Jameson argues, is the axonometric drawings of architects.[9] In this way, abstraction is taken to the "second power."[10] This second level of abstraction turns what could otherwise be taken as a lapse into cliché into a more complex figuration, directing our attention beyond either mimetic/metonymic presentation or reified data and toward a complex totality, whose complexity stems from the sheer number of relationships involved and this material's constant state of flux. To the extent that this is a figure for the "real foundation" or at least a novel dimension of late capitalism, Jameson suggests it involves finance capital.

I infer a related concept from Jameson's point about numbers. Marx uses the phrase "behind the backs" to explain the concept of simple average labor, by which he explains how value is determined. In Marx's analysis value can only be created by labor power, and its numerical equivalent is equal to an average level of productivity across the entirety of production. He writes: "A commodity may be the outcome of the most complicated labour, but through its value it is posited as equal to the product of simple labour, hence it represents only a specific quantity of simple labour. The various proportions in which different kinds of labour are reduced to simple labour as their unit of measurement are established by a social process that goes on behind the backs of the producers."[11] The determination of simple average labor takes place on a scale too vast for anyone to see locally and would be constantly changing. This complexity would obviously be greatly increased in our own time as more material inputs to make new commodities are commodities resulting from complex production processes. Jameson's description of the cyberspace "camera eye" is analogous to scanning financial tables: "following their openings and canyons, skirting their barriers, moving deeper into the nonexistent space of these new systems."[12] The stock market, then, could be thought of as a representational figure for precisely this impossible-to-capture complexity, but here with a further layer of mediation, in that the numbers do not express quantities of things, production rates, changes in the education of the work force, and so forth. The bulk of the stock market numbers, especially in common cultural understanding, stand for companies. This gives cause to a further twist of abstraction involving the simulation and dissimulation of values.

As the Sprawl trilogy ends with *Mona Lisa Overdrive*, in addition to the familiar imagery of abstract, volumetric architecture, Gibson emphasizes this politics of representation first by reminding us that it is a representation—"iconics," as Gentry refers to it—and second by illustrating that what it shows has to be taught, as Kumiko recalls her tutor's lectures explaining "humanity's need for this information-space. Icons, waypoints, artificial realities."[13] The ideological lesson, remembered years later by Gentry: "People jacked in so they could hustle. Put the trodes on and they were out there, all the data in the world stacked up like one big neon city, so you could cruise around and have a grip on it, visually anyway, because if you didn't, it was too complicated."[14] The fact that Angie and Kumiko recall being taught as children about the need for cyberspace taints it as a transmission of ideology. Media theorist Friedrich Kittler describes schools the same way in his description of the city as a computer, where schoolchildren are the functional equivalent of RAM (thus the visual representation suggested earlier of moving traffic and skyscrapers becomes less metonymic).[15] In this way, cyberspace is an analog for the market, where the ideology that may appear superstructural is in fact internal to the thing, required and generated by it.[16] The two characters through whom Gibson reflects on cyberspace are skeptical of this understanding of it. Gentry tries to discern the shape of the whole, suspecting a more complex, abstract pattern (an idea that anticipates Laney's pattern recognition in the Bridge trilogy and Bigend's order flow in the Blue Ant trilogy). Meanwhile, Slick ponders the politics of it, dismissing both the school lesson and Gentry's attempt to make it into a philosophical totality: "But Slick didn't think cyberspace was anything like the universe anyway; it was just a way of representing data. The Fission Authority had always looked like a big red Aztec pyramid, but it didn't *have* to; if the Fission Authority wanted it to, they could have it look like anything. Big companies had copyrights on how their stuff looked. So how could you figure the whole matrix had a particular shape? And why should it mean anything if it did?"[17]

Cyberspace in the Blue Ant Trilogy

One way to think of cyberspace today, removed from its science fiction projection as an actual space, is as a way of seeing already apparent in the Sprawl trilogy's geometric abstraction that is functionally similar to axonometric drawing but also as a representational scheme related to the production of space. In *The Production of Space*, Henri Lefebvre describes a shift in the second half of the twentieth century away from the production of things in space (industrialism) to the production of space itself.[18] The idea of cyberspace points toward a new production of space that serves what Gibson refers to as a "post-geographic" landscape. Lefebvre's narrative converges with Jameson's reading of cyberspace in the history of linear perspective. Axonometric drawing (like other forms of descriptive geometry) can be connected historically with the invention of linear perspective as the development of technical standards, as Kittler shows in *Optical Media*. Kittler begins in the Italian Renaissance. In 1425, Filippo Brunelleschi, an engineer who built domes and fortresses, began a "revolution in seeing"[19] by painting a church exterior using the camera obscura technique to achieve unprecedented accuracy. Leon Battista Alberti advanced this technique in his treatise on painting, which he dedicated to Brunelleschi. Alberti adopted the perspective of an ideal window shaped like a rectangle, demonstrated by a "semi-transparent veil" with vertical and horizontal threads forming a grid.[20] Kittler observes that the "pattern then allowed geometrical constructions to be performed—in other words, operations with Dürer's ruler and compass—to such a high degree of accuracy that the resulting drawing obeyed all the laws of linear perspective."[21] Kittler stresses the technological invention, but Lefebvre observes that this vision was already in place in the new spatial organization of wealth accumulation, based on the *métayage* system, that emerged in Italy in the prior century. He writes: "Luxurious spending on the construction of palaces and monuments gave artists, and primarily painters, a chance to express, after their own fashion, what was happening, to display what they perceived. These artists 'discovered' perspective and developed the theory of it because a space in perspective lay before them, because such a space had already been produced."[22] Perhaps anticipating the Protestant work ethic, this new, literally mundane vision revolutionized the gaze. Before the development of linear perspective, images such as paintings and stained glass windows identified the gaze with God, who presents "himself" to the viewer via the divine visual ray (Kittler points out the style of Byzantine painting in which gold light casts from its icons toward the viewer).[23] Now an abstract (geometric and free-floating) gaze presents accumulated wealth to the viewer. Light casts in rather than out. Although Alberti is still bound by geometry (as is Gibson's visualization), Kittler refers to it as the first "mathematization of painting,"[24] especially for the scanning pattern that breaks the window into smaller windows, like so many virtual eyes. If the technique makes it possible to paint nature that does not exist, as Kittler argues, it seems possible for the patrons in Lefebvre's narrative to aspire to new scenes of accumulation.

Linear perspective's successors today form one component of a cyberspace gaze in computer drawing programs used in the urban planning that steers the production of space as means of production. New forms of the gaze find linear perspective too subjective for design tools, for the vanishing point hints at an observer. The orthographic gaze used in design applications imagines the viewer as a kind of free-floating camera that can zoom in and out of the drawing. This new space, Damjan Jovanovic explains, "can thus be described as a disassociated, fragmented space that had to be *stitched* together."[25] Yet Jovanovic also points out the prevalence of Alberti's rectangles in the flat ground grid in design applications and especially gaming. Thus, we have a free-floating and disinterested subject with full access to move in and out of the volumetric diagram, whose foundation is the grid. The wealthy patrons of such images would be a combination of cyber-cowboy and Thomas Piketty's rentier. As David Harvey writes, "capital is building cities for people and institutions to invest in, not cities for common people to live in."[26] Cyberspace as a vision of space, and the types of encounter or exchange that can happen in it, in this way may lead to what Lefebvre described as a production of space rather than things in space.

I focus now on three aspects of Gibson's writing in the Blue Ant trilogy that may offer a renewed cyberspace figuration based on this technological development, though now incorporating the author's focus on advertising and fashion. First, Gibson depicts advertising as a pervasive climate, or total environment, part of constructing a new space of capital accumulation. Second (zooming into this space), Gibson's sentences exhibit a dense, referential—spatial—style that depicts the city as an intermingling of space and digital information. Third, as the trilogy progresses, Gibson's characters increasingly move through, observe, and access the city as data, as if punching through cyberspace.

Total Environment

Descriptions of space in the Blue Ant trilogy recall some of the emphasis on abstract spatial representation in the original description of cyber-space, as well as the communication and control associated with cybernetics. Gibson's shift of setting from the future to the present has often been explained with reference to technoscience and technoculture, usually with emphasis on particular advances that would have "seemed" futuristic to earlier generations of science fiction writers.[27] The term "technoscience" itself, however, refers not simply to a rate of advancements but to the intermingling of technology with modern scientific method, where the development of particular technologies is inextricably linked to, and perhaps confused with, the development of science. Writing a few years before the publication of *Pattern Recognition*, Paul Virilio begins *The Information Bomb* by defining technoscience as "the product of the fatal confusion between the operational instrument and exploratory research," and noting that it has essentially become science itself in our time.[28] This confusion consequently shifts science's emphasis from truth to effectiveness, and thus to digital procedures and cybernetic methods, as computing and optical technologies, now combined into a vision-machine, are used to observe, measure, and shape our behaviors with our coerced participation. Virilio finds the advertising industry exemplary of this change, observing that in the nineteenth century, advertising existed simply to cast light on a product, whereas in the twentieth it became an industry for producing desire. In the twenty-first, it will "become pure communication. To this end it will require the unfurling of an advertising space which stretches to the horizon of visibility of the planet."[29] "Global advertising," he continues, will no longer exist in the "breaks" between content but will encompass us in a "single world advertising market," or "environment."[30] What matters is not the message but the rapidity of the interaction, which, in the production of desire (the consumer), puts the means of communication in the role of the means of transportation.

This total environment is, of course, the setting of the Blue Ant trilogy, its novels unfolding by exploring manifold spaces of advertising as communication. *Pattern Recognition* begins by evoking such an encompassing environment. Cayce's disturbed circadian rhythm suggests something like the postgeographic knowledge worker's postindustrial brand of shift work sleep disorder, which blurs working time and life time. Gibson's gray sky doesn't crackle with the energy of television static as in the opening of *Neuromancer*. Rather, it forms a "gray bowl" that surrounds Cayce.[31] Much of this description at the beginning of the trilogy emphasizes space as a total environment, connecting climate, cartography, and colonialism (e.g., the restaurant Charlie Don't Surf). The immaterial gray boundaries trap Cayce in a stasis, suggestively described through meteorological metaphor: "the trough of soul delay open[s] out into horizonless horse latitudes."[32] The reference to the horse latitudes connotes the British Empire, whose crews could find themselves stalled at sea because of extremely calm winds, and thus be forced to throw horses overboard to conserve water. The connotation further suggests the abstract grid integral to the production of space, as the British Empire mastered maritime measurement when John Harrison created the first clock that could keep time at sea, solving the longitude problem. Gibson invokes souls and horizons in his description of the shopping mall where Cayce speculates about the existence of a "Tommy Hilfiger event horizon."[33] When Cayce performs her peculiar brand of knowledge work by saying "yes" or "no" to a shoe company logo that suggests to her the iconic psychedelic art of American artist Rick Griffin, for a moment "she imagines the countless Asian workers who might, should she say yes, spend years of their lives applying versions of this symbol to an endless and unyielding flood of footwear."[34] Cayce wonders, "What would it mean to them, this bouncing sperm? Would it work its way into their dreams, eventually?"[35] The trademark image (if not the connotation) can travel the length of the commodity chain in this diluvial image, which suggests the product and its communication, at least, will not languish in calm waters.

 The Blue Ant trilogy thus captures the emerging space of empire that subsumes the spaces of the former colonial empires, featuring the loss of distance through speed of transport and communication, the growth of commodity chains that commonly stretch across the globe in nonlinear fashion, the blurring of work and leisure, and the mobilization of a global just-in-time stock of commodities constantly on the move from megaports to superhighways. In *Spook Country*, of course, GPS gridlines and container ships replace the horse latitudes, referencing the contemporary spatial regime of global capital, and connecting the system for the global movement of commodities in container ships to the global movement of communication via the internet. Virilio has written about this "just-in-time and stockless" system in futuristic terms as a "post-urban revolution that will drive the twenty-first century,"[36] the city replaced by a cyberspace-like immersion in the elsewhere of the screen or informational layers of the city, while commodity stocks pick up from docks and warehouses become mobile. Where Alberti's perspective painting fixed the palatial domains of the new town on a grid of points and lines, Virilio sees the city transforming from point to "trajectory."[37] Gibson's writing must be able to "keep up" with this movement.

Writing Posturban Space

Gibson seems to figure out how to make the web surfer's waste of time productive, as one of the pleasures of reading the Blue Ant trilogy is to search for the proper name references and track them to what I sometimes imagine is the webpage he used in writing a particular passage. Although some references may be details or asides unnecessary to the plot, the writing strategy can formally enact Blue Ant's branding and coolhunting work and the reading strategy the information worker's leisure habits. Gibson name-drops brands and other proper nouns, adds manufacturing and purchase backgrounds about objects, and describes textures and spaces in which the action takes place. Adding to the effect, the action is often observation, as characters move like camera-eyes across global cities such as London and Los Angeles (a point I return to later)—akin to the virtual eyes in postperspectival digital drawing software. Critical essays on the trilogy often cite Gibson's prose style, which maintains at least some estrangement despite the lack of a novum. Lee Konstantinou describes Gibson's style in *Pattern Recognition* as "maximalist" in counterpoint to its main character's logo-aversive minimalism.[38] Jameson calls it "hyped-up name dropping."[39] Writing about the whole trilogy, Jaak Tomberg observes its "dense concentration of descriptive words."[40] Veronica Hollinger uses the more familiar word "texture,"[41] which takes on an added layer of meaning considering the novels' descriptions of spaces and objects that often evoke tactility through the references to materials that compose, for example, hotel lobbies and shop counters. Tomberg refers to the prose as "over-accelerated,"[42] but in these textural sentences it slows down, giving the prose as a whole a variety of speeds in addition to camera-eyes.

I agree with Tomberg that many of these stylistic features are not novel to the Blue Ant trilogy but are evident in Gibson's writing from the beginning. I would add that the style seems more dominant in the Blue Ant trilogy. One way to think of this technique is as Jameson writes of

Rem Koolhaas's "Junkspace" sentences.[43] Here "it is the new language of space which is speaking through these self-replicating, self-perpetuating sentences, space itself become the dominant code or hegemonic language of the new moment of History—the last?—whose very raw material condemns it in its deterioration to extinction."[44] We can construct an effective homology between Koolhaas's language of space and Gibson's descriptions, finding equivalence between Gibson's informational density and Koolhaas's perpetuum mobile. Where Koolhaas replicates a phrasing or image as a formal idea, creating unified thematic or imagistic blocks within the essay's flow (the text appears as a monolithic block, perhaps like a cyber-stack, lacking indentation, section breaks, subtitles, or architectural photographs, divided only by ellipses), Gibson's material descriptions seem to propel headlong on the momentum of the method, in this case an observational exhaustion. Gibson's descriptions, like Koolhaas's, are not simple denotations and use a complex referential code that can focus on embedded information. For instance, a recurring sentence, going back even to his early cyberpunk writing, describes the smell of plastic in terms of chemical components, seemingly making reference to the object's materiality at a deeper, informational level, implying a form of immaterial property. A refrigerator is "so new that its interior smells only of cold and long-chain monomers."[45] The observation penetrates the visible surface of things while remaining in the physical rather than editorializing or romanticizing. At other times, space itself is seen in terms of products. In *Zero History*, a building appears to Hollis as "a European countertop appliance from the Nineties, something by Cuisinart or Krups, metallic gray plastic, its corners blandly rounded." Its interior surfaces appear made "of the same metallic-looking plastic, or plastic-looking metal."[46] Thus, as with advertising, connotation is raised up as the primary level of the message for the reader as hyperinformed consumer.

Gibson's references are often to cultural texts, such as paintings, film, or fashion, and he often describes a scene through reference to the artistic portrayal of another. In the first scene where Cayce flexes her unusual powers for the readers, Gibson describes Blue Ant employee Bernard Stonestreet (or Cayce describes him) as having "carroty hair upswept in a weird Aubrey Beardsley flame motif."[47] The logo she has been hired to observe looks like "syncopated sperm, as rendered by the

American underground cartoonist Rick Griffin, circa 1967."[48] It is hard to see why most readers would need these proper references to make sense of the passages in a way that, say, "carroty hair upswept like a flame" or "syncopated sperm" would not signify. Descriptions of space follow the same pattern. In one scene, he writes that the sky was "like a gray-scale Cibachrome of a Turner print, too powerfully backlit."[49] In another, "the street was as empty as that moment in the film just before Godzilla's first footfall."[50] In a film reference particularly relevant to Gibson, Cayce is in the Roppongi district in Tokyo:

> where she's had the cab drop her into the shadow of the multi-tiered expressway that looks like the oldest thing in town. Tarkovsky, someone had once told her, had filmed parts of Solaris here, using the expressway as found Future city.
> Now it's been Blade Runnered by half a century of use and pollution, edges of concrete worn porous as coral.[51]

As connotations in the sense of ideological or cultural meanings, they seem to be just unfamiliar enough not to work precisely in that way. I imagine this scene in the way Gibson's early short story "The Gernsback Continuum" flashes for its protagonist between abandoned retro–space age architecture and the imagined future that architecture at one time represented.[52] As the story's title suggests, the architecture of this imagined future was called forth by the pulp sci-fi of Hugo Gernsback's *Amazing Stories*, the first science fiction magazine. In this case, the entire freeway scene, once conjured up, should strike a mood conveyed by the hypnotic way it builds up to its final image of the multiple tiers while focusing on the single rider, former cosmonaut Berton. As Cayce embarks on this leg of her journey to find the maker of the mysterious video footage, the reader keeps in mind these cultural creations of the future, powerful as imaginations of the future and as distorted images of their own present tenses, now ancient history for the reader. Taken together, these close readings of Gibson's prose capture one way the content of the form lies in the importance of information and immaterial labor to create and circulate commodities. Yet they also suggest subterranean possibilities, as one might rediscover a path not taken through the communication of moods via connotation.

Punching

As the trilogy progresses, Gibson writes with more of what I call a hypermediated description of the city, probably influenced by contemporary writing on London (Gibson refers to it as "The London Project"), including Peter Ackroyd's *London: A Biography* and Alan Moore's *From Hell*.[53] In *Zero History* especially, Gibson appears to combine his web surfer's writing technique with the first trilogy's movement through cyberspace, called "punching." Moreover, the descriptive penetration of objects in space suggests the intermingling of information with the production of space. As Joe Shaw and Mark Graham observe in "An Informational Right to the City,"[54] this is a new aspect of urban spatial production different from Lefebvre's emphasis on urban planning and architecture (and digital information was peripheral to the production of space in Lefebvre's time). They argue that urbanization today reproduces the city through digital information, bringing together "ICTs and people as a productive force," producing information and space that can be accumulated as capital. They point to how users of the city interact with ICTs, providing geospatial information, a process through which companies like Google produce the urban environment by gathering information and re-directing flows of information, capital, and people. As they point out, Google dominates urban space through their maps and search queries, and it "often outputs geographic information that displays a loss of nuance, an obscure provenance, hidden personal filtering, and an increasingly complex technical operation behind the process."[55] Thus users of such electronic platforms produce space that serves capital. Moreover, their prosumption may seem to offer access and be participatory, but it also reduces interaction with the city to commodification and simulation of social relations while reducing the city to a market.

Although the Blue Ant trilogy's thematic emphasis on marketing would appear to cover related territory, very little of the content directly connects to this particular type of spatial production that, as Shaw and Graham show, is a key method in the spatial accumulation of wealth. It does not appear as a new space extensively like the perspectival spaces of thirteenth century Italy. It appears intensively, as in the ground grid of digital modeling applications and the product and spatial descriptions in Gibson's prose that penetrate to the informational property. In *Zero History*, transitions between the action often involve Hollis or Milgrim being transported, allowing them to observe the built space that surrounds them: buildings, infrastructure, signage. Although these movements are not slow enough that moments of extended observation between points is possible, they can work through juxtaposition, similar to the hyperjump punching of cyberspace movement. For instance, like the original book jacket for *Zero History*—which depicts an abstract railway tunnel (or fiber-optic cable?) impelling the observer around the bend and into the vanishing point—as Milgrim arrives in London, the city is seen as a medium, resembling the barely fleshed-out vistas of early video games. "Like entering a game, a layout, something flat and mazed, arbitrarily but fractally constructed from beautifully detailed but somehow unreal buildings, its order perhaps shuffled since the last time he'd been here. The pixels that comprised it were familiar, but it remained only provisionally mapped, a protean territory, a box of tricks, some possibly even benign."[56] In part, the details of the metaphor are recognizable throughout the trilogy, as when hotel furniture veneer is described in terms of relative pixelation. Here the entrance into the game-city recalls the moment hackers jack into cyberspace. The description of the building layout as "perhaps shuffled" calls to mind late capitalism's building and rebuilding in search of marginal value (or the "spectacular urbanization"). Moreover, the construction is more protean than solid, or perhaps exists as an illusion or perspective trick, more like a digital model to be observed and manipulated on a screen.

In other moments, Gibson fills in the cyberspace layout, as a montage of proper names moves the characters through space in a series of cuts: "Pentonville Road, on a sign, though he didn't know whether they were on it or near it. Midmorning traffic, though he'd never seen it from a motorcycle. . . . More signs, blurry, through the plastic: King's Cross Road, Farringdon Road."[57] The verb-less, fragmented syntax puts the focus on the urban space while detaching orientation or praxis from the subject's actions in the space. Movement through the space is purely visual (like a video montage) and proceeds by jumps between images, as a hacker might punch his way through the abstract cyberspace layout. The cyber- prefix remains, literally, in the sense of being steered. The cityspace remains abstract, lacking detail due to the speed of the motorcycle, which reduces the city to jumps. It reads similar to passages from *Neuromancer*:

> The transition to cyberspace, when he hit the switch, was instantaneous. He punched himself down a wall of primitive ice belonging to the New York Public Library automatically counting potential windows. Keying back into her sensorium, into the sinuous flow of muscle, senses sharp and bright.[58]
>
> Case's virus had bored a window through the library's command ice. He punched himself through and found an infinite blue space ranged with color-coded spheres strung on a tight grid of pale blue neon. In the nonspace of the matrix, the interior of a given data construct possessed unlimited subjective dimension; a child's toy calculator, accessed through Case's Sendai, would have presented limitless gulfs of nothingness hung with a few basic commands.[59]

The proper names function as signs or iconic nodes for hypertextual interaction, as when Milgrim recognizes Blackfriars Bridge on this trip: "Eventually, a bridge, low railings, red and white paint. Blackfriars, he guessed, remembering the colors. Yes, there were the tops of the very formal iron columns that had once supported another bridge, beside it, that red paint slightly faded."[60] When Fiona cuts the engine and kicks the kickstand, Milgrim jacks out. Cyberspace in *Zero History* is thus a mode of observation rather than a separate space, which of course is all cyberspace is.

It may be useful to think of cyberspace as a concrete abstraction, a category taken from Marx's method to describe commodity exchange. Lefebvre defines it as a mental concept developed by thought until it becomes concretized as a form in social practice, and he uses the concept to describe the production of space out of social space. Social space has a form, which Lefebvre calls "encounter, assembly, simultaneity."[61] Anything produced in space by living beings, whether through cooperation or conflict, assembles in social space and implies accumulation around a point. As productive forces have developed and capitalism expanded, Lefebvre sees the concretization of social space expanded, creating manifold spaces of production, consumption, leisure, and so on. As a heuretic exercise, I borrow Lefebvre's formula and suggest that Gibson's concept of cyberspace may fill one of the slots in a new formula, now updated for twenty-first-century capitalism. The Electronic Frontier Foundation, after all, described it as a "Platonic realm."[62] Is cyberspace a figure for an emerging form of spatial representation that coincides with the creation of new spaces of accumulation, as in the history of linear perspective? This way of understanding cyberspace could explain more satisfactorily why Gibson's writing evolves from science fiction to the science-fictionalized present: it follows the emergence of cyberspace from mental concept to concrete production and accumulation. Moreover, from this perspective, it may indicate a set of strategies for recording this hidden abode in the novel form, arresting this new spatial production in a place for reflection and suggesting ways to navigate it.

CHAPTER 11 . . . **CHRISTIAN P. HAINES**

"JUST A GAME"

BIOPOLITICS, VIDEO GAMES, AND FINANCE
IN WILLIAM GIBSON'S THE PERIPHERAL

In January 2018, the World Health Organization (WHO) added the diagnosis of "gaming disorder" to its eleventh revision of the International Classification of Diseases. WHO defines the disorder as "a pattern of gaming behavior (digital-gaming or video-gaming) characterized by impaired control over gaming, increasing priority given to gaming over other activities to the extent that gaming takes precedence over other interests and daily activities, and continuation or escalation of gaming despite the occurrence of negative consequences."[1] Instead of the moral panic linking video games to violence, this diagnosis emphasizes the disruption of daily routines because of an inability to properly manage one's time. However, gaming disorder isn't pure disruption, for, as the WHO suggests, it has its own pattern. The problem is that gaming threatens to go viral, subsuming the rest of life and colonizing the pleasures and obligations of the everyday with the yearning to escape into digital fantasies. That the threat gaming presents is not only psychological but also economic can be seen in think pieces that worry over gaming's contribution to rising rates of unemployment, especially among young men.[2] The specter of young men opting out of the labor force in favor of digital play indexes a more general fear of economic stagnation and political disaffection, an anxiety that so much time might go to waste and that this waste might return to haunt the social body of capitalism. To his credit, Ryan Avent, an editor for *The Economist*, recognizes that this social pathology is less cause than symptom of an economy in which long-term careers have been replaced with contingent employment and consumer credit: "A life spent buried in video games, scraping by on meagre pay from irregular work or dependent on others, might seem empty and sad. Whether it is emptier and sadder than one spent buried in finance, accumulating points during long hours at the office while neglecting other aspects of life, is a matter of perspective."[3]

Gaming disorder is a symptom of financialized capitalism. It is less a suspension of capitalist temporality than an element of the more general transition toward an economy in which temping (temporary labor) has become the norm.[4] Financialization is, at least, a twofold phenomenon. First, it is, in Greta Krippner's words, "a pattern of accumulation in which profits accrue primarily through financial channels rather than trade and commodity production."[5] This aspect of financialization pertains not only to the restructuring of corporations so that they are more responsive to the interests of shareholders but also to how companies not traditionally associated with finance increasingly rely on financial revenue streams. Since the 1970s, corporations and nation-states have relied more and more on financial speculation to compensate for declining profit rates. Second, financialization also names the spread of financial techniques into everyday life. Randy Martin writes: "Financialization integrates markets that were separate, like banking for business and consumers, or markets for insurance and real estate. It asks people from all walks of life to accept risk into their homes that were hitherto the province of professionals. Without significant capital, people are being asked to think like capitalists."[6] Financialization generalizes the ethos of speculation so that it encompasses all kinds of social conducts, from parenting to leisure activities. It replaces the ascetic worker-subject described by Max Weber with an opportunistic freelancer always seeking to transform a situation into another revenue stream. Opportunism is the mood of financialization; it's the background hum of subjects compelled to speculate on contingent possibilities to survive in conditions of economic stagnation.

Gaming disorder is financialization's fallout: the disaffected young men about whom capitalist intellectuals worry so much are a consequence of financialization—an inverted figure of the financial opportunist, a sign of what happens when speculation breaks the economic motivation of subjects. However, gaming is also inextricable from finance. The connection between video games and finance is obvious on the side of production. The global games industry generated US$109 billion in revenues in 2017 alone.[7] Game development is intimately bound up with financial speculation, not least because the video game industry is dominated by large publishing corporations beholden to shareholders. Games are regularly canceled mid-development due to worries about projected profits and developers are forced to "crunch" (work prolonged periods of overtime) to release games during optimal sales windows. Financialization determines what kinds of games get made and how they get made.

The most pervasive financial element of gaming has less to do with development than with how playing games cultivates a financialized form of subjectivity. Gaming models financial subjectivity by compelling players to act on the basis of risk assessment, to parcel out time in a manner corresponding to the rhythms of the gig economy, and to compete against others for access to credit. In short, gaming trains players to act like subjects of speculation. Gaming draws out the biopolitics of gaming—the manner in which the logic of digital games has become synonymous, at least tendentiously, with the governance of social life. Gaming may involve a sense of escape, but it also asks gamers to attune themselves to the rhythms of speculation.

It should come as no surprise that one of the most incisive critiques of gaming and financialization comes from William Gibson, whose fiction has examined the nexus of politics, society, economy, and technology for decades. Gibson's 2014 novel *The Peripheral* takes place during two historical periods—a near future (in the twenty-first century) and a far future (the twenty-second century)—linked through an unconventional form of time travel: information exchange across timelines via mysterious computer servers. In Gibson's fiction, time travel doesn't involve transporting a physical person to another time but exchanging data between discrete historical periods through a digital medium. Moreover, the act of establishing this connection introduces a fissure between the timelines, so the past to which the future connects is no longer that future's past because it has branched off to constitute another temporal continuum. This image of bifurcating timelines is more than analogous to financial speculation. In Gibson's fictional world, it's a conduit for it: many of the novel's central plot points turn on the efforts of the far future to manipulate the financial markets of the near future. One might think of these as attempts to game the markets, first, because such markets are already game-like (they involve investors evaluating one another's moves or wagers in a rule-governed space of possibilities) and, second, because *The Peripheral* transposes the register of finance into the domain of digital games. Gaming isn't merely the novel's content; it's the model through which Gibson articulates a critical account of neoliberalism, militarism, digital technology, and precarious labor. Some of *The Peripheral*'s characters are literally gamers, but all of the characters have to negotiate complex passages between the digital and the physical, the virtual and the actual, the future and the present, as if they were playing a high-stakes game.

Gaming and the Speculative Subject

The Peripheral begins with a game. Flynne, also known by her gamer tag, Easy Ice, agrees to fill in for her brother, Burton, playing a "beta of some game."[8] Burton knows little about the game, only that he's being paid by a company, Milagros Coldiron SA, and that the action involved in playing is minimal: "Nothing to shoot. Work a perimeter around three floors of this tower, fifty-fifth to fifty-seventh. See what turns up" (3). In the game, Flynne spends her time chasing off "bugs" (aerial drones) from a loft apartment in a futuristic high-rise, until she witnesses another woman (whom she assumes to be a digital avatar) being killed by a strange mobile entity deploying "directed swarm weapons. Flesh-eaters, in the trade" (418). The novel's description of the woman's death reads:

> The woman never moved, as something tiny punched out through her cheek, leaving a bead of blood, her mouth still open, more of them [nanobots composing the swarm weapon] darting in, almost invisible, streaming over from the pale-edged slit. Her forehead caved in, like stop-motion of Leon's pumpkin of the president, on top of the compost in her mother's bin, over days, weeks. As the

brushed-steel railing lowered, behind her, on the soap-bubble stuff that was no longer glass. Without it to stop her, the woman toppled backward, limbs at angles that made no sense. Flynne went after her.

She was never able to remember any more blood, just the tumbling form in its black t-shirt and striped pants, less a body every inch it fell, so that by the time they passed the thirty-seventh, where she'd first noticed the thing, there were only two fluttering rags, one striped, one black. . . .

"Just a game," she said, in the trailer's hot dark, her cheeks slick with tears. (56)

This passage merges the digital and the physical, the virtual and the actual, so that the apparently fictional death of a woman becomes a visceral event. Although the text leaves the details of the gaming system vague, it seems as though it's a virtual reality rig, involving a high-resolution screen, ergonomic chair, and intuitive controller. Whatever its technical specifications, the system generates a degree of immersion high enough to elicit intense emotion, registered in Flynne's face becoming "slick with tears." There's little in the text's description of gameplay to mark a clear distinction between the virtual world and the actual world, except that Flynne's body has been replaced by a kind of quad copter with "gyros" and the surreal way the woman's body decomposes at an accelerated rate. Gibson's description echoes Brendan Keogh's phenomenology of video games, according to which "the videogame experience" is "a *coming-together* of the player and the videogame not as preexisting, separate, distinct subjects or objects but as a cybernetic assemblage of human body and nonhuman body across actual and virtual worlds."[9] Gaming is a feedback loop in which the embodied player and digital game constitute a semi-autonomous material experience—a blur of digital technology, virtual play, and human flesh. In this posthuman vision of play, the game modifies the player on an affective level—a visceral reprogramming of subjectivity through gameplay—but even so, the player remains inoculated from material trauma by the ontological distinction of virtuality. It is, Flynne reminds herself, "Just a game."

Material realities intrude into the game, however. These realities include the fact that Flynne's gaming is gig work, or contract employment; Flynne's geographic position in the impoverished landscapes of rural

America; and the narrative reveal that the woman in the "game" was a real person in the twenty-second century. Flynne was actually performing security, and the woman was really assassinated. The text introduces an indistinction between gaming and everyday life, so the ludic experience is workerly not only in its rhythms and goals but also in its capacity for producing effects in the nongame world. It might be tempting to read this indistinction as the erasure of the ludic, or the negation of the game by the exigencies of real life, but *The Peripheral* poses it in precisely the opposite terms as the conversion of everyday life into a game. The game doesn't dissolve, it spreads, transforming from a sealed-off domain of play into a neoliberal hub of economic competition. The novel encapsulates this mutation when Wilf Netherton, a far-future character, responds to Flynne's question—"Is it a game?"—by saying, "It's a gamelike environment" (82). Netherton dissimulates in respect to the corporate intrigue into which Flynne has become mired, but he's also speaking a certain truth: the logic of digital games cannot be confined to a distinct space of gameplay because social life has come to be governed by the kinds of algorithms—procedural, rule-based systems of conduct—we typically find in games.[10]

The idea that the world we live in has become "gamelike" suggests two significant points. First, it implies a historical trajectory in which electronic games emerge from the research efforts of corporations and the military after World War II, then migrate into the entertainment industry, only to become generalized beyond conventional leisure through trends that include gamification (the application of digital game elements—especially scoring and ranking—to other aspects of life, such as physical exercise and romance) and casual games (games emphasizing short, intermittent bursts of play, usually on mobile devices, and often played between one task and another).[11] Material reality becomes "gamelike" to the degree that the boundaries between work and leisure, military and civilian life, algorithm and social custom, the digital and the analog, have eroded. Gaming "reveal[s] itself as a school for labor, an instrument of rulership, and a laboratory for the fantasies of advanced technocapital."[12] Implicit in gaming's tendency to encompass every dimension of social life is its tendency to subsume subjectivity in an ideological and biopolitical way. It's not just the world that becomes gamelike but the thought processes, feelings, and activities of subjects. More specifically, the conversion of social space into gamespace entails producing neoliberal subjects for whom every practice, recreation included, belongs to a competitive arena in which the goal is to outperform other players.

Gaming and financialization converge in the concept of a scored life—a life organized around rating and being rated and around the ethos of competition associated with ratings. It's a genre of life that corresponds to Michel Foucault's analysis of neoliberal society as an "enterprise society" ("not a society subject to the commodity-effect but a society subject to the dynamic of competition") and of the neoliberal subject as human capital ("*homo oeconomicus* as entrepreneur of himself, being for himself his own capital").[13] Neoliberalism transposes the form of the market onto the entirety of social relations—a marketization of social life analogous to the gamification of social life. According to Foucault, US neoliberal intellectuals formulate society less as an object of discipline than as a game, "an optimization of systems of difference, in which the field is left open to fluctuating processes, in which minority individuals and practices are tolerated, in which action is brought to bear on the rules of the game, rather than on the players, and finally in which there is an environmental type of intervention instead of the internal subjugation of individuals."[14] In this interpretation, neoliberalism does not compel subjects to conform to an extrinsic norm; instead, it cultivates an environment in which certain kinds of actions—marketable ones—are more likely to meet with success. Foucault's analysis could easily be transposed to digital games, especially so-called open-world games, which accommodate player freedom by including nonlinear and emergent gameplay alongside linear narrative structures. For example, in *Red Dead Redemption 2* (Rockstar Games, 2018), players might choose to spend hours playing poker or fishing instead of pursuing the story missions. Of course, power isn't absent from neoliberalism; it takes the form of market transactions. In gaming terms, the player has freedom only to the extent that the rules of the game afford it—the open world is only as open as the developer's code permits.

Foucault's analysis of neoliberalism has its limits. As Wendy Brown, Melinda Cooper, and Randy Martin have argued, Foucault doesn't account for the constitutive exclusions of neoliberalism—the production of subjects deemed unworthy of investment—nor does he anticipate the transition toward a speculation-driven model of subjectivity.[15] These shortcomings are partly because Foucault's theorization of neoliberalism preceded current conditions of financialization and partly an effect of his methodological commitment to describing operations of power in an immanent manner. In Brown's words, moving beyond these limitations means considering how financialization has "altered the figure of human capital from an ensemble of enterprises to a portfolio of investments."[16] Financialized subjects are less interested in producing commodities than in pursuing lines of credit. They are investees or, as Michel Feher writes, "bearers of projects in search of investment. As such, the fate of their initiatives depends on whether they succeed in earning the confidence of individuals or institutions capable of sponsoring them."[17]

Financialized subjects are surrounded by a host of rating mechanisms, from credit scores to "likes" on social media, which rank the subject on the basis of their history and in light of their potential for future earnings. The result is that every subject is compelled to bear the risk of investment, whether or not they can weather the consequences. As Martin explains, we become creatures of risk, measured with regard not only to our capacity to bear risk but also our willingness to do so: "Risk also performs a moral function, by sorting out those with the disposition to embrace it from those relegated to being bad risks. The risk taker is a righteous agent of history; those at risk are left in the ashcan."[18] The good speculative subject takes on risk, meaning she is willing to accept the terms of accreditation. She operates as a conduit for financial flows in the hope of ever-greater returns, while at the same time exorcising the constant specter of failure. She cultivates herself as an attractive portfolio of opportunities—a credit-worthy creature—even as she knows that beneath every speculative subject lurk the subprime: those who have taken on lines of credit but have failed to meet expected returns; those who have never been deemed worthy of credit because of race, geography, or other social conditions—in short, everyone who has been sacrificed to the altar of risk.[19]

A description of Flynne readying herself for a gaming session calls attention to the intimate connections between gaming and risk management:

> Something she'd gotten from Burton and the [Marine] Corps, that you didn't do things in clothes you sat around in. You got yourself squared away, then your intent did too. When she'd been Dwight's recon point, she'd made sure she got cleaned up. Doubted she'd be

doing that again, even though it was the best money she'd made. She didn't like gaming, not the way Madison and Janice did. She'd done it for the money, got so good at one particular rank and mission in Operation Northwind that Dwight wouldn't have anyone else. Except that he would by now. (42)

The passage distinguishes Flynne's object—money, not fun—and indicates how gaming requires a labor of preparation, of readying one's body and mind for the concerted effort of gameplay. One has to get "squared away," which is to say that one has to sand off the uneven edges of perception, feeling, or thought that might intrude on the attention the game demands. It's a process of attuning the self to the fundamentally quantitative values constituting the algorithmic basis of gameplay. A flashback to another gaming session highlights the quantitative measure of what might be called gig play: "Players like Flynne were paid on the basis of kills, and on how long they could survive in a given campaign" (47). Flynne takes amphetamines on a "dosing schedule" to optimize her kill and survival rates. Gaming requires an enhanced state of awareness—an alertness in regard to perception (the ability to quickly pick out an enemy in the midst of other stimuli) and reflexes (the ability to rapidly translate perception into manual action). The goal is to enter into a state of "flow," which is the opposite of reflective thought. "Not to learn it, [Burton] said, because it couldn't be taught, but to spiral in with it, each turn tighter, further into the forest, each turn closer to seeing it [the state of 'hunting'] exactly right. Down into that one shot across the clearing she found there, where the sudden mist of airborne blood, blown with the snow, was like the term balancing an equation" (48). The casual player becomes the hardcore gamer by entering a "spiral" with the algorithms of the game. It's a matter of eliminating qualitative difference, critical distance, and lag from a loop in which the stimuli produced by the game's code elicits physical input. It's also a process of reduction, as the variability of play—the possibility space enabled by the game—gives way to the act of destroying the target, "like the term balancing an equation."

Underlying this process of becoming a hardcore gamer is a general sense of economic precarity, the awareness that despite Easy Ice's skill, she can always be replaced. The novel registers this precarity through the lengths Flynne goes to adapt herself to the game and through her assessment of what motivates the accountant against whom she competes.

"She'd gotten to feeling that what the accountant most liked, about killing them, was that it really cost them. Not just that he was better at it than they were, but that it actually hurt them to lose. People on her squad were feeding their children with what they earned playing, and maybe that was all they had, like she was paying Pharma John for her mother's prescriptions" (48). *The Peripheral* represents gameplay only insofar as it interrupts the seamlessness of the digital by calling attention to the material conditions of gaming. Class division may not appear in the virtual domain of the game, but it structures the feeling of play. For Flynne, what's at stake is her mother's survival via access to medicine; for the accountant, what's at stake is a pleasure grounded in dominating other players. Differentials of risk mediate the experience of the game so that play always already harbors the constraints of capitalism.

Like neoliberalism, digital games involve a fantasy of equality: a vision of the gamespace as a perfect meritocracy in which skill and effort are the ultimate factors in deciding success.[20] Ivan Ascher compares financialized class division to a horse race, reminding readers that "the ideological cover provided by neoliberalism cannot entirely conceal the fact that investors depend on other investors in relations that are at once reciprocal and thoroughly asymmetrical."[21] He explains that this division is not between borrowers and creditors, or investment bankers and laypeople, but "between those whose lives keep placing them at risk and having thus to seek protection (say, in the form of a loan or an insurance policy) and those whose position of relative security, by contrast, gives them the opportunity to take risks—say, by lending to others or betting on their probability of default."[22] The formal equality of players, epitomized by the relative equivalence of their in-game avatars, belies the embodied inequalities of speculative subjects, some of whom have the means to enjoy the game, whereas others need it to survive. If Gibson represents this class division through a first-person shooter (*Operation Northwind*), it's not only because that genre is so popular but also because its primary gameplay mechanism—what Mackenzie Wark calls targeting—captures the economic and libidinal appeal of online multiplayer gaming.[23] These games depend on the collaborative efforts of players to transform virtual environments into arenas of lively competition, but they also require the disavowal of collaboration, because they privilege victory conditions based on eliminating competitors. As Wark explains, it's also a matter of time: "Time is the enemy. Targeting attempts to transform time from a medium of events, where one thing alternates with another, to a medium of self-fulfillment, where, by picking out a deliberative line across its surface, you can make time register the integrity and significance of your character—and by proxy yourself—and reward it with the next level."[24] The hardcore gamer transforms time into a medium through which to accumulate profit and prestige; she invests her energy and skill into gameplay, speculating on the possibility of victory, or at least avoidance of the subprime condition.

Speculative Time

In *The Peripheral*, gaming is a way of thinking about the colonization of time by finance capital. The novel's central conceit—digital time travel—transforms history into a game of speculation. The far-future denizens extract information from the past as a way of gaining advantage against competing corporate and governmental interests. In turn, the near-future characters leverage their own positions through the information they receive from the far future (especially information about technological innovations and market trends). There is, however, a fundamental fissure between the timelines, caused by the very act of producing "stubs." "When we sent out first e-mail to their Panama, we entered into a fixed ratio of duration with their continuum: one to one. A given interval in the stub is the same interval here, from first instant of contact. We can no more know their future than we can know our own, except to assume that it ultimately isn't going to be history as we know it. And, no, we don't know why. It's simply the way the server works, as far as we know" (92). The gap between timelines introduces epistemological uncertainty, as well as historical indeterminacy, the former being a corollary of the latter: time travel doesn't lead to sovereignty over history because both content (the stub) and platform (the server) are opaque. This opacity enables speculation by creating a margin between the predictable and the unpredictable, a space where wagers on possible futures can occur. It's what Lisa Adkins calls "speculative time," operating not on the basis of "calculations of the probable, predicted, and projected from the present into the future" but through "calculations of the possible." "In this calculus futures do not unfold from the known present, but the present is remediated by futures that have not yet and might never arrive."²⁵ In a sense, *The Peripheral* does little more than figure the time of speculation, using science fiction to represent the obscure complexities of high finance. On the other hand, the novel offers its own gaming of finance, not an opportunistic leveraging of history but an attempt to imagine a life beyond the biopolitical pincers of the good speculative subject and the subprime rabble.

The far-future characters of *Peripheral* are good speculative subjects insofar as they successfully manage to leverage their position in history. They are what J. Paul Narkunas calls "market humans." "Market humans believe in their own powers of self-creation, with free will and an individuality that is supplemented only by a sense of community based on the freedom to innovate."²⁶ Market humans have faith in their own powers because they frame history as an engine of innovation: a temporal continuum whose units of measure are financial opportunities. This faith requires speculative subjects to immunize themselves from the negative consequences of risk. In Gibson's novel, they do so through several means, including biotechnology, labor automation, and humanoid drones ("peripherals"), but the practice of constructing stubs is the pinnacle of this immunitary logic, as it allows market humans to exercise almost god-like power over subjects that cannot strike back. The "enthusiasts" of this genre of time travel operate as if the temporal continuum they connect to were a discrete unit of time, entirely knowable by virtue of hindsight. The dismissive terminology of "stubs" alludes to the fact that this kind of time travel introduces a rupture between timelines. It also indicates the potential for manipulation, the far future's ability to leverage its knowledge of the past without needing to worry about blowback. It's a form of temporal imperialism, or, as one character puts it, "We're third-worlding alternate continua. Calling them stubs makes that a bit easier" (103). From the perspective of the far future, the stub dwellers are disposable avatars, less subjects of history than pieces in a game. Flynne makes this point directly: "It was like a game . . . We aren't their past. We go off in some different direction because they've changed things here. . . . Their world's not affected by what happens here, now or going forward" (192–93).

If the stubs exemplify the temporal dimension of speculative subjectivity, then the peripherals exemplify its spatial dimension. A peripheral is an "anthropomorphic drone" or "telepresence avatar"—a humanoid automaton controlled through a digital device connected directly to the human brain (175). Peripherals abolish the gap between embodied player and in-game avatar in a paradoxical manner: the player becomes her avatar by coming into the possession of another body—a machine body. It's an extreme version of virtual reality, premised on the transformation of everyday life into a gamespace. Like in-game avatars, peripherals can even be upgraded. The peripheral literalizes the neoliberal articulation of society in terms of human capital, remaking the person into a bundle of technical capacities capable of being updated for a price. Even the substrate of these capacities is disposable, since the death of a peripheral isn't synonymous with the death of its operator. Instead, the destruction of a peripheral is "game over"—not a final resting place but a temporary terminus in a loop designed to be repeated. As Keogh suggests, "game over" (avatar death) enables video games to complicate time by engendering loops in which players can learn from past gameplay experiences and experiment with different actions.[27] However, *The Peripheral* suggests that this kind of inconsequential death—this immunity from risk—is synonymous with "third-worlding" stubs: it's part and parcel of a system designed to concentrate power in the hands of the wealthy by outsourcing vulnerability to subprime subjects.[28] Indeed, one of the novel's antagonists, Hamed al-Habib, uses a peripheral to fake his own death as part of a scheme to monetize a floating island of trash. Whereas al-Habib's death is only temporary, the deaths of the "patchers" (a kind of posthuman rabble following him) are quite permanent.

The Peripheral allegorizes the conversion of social space into gamespace through its narrative structure and style, as well as its content. The novel alternates between the near-future and far-future timelines from one chapter to the next. This alternation takes place quickly, most chapters not exceeding ten pages, some as short as two pages. What results is a formal analogue to the construction of stubs: the transition between chapters marks the contingency of historical conditions, the mutability of gamespace. Gibson's prose style echoes this narrative speed: his sentences are modular and clipped, dropping subjects or verbs, coining neologisms that collapse ideas together. It's as if the novel were trying to model itself after the rhythm of financialized capitalism, transforming the act of reading into a neoliberal training regimen: in learning to negotiate the rapid turnover of timelines and accept the disposability of bodies (peripherals), Gibson's reader becomes a good speculative subject—a creature for whom the future is a source of profit accessed by means of credit (or fiction). Gibson's novel could be compared to action games, described by Claus Pias as "time-critical" systems in which "play consists of producing temporally optimized sequences of action out of determined options." "To play an action game means to perform a permanent act of accommodation [to the machine], the end of which is no longer the symbolic death of the player, who in his or her non-conformity has failed to be resurrected with a 'sublime body.' Rather, the process ends with a 'victory' over a machine."[29] Stuck in an age in which the digital is dominant, the novel does the only thing it can: it offers the fantasy of the hardcore gamer, that is, the promise of victory over one's competitors, provided one is willing to surrender to the rules of the game.

The Peripheral may allegorize gamespace, but it also marks the irreducibility of social life to the digital. It emphasizes how digitization is a technological fact and a social process involving the separation of subjects of information from the nuisance of noise. It's what Seb Franklin calls "control": an episteme and set of technical procedures introducing "a break into the realms of both individual human activity and social formations, so that behavior, affects, and capacities appear as either (1) productive and representable (information) and thus deemed existent or (2) nonproductive and unrepresentable (not information) and thus denied existence."[30] The overlap between this opposition and that between good subjects of speculation and the subprime is not an accident but a consequence of the historical dovetailing of financialization and digitization. As a number of scholars have recounted, financialization has used digital technologies (as exemplified by high-frequency trading) and drawn on the conceptual frameworks of information science (not least of all game theory) to reformat the world as a competitive arena of speculation.[31] Gibson responds to this arena by representing the noise of social life not as a residue of historical progress but as another way of dwelling in time. For example, the novel emphasizes the dissonance between Flynne's embodiment and her use of the peripherals: "The more time you spend here [in the far future], the more likely you are to notice dissonance on returning. Your peripheral's sensorium is less multiplex than your own. You may find your own sensorium seems richer, but not pleasantly. More meaty, some say. You'll have gotten used to a slightly attenuated perceptual array, though you likely don't notice it now" (225–26). The felt difference between avatar and flesh implies an excess of the qualitative over the quantitative—a multiplicity irreducible to the discrete terms of financial and digital culture. This experience may seem minor, but the novel is replete with descriptions of characters suffering from a "surfeit of information, oceanic to the point of meaninglessness," covered in tattoos of extinct creatures meant to memorialize what's been lost to speculation, and reveling in being "chronic malcontent[s]" (383, 282). Gibson's fiction doesn't so much simulate an action game as teach readers how to recognize what is lost in the transition to gamespace: it cultivates an awareness of what fails to accommodate itself to the score.

The Peripheral is a metagame as much as it is a representation of gamespace. In general terms, "metagaming" means everything surrounding a digital game—all of the various activities, information, communities, and programs that exceed the actual playing of the game yet affect or build on the game in some way. The "meta," as it's also called, includes strategies for competing in multiplayer games, "mods" that hack games to change how they play or transform them into new games, online forums for sharing game tips, and "achievements" (digital trophies) for accomplishing specific goals in games. Stephanie Boluk and Patrick Lemieux argue that metagaming denaturalizes our experience of games and, in doing so, creates critical potential for intervening into gamespace. They contend that "videogames operate as the ideological avatar of play: a widely held, naturalized system of beliefs that conflates the fantasy of escapism with the commodity form and encloses play within the magic circle of neoliberal capital." In contrast, metagames "articulate a ludic practice that profanes the sacred, historicizes art, mediates technology, and de-reifies the fetish."[32] There are ideological metagames, of course, or practices that operate as alibis for the military-industrial-entertainment complex—one thinks, for example, of the secret strategies that allow professional teams of gamers to compete successfully in high-stakes tournaments—but there are also metagames that ask how gaming might move beyond competition. These subversive metagames range from avant-garde games that overturn the dominant conventions of digital games to online activism that combats sexism in gaming culture.

The Peripheral is a subversive metagame not only because it criticizes the gamification of social life but also because it draws on gaming to imagine systemic change. To think of the novel as a metagame is not to suggest that it transcends gamespace. On the contrary, *The Peripheral* seems to say that the best we can hope for is not redemption but something like repair, or what the novel describes as "steer[ing]" history away from disaster, "no guarantee of what we'll ultimately produce" (378). One probably would not call this approach utopian, but it does speak to a desire to reclaim our investment in the future, to conceive of time as something more than a medium of competition. Gibson asks us to speculate with him on the possibility not of escaping the game but of a "game changer": the emergence of a world irreducible to the oppositions between digital information and noise, good speculative subjects and the subprime, capitalist futurity and the dustbin of history (442). *The Peripheral* knows the score, but it also believes in truly unpredictable possibilities.

CHARLES YU

AFTERWORD

THE WORLD IMPLIED

To read William Gibson is to be a step behind.

That feeling of someone, very fast, running stride for stride with you. You are exerting yourself right up to the limit of your ability; he is not. You are close but only because he is allowing you to stay close. If you reach out, you think, you might be able to grasp him, to catch him, if only for a second. How gratifying that would be, to pull even, be in step. To move through the world alongside him, seeing it as he does. Except you never quite manage to close that final step. And it's a wonderful feeling.

To read Gibson is to constantly feel as if you are about to lose your footing, to tumble into the dirt, head over tail, spinning into disorientation. To read Gibson is to get faster, his mind training yours, with each turn of the page, each new shift in perspective, each new corner of a universe being revealed. To read Gibson is bewilderment and exhilaration.

Think pieces, profiles, book reviews, scholarly essays, message board posts, midnight yawps of awe and admiration—how many thousands, millions of words have been written about Gibson's work? How many of those words focus on Gibson's uncanny knack for accurately imagining the future?

And for good reason. He nailed it, okay? In about a thousand ways, from nano to macro. Gibson wrote stuff thirty years ago that, when you read it today, feels fresher than the nth generation of his literary offspring and imitators. He's the before and the after and the during, he's the origin story and today's news.

He was a piece of twenty-first-century fiction dropped into the twentieth. Genius here, just unevenly distributed, a disproportionate share of it clumped into his brain. He has said he's not predicting the future so much as generating scenarios, which is a graceful way of being both modest and precise. To say Gibson predicted the future mischaracterizes and underestimates his contributions. He didn't just point us in the right direction, he created the map. He didn't anticipate the future so much as he brought it into being. He didn't pick a possibility but swept out the range of possibility space. Not the furniture but the architecture. Not the fish in the tank but the tank itself. It's his water and we're swimming in it.

· · · · ·

If Gibson is properly appreciated in his capacity as a visionary, it may have come at the expense of his other gifts. Namely, as a writer of prose. As odd as it is to think of someone of his stature as somehow underrated, in Gibson's case, his otherworldly ability to extrapolate possible futures can often overshadow his actual writing.

As good as he is at writing novels, he is even better at writing sentences.

Not that the two are unrelated, of course. Worldbuilding is sometimes thought of as requiring mythologies, back stories, or paratextual material, making worlds out of maps or timelines or family histories (not that there's anything wrong with any of that!). But in Gibson's work, worldbuilding is practiced in its purest, highest form: at the level of fundamental particles, in the language itself. Realities built word by word, through syntax, through patois, through granular detail accumulating into pictures, images clicking by at a high frame rate, his expertly operated camera whooshing us into, through, and then up out of the scene before we can fully process what we have heard and seen. By the time we are starting to catch on, he's already onto the next scene; meanwhile, what our brains are registering is an undeniable, rich, dense, populated, believable universe. His worldbuilding seldom exposits for the audience's benefit; explanation is kept to the necessary minimum. From this lack of exposition, from the velocity of speech and action, from the way his characters interact, we get not just plausibility but actual immersion.

We don't visit Gibson's cities, strolling in for a look. We are dropped in, no map or translator.

From Chiba City to London. Five blinks into the future or the post-Jackpot twenty-second century. Time, continuous or stubby. Space of various flavors, meat- or cyber- or something else yet to be conceived of. All of it rendered in prose constructed of Gibsonium, a gleaming alloy, airtight, strong, light, shimmery, ductile strength off the charts. Never straining or creaking under the narrative burden.

Plus another thing: he's funny.

"A middleman's business is to make himself a necessary evil."[1]

"Shaylene had big hair without actually having it, Flynne's mother had once said."[2]

"Like a model from an ad where they didn't want to stress ethnicity."[3]

Gibson's wit is a hidden blade, making surgical slices so thin you sometimes don't notice until you look harder.

· · · · ·

In an interview Gibson once said, "What would any given SF favorite look like if we could crank up the resolution? As it was then, much of it was like video games before the invention of fractal dirt. I wanted to see dirt in the corners."[4]

Well he showed us the dirt.

And underneath the dirt, the world implied.

NOTES

Foreword

1. Marcel Proust, *Remembrance of Things Past, Volume 1: Swann's Way*, trans. C. K. Scott Moncrieff and Terence Kilmartin (New York: Random House, 1981), 5–6.
2. William Gibson, "An Interview with William Gibson," interview by Jesse Hicks, *The Verge*, January 24, 2012, https://www.theverge.com/2012/1/24/2724370/william-gibson-interview.
3. William Gibson, *Mona Lisa Overdrive* (New York: Bantam, 1988), 71.
4. William Gibson, *Pattern Recognition* (New York: Berkley, 2003), 6 and 106.
5. Michael Schulson, "William Gibson: I Never Imagined Facebook," *Salon*, November 10, 2014, https://www.salon.com/2014/11/09/william_gibson_i_never_imagined_facebook/.
6. Ibid.
7. Tsvetan Todorov, "The Typology of Detective Fiction," in *The Narrative Reader*, ed. Martin McQuillan (New York: Routledge, 2000), 120–27.
8. Ibid., 122.
9. A. S. Byatt, *Possession* (New York: Vintage, 1991), 253.
10. Karl E. Weick, "Enacted Sensemaking in Crisis Situations," *Journal of Management Studies* 25, no. 4 (1988): 305.
11. See David Comer Kidd and Emanuele Castano, "Reading Literary Fiction Improves Theory of Mind," *Science Magazine*, October 18, 2013, 377–80.

Introduction

1. Stephen Poole, "Nearing the Nodal," *Guardian*, October 30, 1999, https://www.theguardian.com/books/1999/oct/30/sciencefictionfantasyandhorror.williamgibson.
2. See recent films *Bladerunner 2049* (2017) and *Ready Player One* (2018), not to mention CD Projekt Red's upcoming role-playing game *Cyberpunk 2077*, to

which Keanu Reeves—star of Robert Longo's 1995 film adaptation of Gibson's "Johnny Mnemonic"—lends his likeness and voice acting.

3. Tim Adams, "Space to Think," *Observer*, August 12, 2007, https://www.theguardian.com/books/2007/aug/12/sciencefictionfantasyandhorror.features.

4. Rachel Greenwald Smith, ed., *American Literature in Transition, 2000–2010* (Cambridge: Cambridge University Press, 2018).

5. For more information on *Agrippa*, visit the online archive the Agrippa Files at http://agrippa.english.ucsb.edu/.

6. On *Agency*, see Mitch R. Murray, "The Worst of All Possible Worlds?" *Public Books*, July 20, 2020, https://www.publicbooks.org/the-worst-of-all-possible-worlds/.

7. William Gibson, Michael St. John Smith, and Butch Guice, *William Gibson's Archangel* (San Diego: IDW, 2017); William Gibson, Johnnie Christmas, and Tamra Bonvillain, *Alien 3: The Unproduced Screenplay* (Milwaukie, OR: Dark Horse Comics, 2019).

8. See Mathias Nilges, "William Gibson," in *Oxford Bibliographies in American Literature*, ed. Sherryl Vint (New York: Oxford University Press, 2019), n.p.

9. See Neil Easterbrook, "William [Ford] Gibson (1948–)," in *Fifty Key Figures in Science Fiction*, ed. Mark Bould et al. (New York: Routledge, 2020), 86–91.

10. Fredric Jameson, "Fear and Loathing in Globalization," in *Archaeologies of the Future: The Desire Called Utopia and Other Science Fictions* (London: Verso, 2007), 384–92; Tom Moylan, "Global Economy, Local Texts: Utopian/Dystopian Tension in William Gibson's Cyberpunk Trilogy," *Minnesota Review* 43/44 (1995): 182–97; and Lee Konstantinou, "The Brand as Cognitive Map in William Gibson's *Pattern Recognition*," *boundary 2* 36, no. 2 (2009): 67–97.

11. See Sherryl Vint, *Bodies of Tomorrow: Technology, Subjectivity, Science Fiction* (Toronto: University of Toronto Press, 2007); and Timo Siivonen, "Cyborgs and Generic Oxymorons: The Body and Technology in William Gibson's Cyberspace Trilogy," *Science Fiction Studies* 23, no. 2 (1996): 227–44.

12. See Lauren Berlant, "Intuitionists: History and the Affective Event," *American Literary History* 20, no. 4 (2008): 845–60; Robert Briggs, "The Future of Prediction: Speculating on William Gibson's Meta-Science Fiction," *Textual Practice* 27, no. 4 (2013): 671–93; Veronica Hollinger, "Stories about the Future: From Patterns of Expectation to Pattern Recognition," *Science Fiction Studies* 33, no. 3 (2006): 452–72; Lisa Swanstrom, "External Memory Drives: Deletion and Digitality in *Agrippa (A Book of the Dead)*," *Science Fiction Studies* 43, no. 1 (2016): 14–32.

13. See Darko Suvin, "On Gibson and Cyberpunk," *Foundation: The Review of Science Fiction* 46 (1989): 40–51; Jaak Tomberg, "On the 'Double Vision' of Realism and SF Estrangement in William Gibson's Bigend Trilogy," *Science Fiction Studies* 40, no. 2 (2014): 263–85; Sherryl Vint, "The World Gibson

Made," in *Beyond Cyberpunk: New Critical Perspectives*, ed. Graham J. Murphy and Sherryl Vint (New York: Routledge, 2010), 228–33; Phillip E. Wegner, "Recognizing the Patterns," *New Literary History* 38, no. 1 (2007): 183–200.

14. See Neil Easterbrook, "Recognizing Patterns: Gibson's Hermeneutics from the Bridge Trilogy to *Pattern Recognition*," in *Beyond Cyberpunk: New Critical Perspectives*, ed. Graham J. Murphy and Sherryl Vint (New York: Routledge, 2010), 46–64; Veronica Hollinger, "Cybernetic Deconstructions: Cyberpunk and Modernism," *Mosaic* 23, no. 2 (1990): 29–44; Larry McCaffery, ed., *Storming the Reality Studio: A Casebook of Cyberpunk and Postmodern Science Fiction* (Durham, NC: Duke University Press, 1991); Claire Sponsler, "Cyberpunk and the Dilemmas of Postmodern Narrative: The Example of William Gibson," *Contemporary Literature* 33, no. 4 (1992): 625–44.
15. Fredric Jameson, *Marxism and Form: Twentieth-Century Dialectical Theories of Literature* (Princeton, NJ: Princeton University Press, 1971), 306.
16. Andrew Hoberek, "Literary Genre Fiction," in *American Literature in Transition, 2000–2010*, ed. Rachel Greenwald Smith (Cambridge: Cambridge University Press, 2018), 70.
17. On this latter genre, see Caren Irr, *Toward the Geopolitical Novel: U.S. Fiction in the Twenty-First Century* (New York: Columbia University Press, 2014).
18. Gibson quoted in Adams, "Space to Think."
19. Jeremy Rosen, "Literary Fiction and the Genres of Genre Fiction," *Post45*, August 7, 2018, http://post45.research.yale.edu/2018/08/literary-fiction-and-the-genres-of-genre-fiction/; emphasis in original.
20. Ibid., note 3; emphasis in original. It is important to note that these authors are not just Rosen's examples but a fairly routine list for scholarship on the genre turn. The fact that these authors all made their careers by writing distinctly literary novels is key here. Gibson, as masterful a literary stylist as any, would be a weird omission if not for the fact that literary criticism still often understands itself doing something distinct from what science fiction studies do.
21. Carl Freedman, *Critical Theory and Science Fiction* (Hanover, NH: Wesleyan University Press, 2000), 29; emphasis in original.
22. William Gibson, "The Art of Fiction No. 211," interview by David Wallace-Wells, *Paris Review* 197 (2011): 109.
23. See Mark McGurl, *The Program Era: Postwar Fiction and the Rise of Creative Writing* (Cambridge, MA: Harvard University Press, 2009), 409. The program era of American literature might also be described as the rise of "literary fiction" and its place as the metrological standard for the literary.
24. Phillip E. Wegner, *Shockwaves of Possibility: Essays on Science Fiction, Globalization, and Utopia* (Oxford: Peter Lang, 2014), xiii.
25. Ibid., xiv.

26. Hoberek, "Literary Genre Fiction," 73. Hoberek emphasizes that this embrace of genre is strongly and problematically gendered, with women's writing marking "the outer limits of what counts as literary" (71). Indeed, the arrival of cyberpunk in 1984 could be read similarly as an epitaph to the radical feminist science fiction of the 1960s and 1970s, which includes landmark novels by Ursula K. Le Guin, Joanna Russ, Marge Piercy, and Octavia Butler.
27. Fredric Jameson, *Postmodernism, or, The Cultural Logic of Late Capitalism* (Durham, NC: Duke University Press, 1991), 419, n.1; emphasis in original.
28. William Gibson, *Idoru* (New York: Berkley, 1996), 26.
29. Gordon Hutner, "Historicizing the Contemporary: A Response to Amy Hungerford," *American Literary History* 20, nos. 1–2 (2008): 420–24. See also Theodore Martin, "The Currency of the Contemporary," in *Postmodern/Postwar—And After: Rethinking American Literature*, ed. Jason Gladstone, Andrew Hoberek, and Daniel Worden (Iowa City: University of Iowa Press, 2016), 227–39.
30. Fredric Jameson, *The Ancients and the Postmoderns: On the Historicity of Forms* (London: Verso, 2015), 234.
31. Ibid.
32. William Gibson, *Spook Country* (New York: Berkley, 2008), 25.

Chapter 1

1. The phrase "critical utopia" comes from Tom Moylan's classic 1986 study, *Demand the Impossible*, which has recently been republished in an expanded edition. See Tom Moylan, *Demand the Impossible: Science Fiction and the Utopian Imagination* (Oxford: Peter Lang, 2014). I touch on Russ's work as well and the emergence of the critical utopia in Phillip E. Wegner, "Introduction," in Robert C. Elliott, *The Shape of Utopia: Studies in a Literary Genre* (Oxford: Peter Lang, 2013), xiii–xxx. The first version of this essay was presented in spring 2016 at Columbia University's Temple Hoyne Buell Center for the Study of American Architecture, and I thank the center's director, Reinhold Martin, for his generous invitation to speak.
2. Joanna Russ, "When It Changed," in *Again, Dangerous Visions*, ed. Harlan Ellison (New York: Doubleday, 1972), 258.
3. I discuss *The Word for World Is Forest* and its influence in Phillip E. Wegner, *Shockwaves of Possibility: Essays on Science Fiction, Globalization, and Utopia* (Oxford: Peter Lang, 2014), chap. 1.
4. I discuss *Nineteen Eighty-Four* in some detail in Phillip E. Wegner, *Imaginary Communities: Utopia, the Nation, and the Spatial Histories of Modernity* (Berkeley: University of California Press, 2002), chap. 6.
5. Wegner, *Shockwaves of Possibility*, 110.
6. David Langdon, "AD Classics: AT&T Building / Philip Johnson and John

Burgee," *Arch Daily*, January 12, 2019, https://www.archdaily.com/611169/ad-classics-at-and-t-building-philip-johnson-and-john-burgee.
7. Michael Azerrad, *Our Band Could Be Your Life: Scenes from the American Indie Underground, 1981–1991* (New York: Back Bay Books, 2001), 8; Alan Light, "Why 1984 Was Pop Music's Best Year Ever," *Billboard*, October 24, 2014, https://www.billboard.com/articles/news/6296392/1984-best-year-of-pop-music-ever-essay. After listing some of the crucial works to appear in 1922—among others, T. S. Eliot's *The Waste Land*, James Joyce's *Ulysses*, Ranier Maria Rilke's *Die Sonette an Orpheus*, and Virginia Woolf's *Jacob's Room*—Levin concludes, "Though I have been highly selective, the list is sufficient to justify an *annus mirabilis*." Harry Levin, "What Was Modernism?," *Massachusetts Review* 1, no. 4 (1960): 619.
8. Fredric Jameson, "Postmodernism, or the Cultural Logic of Late Capitalism," *New Left Review* 146 (1984): 53–92. Also see Fredric Jameson, "The Politics of Theory: Ideological Positions in the Postmodernism Debate," *New German Critique* 33 (1984): 53–65; Fredric Jameson, "Exoticism and Structuralism in Wallace Stevens," *New Orleans Review* 11, no. 1 (1984): 10–19; Fredric Jameson, "Foreword," in Jean-François Lyotard, *The Postmodern Condition: A Report on Knowledge*, trans. Geoff Bennington and Brian Massumi (Minneapolis: University of Minnesota Press, 1984), vii–xxi; and Fredric Jameson, "Periodizing the 60s," *Social Text* 9/10 (1984): 178–209.
9. Perry Anderson, *The Origins of Postmodernity* (New York: Verso, 1998), 54.
10. Jameson, "Postmodernism," 88. Reprinted, with minimum modifications, in Fredric Jameson, *Postmodernism, or, the Cultural Logic of Late Capitalism* (Durham, NC: Duke University Press, 1991), 49. For his arguments for the shift from the notion of postmodernism to postmodernity, see Fredric Jameson, "The Aesthetics of Singularity," *New Left Review* 92 (2015): 101–32.
11. Jameson, "Postmodernism," 78; Jameson, *Postmodernism*, 36.
12. Doug Henwood, *After the New Economy* (New York: New Press, 2003), 146.
13. Fredric Jameson, "Notes on Globalization as a Philosophical Issue," in *Valences of the Dialectic* (New York: Verso, 2008), 435–55.
14. Jameson, "Postmodernism," 71; Jameson, *Postmodernism*, 25.
15. Jameson, "Postmodernism," 64; Jameson, *Postmodernism*, 16.
16. Jameson, "Postmodernism," 89; Jameson, *Postmodernism*, 50–51; emphasis in original.
17. See Jameson, "Postmodernism," 89–90; Jameson, *Postmodernism*, 51–52, 415–17; Wegner, *Imaginary Communities*, chap. 2. I discuss the notion of cognitive mapping in Phillip E. Wegner, *Periodizing Jameson: Dialectics, the University, and the Desire for Narrative* (Evanston, IL: Northwestern University Press, 2014), chap. 3.
18. Jameson, "Postmodernism," 92; Jameson, *Postmodernism*, 54.

19. Fredric Jameson, *Allegory and Ideology* (New York: Verso, 2019), 190.
20. Jameson, *Postmodernism*, 407.
21. Interestingly, this is the same weekend that the second season of the Netflix series *Stranger Things* (2016–present) purports to begin.
22. Jameson, "The Aesthetics of Singularity," 103.
23. See Wegner, *Shockwaves of Possibility*, chap. 1. The notion of the 1960s as a belated upsurge of the radical utopia energies of modernism is first developed by Perry Anderson in his landmark essay, also first published in 1984 in the pages of *New Left Review*, "Modernity and Revolution," *New Left Review* 144 (1984): 96–113.
24. Veronica Hollinger, "Science Fiction and Postmodernism," in *A Companion to Science Fiction*, ed. David Seed (Oxford: Blackwell, 2005), 236.
25. Carl Freedman, *Critical Theory and Science Fiction* (Hanover, NH: University Press of New England, 2000), 147; and Steven Shaviro, *Connected, Or, What It Means to Live in the Networked Society* (Minneapolis: University of Minnesota Press, 2003).
26. Jameson, *Postmodernism*, 38.
27. Larry McCaffery, "The Fictions of the Present," in *Columbia Literary History of the United States*, ed. Emory Elliot (New York: Columbia University Press, 1988), 1164.
28. William Gibson, *Neuromancer* (New York: Ace, 1984), 3.
29. Brian McHale, *Constructing Postmodernism* (London: Routledge, 1992), 226.
30. Mark McGurl, *The Program Era: Postwar Fiction and the Rise of Creative Writing* (Cambridge, MA: Harvard University Press, 2009), 103.
31. Thomas Disch underscores the New Wave's link to and distinction from modernism in *The Dreams Our Stuff Is Made Of: How Science Fiction Conquered the World* (New York: Simon and Schuster, 1998), 108.
32. Jameson, *Postmodernism*, 286.
33. Fredric Jameson, *The Ancients and the Postmoderns: On the Historicity of Forms* (New York: Verso, 2015), 229. Also see Scott Bukatman, "Gibson's Typewriter," in *Matters of Gravity: Special Effects and Supermen in the Twentieth Century* (Durham, NC: Duke University Press, 2003), 32–47.
34. Jameson, *Ancients and the Postmoderns*, 230.
35. Ibid.
36. Ibid., 234.
37. Ibid., 235.
38. Ibid., 237.
39. Jameson, "Postmodernism," 91; Jameson, *Postmodernism*, 53.
40. Jameson, "Postmodernism," 91–92; Jameson, *Postmodernism*, 53–54.
41. Fredric Jameson, "Third World Literature in the Era of Multinational Capitalism," *Social Text* 15 (1986): 87–88. Reprinted with a new commentary in Jameson, *Allegory and Ideology*, chap. 5.

42. Jameson, *Ancients and the Postmoderns*, 225.
43. Fredric Jameson, *Signatures of the Visible* (New York: Routledge, 1990), 2–26.
44. Gibson, *Neuromancer*, 37.
45. Tom Moylan, "Global Economy, Local Texts: Utopian/Dystopian Tension in William Gibson's Cyberpunk Trilogy," *Minnesota Review* 43/44 (1995): 191.
46. For a superb analysis of the effects of this reorganization on the university, see Herb Childress, *The Adjunct Underclass: How America's Colleges Betrayed Their Faculty, Their Students, and Their Mission* (Chicago: University of Chicago Press, 2019).
47. Gibson, *Neuromancer*, 7.
48. Michel Aglietta, *A Theory of Capitalist Regulation: The US Experience*, trans. David Fernbach (London: Verso, 1987); David Harvey, *The Condition of Postmodernity: An Enquiry into the Origins of Cultural Change* (Oxford: Basil Blackwell, 1989); Yanis Varoufakis, *The Global Minotaur: America, Europe and the Future of the Global Economy* (London: Zed Books, 2015), 99; and William Davies, "The New Neoliberalism," *New Left Review* 101 (2016): 124.
49. Gibson, *Neuromancer*, 43 and 77.
50. Ibid., 85.
51. Andrew Ross, *Strange Weather: Culture, Science and Technology in the Age of Limits* (New York: Verso, 1991), 146. For Delany's reflections on cyberpunk more generally, and in particular the representation of racial difference in *Neuromancer*, see Mark Dery, "Black to the Future: Interviews with Samuel R. Delany, Greg Tate, and Tricia Rose," in *Flame Wars: The Discourse of Cyberculture*, ed. Mark Dery (Durham, NC: Duke University Press, 1994), 193–201. Delany notes, "For most of us in the science fiction world, the cyberpunk movement was a vigorous, interesting—and extremely short-lived—moment.... But the continuing interest in the cyberpunks by academics, as something they persist in seeing as alive and still functioning, strikes me— I must confess—as a largely nostalgic pursuit of a more innocent worldview, which, as I said, to me has no more active historical validity once we pass the Los Angeles King riots" (199–200). I similarly discuss the 1992 Los Angeles uprising as a marker of a significant historical transition in Phillip E. Wegner, *Life between Two Deaths, 1989–2001: US Culture in the Long Nineties* (Durham, NC: Duke University Press, 2009), 115.
52. Ross, *Strange Weather*, 146.
53. Samuel R. Delany, *Stars in My Pocket Like Grains of Sand* (Middletown, CT: Wesleyan University Press, 2004), 203.
54. Ibid., 342–43.
55. Ibid., 225–27.
56. "Relax (Song)," *Wikipedia*, https://en.wikipedia.org/wiki/Relax_(song), last modified January 20, 2020.

57. Samuel R. Delany, *Times Square Red, Times Square Blue* (New York: New York University Press, 1999), 111.
58. I discuss these three narrative utopias in Phillip E. Wegner, *Invoking Hope: Theory and Utopia in Dark Times* (Minneapolis: University of Minnesota Press, 2020), chap. 7.
59. Delany, *Stars in My Pocket*, 303.
60. Ibid., 66; emphasis in original. Also see the discussion of Delany's notion of the cultural fugue in Shaviro, *Connected*, 243–48.
61. Delany, *Stars in My Pocket*, 209.
62. Jameson, *Postmodernism*, 413.
63. Ibid., 414.
64. Ibid.
65. I discuss the importance of the Lacanian notion of the second death in *Life between Two Deaths*, 28–32.
66. Jameson, "Exoticism and Structuralism in Wallace Stevens," 10.
67. Jameson, *Postmodernism*, 418.
68. Slavoj Žižek, "Afterword: Lenin's Choice," in V. I. Lenin, *Revolution at the Gates: Selected Writings of Lenin from 1917*, ed. Slavoj Žižek (New York: Verso, 2002), 310; emphasis in original.
69. Terry Carr, "Introduction," in Kim Stanley Robinson, *The Wild Shore* (New York: Ace, 1984), vii–viii.
70. Sarah Brouillette, "Corporate Publishing and Canonization: *Neuromancer* and Science-Fiction Publishing in the 1970s and Early 1980s," *Book History* 5 (2002): 205.
71. Gibson, *Neuromancer*, 270.
72. I discuss the value of this modified Greimasian semiotic square for presenting a specific historical situation, one of my case studies being the emergence of the novel form, in *Periodizing Jameson*, 81–117; my introduction to *The Shape of Utopia*, xix–xxvi; and *Invoking Hope*, chap. 1.
73. See Tom Moylan, *Scraps of the Untainted Sky: Science Fiction, Utopia, Dystopia* (Boulder, CO: Westview, 2001), chap. 7. For Moylan's discussion of the other novels in the trilogy, see "Utopia Is When Our Lives Matter: Reading Kim Stanley Robinson's *Pacific Edge*," *Utopian Studies* 6, no. 2 (1995): 1–25; and "Witness to Hard Times: Robinson's Other Californias," in *Kim Stanley Robinson Maps the Unimaginable: Critical Essays*, ed. William J. Burling (Jefferson, NC: McFarland, 2009), 11–47. For Moylan's most recent meditations on Robinson's work, see *Becoming Utopian: The Culture and Politics of Radical Transformation* (New York: Bloomsbury, 2020).
74. Kim Stanley Robinson, *The Novels of Philip K. Dick* (Ann Arbor, MI: UMI Research Press, 1984).
75. I discuss the relationship between dystopia and naturalism in *Life between*

Two Deaths, 117–24; and Phillip E. Wegner, "The British Dystopian Novel from Wells to Ishiguro," in *A Companion to British Literature, Volume 4: Victorian and Twentieth-Century Literature, 1837–2000*, ed. Bob DeMaria, Heesok Chang, and Samantha Zache (Hoboken, NJ: Wiley-Blackwell, 2014), 454–70.

76. Kim Stanley Robinson, *The Wild Shore* (New York: Ace, 1984), 106.
77. George W. Bush, "Transcript of President Bush's Address," CCN.com/US, September 21, 2001, http://edition.cnn.com/2001/US/09/20/gen.bush.transcript/; Colson Whitehead, *Zone One* (New York: Random House, 2011), 99.
78. Robinson, *The Wild Shore*, 202.
79. Ibid., 203–4.
80. Jameson, "Postmodernism," 92; Jameson, *Postmodernism*, 54.
81. Robinson, *The Wild Shore*, 371. I explore the utopianism of the *Künstlerroman* in more detail in *Invoking Hope*, chap. 5.

Chapter 2

1. Jacques Rancière, "In What Time Do We Live," *Politicacomun* 4 (2013), doi: 10.3998/pc.12322227.0004.001.
2. William Gibson, *Pattern Recognition* (New York: Berkley, 2003), 186.
3. Public Art Fund, "Metronome," https://www.publicartfund.org/view/exhibitions/5961_metronome (accessed November 30, 2018).
4. Kristin Jones and Andrew Ginzel, "Metronome," http://jonesginzel.com/project/metronome (accessed December 14, 2018).
5. Robert C. Morgan, "Metronome," *Sculpture* 19, no. 4 (May 2000): 10.
6. Jones and Ginzel, "Metronome."
7. See Related Companies Ltd., "One Union Square South," https://www.relatedrentals.com/apartment-rentals/new-york-city/union-square/one-union-square-south (accessed November 30, 2018).
8. Fredric Jameson, "Fear and Loathing in Globalization," in *Archaeologies of the Future: The Desire Called Utopia and Other Science Fictions* (London: Verso, 2005), 384.
9. Joel Burges and Amy J. Elias, "Introduction: Time Studies Today," in *Time: A Vocabulary of the Present*, ed. Joel Burges and Amy J. Elias (New York: New York University Press, 2016), 3.
10. Ibid., 3.
11. Rancière, "In What Time."
12. Ibid.
13. Ibid.
14. Ibid.
15. William Gibson, *Distrust That Particular Flavor* (New York: Putnam, 2012), 201–9.

16. See Gibson, "Time Machine Cuba," "My Obsession," and "Dead Man Sings," all in Gibson, *Distrust That Particular Flavor*, 199; 133; 52–53.
17. Gibson, *Distrust that Particular Flavor*, 52.
18. Ibid., 1–2.
19. M. M. Bakhtin, "Forms of Time and the Chronotope in the Novel: Notes toward a Historical Poetics," in *Narrative Dynamics: Essays on Time, Plot, Closure, and Frames*, ed. Brian Richardson (Columbus: Ohio State University Press, 2002), 15–25.
20. Ibid., 15.
21. William Gibson, *Neuromancer* (New York: Ace Books, 1984), 51.
22. Bakhtin, "Forms of Time," 17.
23. William Gibson, *Virtual Light* (New York: Bantam Books, 1993), 60, Kindle edition.
24. Bahktin, "Forms of Time," 19.
25. Gibson, *Virtual Light*, 69–70.
26. Burges and Elias, *Time: A Vocabulary*, 3.
27. Gibson, *Distrust That Particular Flavor*, 46.
28. Ibid., 46.
29. Some early reviews champion this as Gibson's first "mainstream novel" or first attempt at contemporary realism. For a critical stance suggesting that *Pattern Recognition* should not be considered science fiction, see Graham Slight, "Review of *Pattern Recognition* by William Gibson," *New York Review of Science Fiction* 15, no. 9 (May 2003): 8–9.
30. For two takes on this reading, see Veronica Hollinger, "Stories about the Future: From Patterns of Expectation to Pattern Recognition," *Science Fiction Studies* 33, no. 3 (November 2006): 452–72; and Phillip E. Wegner, "Recognizing the Patterns," *New Literary History* 38, no. 1 (2007): 183–200. For the Fredric Jameson quote, see "The End of Temporality," *Critical Inquiry* 29, no. 4 (2003): 695–718.
31. Gibson, *Pattern Recognition*, 57.
32. Neil Easterbrook, "Alternate Presents: The Ambivalent Historicism of 'Pattern Recognition,'" *Science Fiction Studies* 33, no. 3 (2006): 493–94. The Swiftian intertext Easterbrook refers to here is none other than Jonathan Swift's *Gulliver's Travels* (1726). When Gulliver visits the island of the Lilliputians, he discovers a satirical faction exists between those inhabitants who break their eggs on the big end and those who practice the reverse.
33. Easterbrook, "Alternate Presents," 495.
34. Hollinger, "Stories about the Future," 463–64.
35. Gibson, *Pattern Recognition*, 143.
36. Ibid., 91–93; emphasis added.
37. Ibid., 245–46; emphasis in original.

38. Rancière, "In What Time."
39. Glyn Morgan, "Detective, Historian, Reader: Alternate History and Alternative Fact in William Gibson's *The Peripheral*," *Polish Journal of Science Fiction* 12 (2018): 312.
40. For a recent discussion of "ecological time" in *The Peripheral*, see Katharine E. Bishop, "Ecological Recentering in William Gibson's *The Peripheral*," *Polish Journal of Science Fiction* 12 (2018): 319–34.
41. John Pier, "Narrative Levels," in *Living Handbook of Narratology*, ed. Peter Hühn et al., last modified October 10, 2016, http://www.lhn.uni-hamburg.de/article/narrative-levels-revised-version-uploaded-23-april-2014.
42. Ibid.
43. William Gibson, *The Peripheral* (New York: Putnam, 2014), 14; emphasis added.
44. Ibid., 15.
45. Ibid., 175, 185.
46. See, for example, Anna McFarlane, "'Anthropomorphic Drones' and Colonized Bodies: William Gibson's *The Peripheral*," *English Studies in Canada* 42, nos. 1–2 (2016): 115–31.
47. Gibson, *The Peripheral*, 179.
48. Ibid., 179.
49. Ibid., 176.
50. Ibid., 179.
51. William Gibson, "William Gibson Interview: Time Travel, Virtual Reality, and His New Books," interview by Adi Robertson, *The Verge*, October 28, 2014, https://www.theverge.com/2014/10/28/7083625/william-gibson-interview-time-travel-virtual-reality-and-the-peripheral.
52. Rancière, "In What Time."
53. William Gibson, "Nostalgia for the Future: William Gibson on *The Peripheral* and His Legacy*,*" interview by Jonathan Sturgeon, *Flavorwire*, November 3, 2014, http://flavorwire.com/486048.
54. Rancière, "In What Time."

Chapter 3

1. Bruce Sterling, "Preface," in William Gibson, *Burning Chrome* (New York: Eos, 2003), xi.
2. Ibid.
3. Ibid.
4. Ibid., xii.
5. Ibid., xi.
6. William Gibson, "The Gernsback Continuum," in *Burning Chrome* (New York: Eos, 2003), 23.

7. Ibid., 28.
8. Ibid., 28.
9. Phillip E. Wegner, "Recognizing the Patterns," *New Literary History* 38 (2007): 187. It is also important to foreground Wegner's suggestion that cyberpunk science fiction can be regarded as "a kind of literary realism" (187).
10. Gibson, "The Gernsback Continuum," 29.
11. Ibid.
12. Ibid., 33.
13. Ibid., 34; emphasis in original.
14. Ibid., 35.
15. Ibid.
16. Ibid., 36.
17. Walter Benjamin, *Understanding Brecht*, trans. Anna Bostock (London: Verso, 1998), 121.
18. Hayden White, "Anomalies of Genre: The Utility of Theory and History for the Study of Literary Genres," *New Literary History* 34 (2003): 598.
19. See Gordon Hutner, "Historicizing the Contemporary: A Response to Amy Hungerford," *American Literary History* 20, nos. 1–2 (2008): 420–24.
20. See Mathias Nilges, *Right-Wing Culture in Contemporary Capitalism: Regression and Hope in a Time without Future* (London: Bloomsbury, 2019).
21. Peter Osborne, *Anywhere or Not at All: Philosophy of Contemporary Art* (London: Verso, 2013), 17; emphasis in original.
22. Richard Terdiman, "From City to Country: An Outline of 'Fluvio-Critique,'" *NOVEL: A Forum on Fiction* 41, no. 1 (2007): 54.
23. Ibid.
24. See, for instance, Tibi Puiu, "Neil DeGrasse Tyson Explains Why 'We Stopped Dreaming,'" *ZME Zine*, March 13, 2012, https://www.zmescience.com/space/neil-degrasse-tyson-why-we-stopped-dreaming-13032012/.
25. Gibson, "The Gernsback Continuum," 25.
26. Ibid.
27. Ibid.
28. Ibid., 26.
29. Ibid.
30. Ibid., 27.
31. Ernst Bloch, *The Utopian Function of Art and Literature: Selected Essays*, trans. Jack Zipes and Frank Mecklenburg (Cambridge, MA: MIT Press, 1987), 217. See Mathias Nilges, "The Realism of Speculation: Contemporary Speculative Fiction as Immanent Critique of Finance Capitalism," *CR: The New Centennial Review* 19, no. 1 (2019): 37–60.
32. Alain Badiou, "Thinking the Event," in *Badiou & Zizek: Philosophy in the Present*, ed. Peter Engelmann (Cambridge: Polity, 2009), 2.

33. Nicholas Brown, "One, Two, Many Ends of Literature," *Mediations* 24, no. 2 (2010): 91.
34. Ibid.
35. Jonathan Arac, "What Good Can Literary History Do?," *American Literary History* 20 (2008): 2.
36. Theodor W. Adorno, *Aesthetic Theory*, ed. Gretel Adorno and Rolf Tiedeman, trans. Robert Hullot-Kentor (Minneapolis: University of Minnesota Press, 1997), 6.

Chapter 4

1. See Thomas Disch, "Queen Victoria's Computers," *New York Times Book Review*, March 10, 1991, http://movies2.nytimes.com/books/98/08/09/specials/disch-gibson.html.
2. D. H. Lawrence, *Studies in Classic American Literature*, ed. Ezra Greenspan, Lindeth Vasey, and John Worthen (Cambridge: Cambridge University Press, 2003), 20.
3. Immanuel Kant, "The Modern Prometheus," 1755, quoted in Angelina Stanford, "Immanuel Kant on Benjamin Franklin," Circe Institute Podcast Network, February 11, 2016, https://www.circeinstitute.org/blog/immanuel-kant-benjamin-franklin.
4. Mary Shelley, *Frankenstein: The 1818 Text* (New York: Penguin, 2018), 29.
5. Ibid., 45; emphasis added.
6. Benjamin Franklin, "Epitaph," in *The Autobiography and Other Writings*, ed. Peter Shaw (New York: Bantam, 2008), 348.
7. Benjamin Franklin, *The Autobiography*, in *The Autobiography and Other Writings*, ed. Peter Shaw (New York: Bantam, 2008), 3.
8. Lawrence, *Studies*, 181.
9. Ibid., 185.
10. Gordon Wood, *The Americanization of Benjamin Franklin* (New York: Penguin, 2004), 55.
11. William Gibson and Bruce Sterling, *The Difference Engine 20th Anniversary Edition* (New York: Ballantine Books, 2011), 191–92.
12. Ibid., 193.
13. Ibid.
14. See Ezra F. Vogel, *Japan as No. 1: Lessons for America* (Cambridge, MA: Harvard University Press, 1979).
15. Gibson and Sterling, *Difference Engine*, 422.
16. Yukichi Fukuzawa, *Gakumon no Susume* (*An Encouragement of Learning*), trans. David A. Dilworth (Tokyo: Keio University Press, 2012), 5.
17. Ralph Waldo Emerson, "The American Scholar," in *Nature and Selected Essays* (New York: Penguin, 2003), 103.

18. Gibson and Sterling, *Difference Engine*, 486; emphasis added.
19. Ralph Waldo Emerson, "Nature," in *Nature and Selected Essays* (New York: Penguin, 2003), 39; emphasis added.
20. See Takayuki Tatsumi, *Young Americans in Literature: The Post-Romantic Turn in the Age of Poe, Hawthorne and Melville* (Tokyo: Sairyusha, 2018).

Chapter 5

1. Maitland McDonagh, "Clive Barker & William Gibson: Future Shockers," *Film Comment* 26, no. 1 (1990): 63.
2. William Gibson, "Academy Leader," in *Cyberspace: First Steps*, ed. Michael L. Benedikt (Cambridge, MA: MIT Press, 1992), 27.
3. Andrew M. Butler, "Journeys beyond Being: The Cyberpunk-Flavored Novels of Jeff Noon," in *Beyond Cyberpunk: New Critical Perspectives*, ed. Sherryl Vint and Graham Murphy (New York: Routledge, 2010), 69.
4. Sarah Chaplin, "Report to Virtual HQ: The Distributed City," *Journal of Architecture* 2, no. 1 (1997): 48.
5. Maria Kaika and Erik Swyngedouw, "Fetishizing the Modern City: The Phantasmagoria of Urban Technological Networks," *International Journal of Urban and Regional Research* 24, no. 1 (2000): 121.
6. Longo had a background in fine arts but had made pop videos and video art and intended to direct a black-and-white low-budget adaptation. He had collaborated with Gibson on the performance piece *Dream Jumbo: Working the Absolutes* (1989) at the UCLA Center for the Performing Arts.
7. Frances Bonner, "Separate Development: Cyberpunk in Film and TV," in *Fiction 2000: Cyberpunk and the Future of Narrative*, ed. George Slusser and Tom Shippey (Athens: University of Georgia Press, 1992), 207.
8. Marc Augé, *Non-Places: Introduction to an Anthropology of Supermodernity*, trans. John Howe (London: Verso, 1995), 52.
9. Ibid., 78.
10. Ibid., 94.
11. McDonagh, "Clive Barker & William Gibson," 62.
12. Brian McHale, "Elements of a Poetics of Cyberpunk," *Critique* 33, no. 3 (1992): 161. The spores eventually appeared in *Alien: Covenant* (Ridley Scott, 2017).
13. William Gibson, *Alien III Revised First Draft Screenplay*, https://www.awesomefilm.com/script/Alien3.txt.
14. William Gibson, "The Gernsback Continuum," in *Burning Chrome* (New York: Ace, 1987), 29.
15. Bruce Sterling, "Preface," in William Gibson, *Burning Chrome* (New York: Ace, 1987), x.
16. Gary Westfahl, "'The Gernsback Continuum': William Gibson in the Context of Science Fiction," in *Fiction 2000: Cyberpunk and the Future of Narrative*,

ed. George Slusser and Tom Shippey (Athens: University of Georgia Press, 1992), 90.
17. Gibson, "Gernsback Continuum," 33.
18. Details of *Tomorrow Calling* were confirmed to me by Leandro, personal communication, October 14, 2018.
19. Augé, *Non-Places*, 4.
20. John Fiske, "Reading the Beach," in *Reading the Popular* (London: Unwin Hyman, 1989), 43–76.
21. Rogier Van Bakel, "Remembering Johnny," *Wired*, June 1, 1995, https://www.wired.com/1995/06/gibson-4/.
22. Arthur Kroker and Marilouise Kroker, "*Johnny Mnemonic*: The Day Cyberpunk Died," in *Hacking the Future: Stories for the Flesh-Eating 90s* (Montreal: New World Perspectives, 1996), 50, 51.
23. Augé, *Non-Places*, 78.
24. Steven Shaviro, *Connected, or What It Means to Live in the Network Society* (Minneapolis: University of Minnesota Press, 2003), 134.
25. Claudia Springer, "Psycho-cybernetics in Films of the 1990s," in *Alien Zone II: The Spaces of Science Fiction Cinema*, ed. Annette Kuhn (London: Verso, 1999), 213.
26. Laurence A. Rickels, "American Psychos: The End of Art Cinema in the '90s," *Art/Text*, no. 67 (2000): 62.
27. McDonagh, "Clive Barker & William Gibson," 62.
28. Gavin Smith, "Dealing with the Now," *Sight and Sound* 7, no. 4 (1997): 9.
29. Paweł Frelik, "'Silhouettes of Strange Illuminated Mannequins': Cyberpunk's Incarnations of Light," in *Cyberpunk and Visual Culture*, ed. Graham J. Murphy and Lars Schmeink (London: Routledge, 2018), 84.
30. Shaviro, *Connected*, 153.
31. Maitland McDonagh, "*New Rose Hotel*," *Film Journal International* (November 2004).
32. Augé, *Non-Places*, 103.
33. Ibid., 117–18.
34. Felix Brinker, "Conspiracy, Procedure, Continuity: Reopening *The X-Files*," *Television & New Media* 19, no. 4 (2018): 329.
35. Bronwen Calvert, "William Gibson's 'Cyberpunk' *X-Files*," *Science Fiction Film and Television* 6, no. 1 (2013): 48.
36. Sue Morris, "First-Person Shooters—A Game Apparatus," in *ScreenPlay: Cinema/Videogames/Interfaces*, ed. Geoff King and Tanya Krzywinska (London: Wallflower Press, 2002), 87.
37. Calvert, "William Gibson's 'Cyberpunk' *X-Files*," 50.
38. Augé, *Non-Places*, 106.
39. Ibid., 102.

40. Mark Bould, "Preserving Machines: Recentering the Decentered Subject in *Blade Runner* and *Johnny Mnemonic*," in *Writing and Cinema*, ed. Jonathan Bignell (Harlow: Longman, 1999), 176.
41. Augé, *Non-Places*, 111.

Chapter 6

1. Zeynep Yenisey, "This Dude Married His Computer, and Is Now Suing Alabama for Not Recognizing His 'Machinist' Sexuality," *Maxim*, September 8, 2017, https://www.maxim.com/news/man-marries-computer-2017-9. Lest one's sympathies be roused by this tale of star-crossed lovers, Sevier really filed this lawsuit, and others in three states, to express his disdain for marriage equality.
2. Lisa Katayama, "Man Marries Video Game Computer," Boing Boing, November 23, 2009, https://www.youtube.com/watch?v=hsikPswAYUM.
3. Elizabeth Zwirtz, "Man, 35, Reportedly Marries Computer Hologram," Fox News, November 14, 2018, https://www.foxnews.com/world/man-35-reportedly-marries-computer-hologram.
4. Max Horkheimer and Theodor Adorno, *The Dialectic of Enlightenment* (Stanford, CA: Stanford University Press, 2002), 3–4.
5. Matthew K. Gold, "Day of DH," in *Debates in the Digital Humanities*, ed. Matthew K. Gold (Minneapolis: University of Minnesota Press, 2012), 67–74.
6. Jason Heppler, "What Is Digital Humanities?," https://whatisdigitalhumanities.com/. As a commentary on this fluid notion of DH, Heppler created the "What Is Digital Humanities?" website, which displays a different definition each time the page loads. There are more than 800 entries.
7. Meredith Hindley, "The Rise of the Machines: NEH and the Digital Humanities: The Early Years," *Humanities* 34, no. 4 (2013), https://www.neh.gov/humanities/2013/julyaugust/feature/the-rise-the-machines. One of the earliest humanities computing projects was undertaken by Father Roberto Busa, a Catholic priest with expertise in the writings of Thomas Aquinas. In the late 1940s, Busa conceived of the Index Thomisticus, a tool to track all word concordances in Aquinas's body of writing. Building the index took him thirty years, even in partnership with IBM, and helped pave the way for future works of the same kind.
8. Matthew Kirschenbaum, "What Is Digital Humanities and What's It Doing in English Classes?," in *Debates in Digital Humanities*, ed. Matthew K. Gold (Minneapolis: University of Minnesota Press, 2012), 3–11.
9. Patricia Cohen, "Digital Keys for Unlocking Humanities' Riches," *New York Times*, November 16, 2010, https://www.nytimes.com/2010/11/17/arts/17digital.html.
10. C. P. Snow, *The Two Cultures* (Cambridge: Cambridge University Press, 1993), 2.

11. Stephen Ramsay, "Who's In and Who's Out," in *Defining Digital Humanities*, ed. Melissa Terras, Julianne Nyhan, and Edward Vanhoutte (New York: Routledge, 2013), 240. In a DH roundtable at the 2011 Modern Language Association's annual meeting, noted DH scholar Stephan Ramsay threw down a gauntlet: "Digital Humanities is not some airy Lyceum," he said. "Do you have to know how to code? I'm a tenured professor of Digital Humanities and I say 'yes'" ("Who's In and Who's Out," 240). This moment illustrates that the tension between these two approaches—to quantitative traditional humanities computing on one hand and to the qualitative domains of cultural studies and aesthetic production on the other—has not yet been resolved. Put another way, we might update Horkheimer and Adorno's statement about "corrosive rationality" in the context of DH, where it would now read that "anything which does not conform to the standard of calculability and utility is [still] viewed with suspicion."
12. William Gibson, *Neuromancer* (New York: Ace, 1984), 193.
13. OED Online, Oxford University Press, "computer, n," http://www.oed.com/view/Entry/37975?redirectedFrom=computer#eid.
14. Arthur C. Clarke, *2001: A Space Odyssey* (New York: Penguin, 2000), 174. Kubrick's ubiquitous *2001* adapted Clarke's "The Sentinel" (1951) for film, and Clarke wrote the novelization to coincide with the film's release.
15. Ibid.
16. Anne McCaffrey, *The Ship Who Sang* (New York: Delray, 1985), 1–3.
17. Robert Heinlein, *The Moon Is a Harsh Mistress* (New York: Tor, 1966), 381–82.
18. William Gibson, "The Winter Market," in *Burning Chrome* (New York: Ace Books, 1987), 118.
19. See N. Katherine Hayles, *How We Became Posthuman: Virtual Bodies in Cybernetics, Literature, and Informatics* (Chicago: University of Chicago Press, 1999), chap. 2.
20. Gibson, "The Winter Market."
21. Kathryn Allan, *Disability in Science Fiction* (New York: Palgrave, 2013), 8.
22. Gibson, "Winter Market," 126.
23. Ibid., 130.
24. Ibid., 125.
25. Ibid., 133.
26. Ibid., 123.
27. Nicola Nixon, "Cyberpunk: Preparing the Ground for Revolution or Keeping the Boys Satisfied?," *Science Fiction Studies* 19, no. 2 (1992): 219–35.
28. Nikkianne Moody, "Untapped Potential: The Representation of Disability/Special Ability in the Cyberpunk Workforce," *Convergence* 3 no. 3 (1997): 90.
29. Gibson, "Winter Market," 150.
30. Alan Liu, "Transcendental Data," *Critical Inquiry* 31, no. 1 (2004): 49–82; Matthew Kirschenbaum, *Mechanisms* (Cambridge, MA: MIT Press, 2007).

31. We are grateful to the editors of *Science Fiction Studies*, who allowed us to digitize all of the journal's content from 1973 onward and provided financial support for these efforts; to Julia Flanders and Élika Ortega for helping us locate the abstracts from the past twelve years of DH conferences; and to Elizabeth Callaway and the members of the DH Collaboratory at the University of Utah, who graciously shared their DH corpus.

Chapter 7

1. William Gibson and Bruce Sterling, "Afterword," in *The Difference Engine 20th Anniversary Edition* (New York: Ballantine Books, 2011), Kindle edition.
2. Ibid.
3. Matthew Kirschenbaum, *Track Changes: A Literary History of Word Processing* (Cambridge, MA: Harvard University Press, 2016), Kindle edition, chap. 5.
4. William Gibson, "William Gibson Talks about 'The Peripheral,' the Power of Twitter, and His Next Book Set in Today's Silicon Valley," interview by Matt Rosoff, *Business Insider*, August 13, 2016, https://www.businessinsider.com/william-gibson-the-peripheral-interview-business-insider-2016-8.
5. Wolfgang Ernst, *Chronopoetics: The Temporal Being and Operativity of Technological Media*, trans. Anthony Enns (New York: Rowman & Littlefield, 2016), 9.
6. Ibid., 9.
7. Jussi Parikka, "Media Archaeology as a Trans-Atlantic Bridge," introduction to Wolfgang Ernst, *Digital Memory and the Archive* (Minneapolis: University of Minnesota Press, 2012), 9.
8. Phillip E. Wegner, *Shockwaves of Possibility: Essays on Science Fiction, Globalization, and Utopia* (New York: Peter Lang, 2014), 206.
9. Benjamin Bratton, *The Stack: On Software and Sovereignty* (Cambridge, MA: MIT Press, 2015), 27.
10. Gibson and Sterling, "Afterword."
11. Roger Whitson, *Steampunk and Nineteenth-Century Digital Humanities: Literary Retrofuturisms, Media Archaeologies, Alternate Histories* (London: Routledge, 2017).
12. Fredric Jameson, *The Political Unconscious: Narrative as a Socially Symbolic Act* (Ithaca, NY: Cornell University Press, 1981), 11.
13. Ibid., 56.
14. Ibid., 35.
15. Ibid., 79, 82.
16. Wolfgang Ernst, "From Media History to Zeitkritik," *Theory, Culture, and Society* 30, no. 6 (2013): 4.
17. Gibson and Sterling, *The Difference Engine*, Third Iteration.
18. Jussi Parikka, *What Is Media Archaeology?* (Cambridge: Polity, 2012), 65.

19. Gibson and Sterling, *The Difference Engine*, Third Iteration.
20. Zieger shows how the proliferation of ephemera like tobacco cards created the same circuit of anxiety in the Victorian period as is experienced in contemporary social media applications. See Susan Zieger, *The Mediated Mind: Affect, Ephemera, and Consumerism in the Nineteenth Century* (New York: Fordham University Press, 2018), 210.
21. See, for instance, Babbage's description of the division of labor in Charles Babbage, *On the Economies of Machinery and Manufacture* (London: John Murray, 1846), and Charles Babbage, *The Ninth Bridgewater Treatise* (London: John Murray, 1837).
22. Gibson and Sterling, *The Difference Engine*, First Iteration.
23. Ibid.
24. Ibid.
25. Ernst, *Chronopoetics*, 78.
26. Roger Whitson, "There Is No William Blake: @autoblake's Algorithmic Condition," *Essays in Romanticism* 21, no. 1 (2016): 69–87. Also see Jerome McGann, *The Textual Condition* (Princeton, NJ: Princeton University Press, 1991), 3.
27. William Gibson, *The Peripheral* (New York: Penguin, 2014), Kindle edition, chap. 18.
28. Ibid.
29. Bratton, *The Stack*, xvii.
30. Karl Marx, *Capital: A Critique of Political Economy*, vol. 3, *The Process of Capitalist Production as a Whole* (New York: International, 1977), 820.
31. Jameson, *Political Unconscious*, 19.
32. Bratton, *The Stack*, 5.
33. Ibid., 76; emphasis in original.
34. Ibid., 77; emphasis in original.
35. Ibid., 116.
36. Ibid., 121.
37. Ibid.
38. Gibson, *Peripheral*, chap. 3.
39. Ibid., chap. 7.
40. Ibid., chap. 15.
41. Ibid.
42. Ibid.
43. Ibid.
44. Ibid., chap. 21.
45. Ibid.
46. Steven Jones, *The Emergence of the Digital Humanities* (London: Routledge, 2014), Kindle edition, chap. 1.

47. Gibson and Sterling, *The Difference Engine*, "Afterword"; emphasis in original.
48. Bratton, *The Stack*, 27–28.
49. William Gibson, "William Gibson on Urbanism, Science Fiction, and Why *The Peripheral* Weirded Him Out," interview by Karin L. Kross, Tor.com, October 29, 2014, https://www.tor.com/2014/10/29/william-gibson-the-peripheral-interview/.
50. Joshua Rothman, "How William Gibson Keeps Science Fiction Real," *New Yorker*, December 9, 2019, https://www.newyorker.com/magazine/2019/12/16/how-william-gibson-keeps-his-science-fiction-real.
51. Bratton, *The Stack*, 353.
52. Gibson, *The Peripheral*, chap. 79.
53. Ibid.
54. Jameson, *Political Unconscious*, 102.
55. Gibson, *The Peripheral*, chap. 79.
56. Ibid., chap. 120.
57. Ibid., chap. 124.
58. Ibid.
59. Ibid., chap. 26.
60. Ibid.
61. William Gibson, "William Gibson on the Apocalypse, America, and *The Peripheral*'s Ending," interview by Analee Newitz, *io9*, November 11, 2014, https://io9.gizmodo.com/william-gibson-on-the-apocalypse-america-and-the-peri-1656659382.
62. Gibson and Sterling, *The Difference Engine*, Third Iteration.
63. Ibid.
64. Gibson, *The Peripheral*, chap. 79.
65. Ibid.
66. Bratton, *The Stack*, 294.
67. Jameson, *Political Unconscious*, 281.
68. Ibid.
69. Ibid., 289.
70. See Karl Marx, *Capital: A Critique of Political Economy Volume 1: The Process of Production of Capital*, Marxists Internet Archive, 1999, https://www.marxists.org/archive/marx/works/1867-c1/.
71. For an account of undersea cables and the ecologies inhabiting them, see Nicole Starosielski, *The Undersea Network* (Durham, NC: Duke University Press, 2015).
72. For a description of control societies and TCP/IP protocol, see Alexander Galloway, *Protocol: How Control Exists after Decentralization* (Cambridge, MA: MIT Press, 2004).

73. For a discussion of how rare-earth metals participate in global politics, see Jussi Parikka, *A Geology of Media* (Minnesota: University of Minneapolis Press, 2015).
74. Bratton, *The Stack*, 351.

Chapter 8

1. As well as the reference to the bailout of banks at taxpayer expense following the 2008 financial crisis, caused by inadequate market regulation of speculative instruments, especially collateralized debt obligations based on mortgages as their underlying asset, the title of my essay also points to the description of Bigend as too big to fail. William Gibson, *Zero History* (New York: Putnam, 2010), 396.
2. Jaak Tomberg, "On the 'Double Vision' of Realism and SF Estrangement in William Gibson's *Bigend* Trilogy," *Science Fiction Studies* 40, no. 2 (July 2013): 263; emphasis in original.
3. Ibid., 274; emphasis in original.
4. William Gibson, *Spook Country* (New York: Putnam, 2007), 100.
5. Guy Debord, *Society of the Spectacle* (Sussex: Soul Bay Press, 2009), dictum 1.
6. Ibid., dictum 4.
7. Ibid., dictum 36.
8. William Gibson, *Pattern Recognition* (New York: Berkley, 2003), 9.
9. Ibid., 86.
10. Ibid., 1.
11. Gibson, *Zero History*, 54.
12. Ibid., 213.
13. Ibid., 21, 213.
14. Ibid., 118.
15. Ibid., 228.
16. Gibson, *Pattern Recognition*, 44.
17. Ibid., 61.
18. Ibid., 254.
19. Debord, *Society of the Spectacle*, dictum 42.
20. Gibson, *Zero History*, 345.
21. Gibson, *Pattern Recognition*, 104.
22. Ibid., 329.
23. Gibson, *Zero History*, 139.
24. Ibid., 31.
25. Ibid., 336.
26. Ibid., 119.
27. Gibson, *Pattern Recognition*, 8.
28. Gibson, *Zero History*, 336.

29. Gibson, *Pattern Recognition*, 104.
30. Ibid.
31. Ibid.
32. Ibid., 194.
33. Debord, *Society of the Spectacle*, dictum 2.
34. Ibid., dictum 17.
35. Ibid., dictum 16.
36. Gibson, *Pattern Recognition*, 340.
37. Ibid., 84.
38. Ibid.
39. Ibid., 17.
40. Debord's work no longer enjoys the centrality to leftist critical tradition that it once had. In his recent *Capital Is Dead: Is This Something Worse?* (London: Verso, 2019), McKenzie Wark makes *détournement* central to their arguments about how best to embody anticapitalist resistance today.
41. Gibson, *Spook Country*, 10.
42. Ibid., 29.
43. Gibson also seems to anticipate how new communication media increasingly isolate rather than connect people, anticipating the divisive consequences of social media such as Facebook or Twitter on the public sphere, visible in recent, polarized US political discourse. Discussing his role in enabling Alberto's locative art, Bobby explains that each server, each augmented version of reality, would show its own preferred reality, "the world we walk around in would be channels" (*Spook Country*, 87).
44. Debord, *Society of the Spectacle*, dictum 226.
45. Ibid., dictum 207. See https://www.adbusters.org for examples of cultural work done by *détournement* of advertisements.
46. Gibson, *Pattern Recognition*, 286.
47. Ibid., 69.
48. Gibson, *Spook Country*, 69.
49. Gibson, *Zero History*, 153.
50. Ibid.
51. The suggestion that the world of global commodities, much more than the world of technological mediation, propels this alienation is apparent in Stella's nostalgic description of the Soviet era as a time of community, compared with a capitalist present in which the rich use police lights to warn others they (the rich) are not required to obey traffic laws: "Once Victor Tsoi sang here, in this room. People had time, in those days. The system was collapsing under its own weight, but everyone had a job, often a pointless one, very badly paid, but one could eat. People valued friendships, talked endlessly, ate and drank. For many people it was like the life of a student. A life of the spirit. Now we say that everything Lenin taught us of communism

was false, and everything he taught us of capitalism, true" (Gibson, *Pattern Recognition*, 301).
52. Gibson, *Pattern Recognition*, 69.
53. Ibid., 67.
54. Gibson, *Spook Country*, 307.
55. Karl Marx and Frederick Engels, *Manifesto of the Communist Party*, 1848, Marx-Engels Archive, https://www.marxists.org/archive/marx/works/1848/communist-manifesto/ch01.htm#007.
56. Gibson, *Pattern Recognition*, 57.
57. Ibid., 1.
58. Gibson, *Zero History*, 335.
59. Gibson, *Pattern Recognition*, 115.
60. Ibid., 292.
61. See Darko Suvin, *Metamorphoses of Science Fiction: On the Poetics and History of a Literary Genre*, ed. Gerry Canavan (Dublin: Ralahine Utopian Studies, 2017); Carl Freedman, *Critical Theory and Science Fiction* (Middleton, CT: Wesleyan University Press, 2000); Fredric Jameson, *Archaeologies of the Future: The Desire Called Utopia and Other Science Fictions* (London: Verso, 2007); and Phillip E. Wegner, *Shockwaves of Possibility: Essays on Science Fiction, Globalization and Utopia* (Oxford: Peter Lang, 2014) for only the most widely cited formulations of this idea. Jameson's essay "Progress vs. Utopia," first published in 1982 and reprinted in *Archaeologies of the Future*, is the most influential formulation of this idea that science fiction is a kind of historical fiction, or at least that it takes over the cultural role previously occupied by historical fiction.
62. For a more detailed discussion of this point, see Sherryl Vint, "Introduction to the Futures Industry," *Paradoxa* 27 (2016), http://paradoxa.com/volumes/27/introduction.
63. See Sherryl Vint, "Promissory Futures: Reality and Imagination in Fiction and Finance," *The New Centennial Review* 19, no. 1 (2019): 11–36.
64. Gibson, *Zero History*, 401; emphasis in original.
65. Gibson quoted in Larry McCaffery, "An Interview with William Gibson," in *Storming the Reality Studio: A Casebook of Cyberpunk and Postmodern Fiction*, ed. Larry McCaffery (Durham, NC: Duke University Press, 1991), 280.
66. Gibson, *Zero History*, 84.
67. Gibson, *Spook Country*, 102.
68. Ibid., 171.

Chapter 9

1. I thank the editors of this volume for allowing me to flesh out my review discussion of *The Peripheral*, Amy J. Elias, "The Futureless Future," *American Book Review* 36, no. 5 (2015): 12–13.

2. See, for example, Istvan Csicery-Ronay Jr., "Antimancer: Cybernetics and Art in Gibson's Count Zero," *Science Fiction Studies* 22, no. 1 (1995): 63–86. Csicery-Ronay correlates different novels in the Sprawl trilogy to different art movements, such as futurism and surrealism.
3. When targeting ontological questions raised by the novels, readers often configure the problem of worlding as the overcoming of humanist mind/body dualism, focus on cognitive processes such as memory as a bridge between differing realities or times, or analyze shifts in ontological status in terms of a mystical/empirical dualism. For example, see Ralph Pordzik, "The Posthuman Future of Man: Anthropocentrism and the Other of Technology in Anglo-American Science Fiction," *Utopian Studies* 23, no. 1 (2012): 142–61. Mojca Krevel understands the attack on mind/body dualism in the Sprawl trilogy in relation to Ray Kurzweil's concept of the singularity, a merging of human mind with AI (Mojca Krevel, "'Back to the Future': Technological Singularity in Gibson's Sprawl Trilogy," *British and American Studies* 20 [2012]: 27–35). Such readings are certainly supported by the ending of *Mona Lisa Overdrive*, when Angie and Bobby upload their consciousness into the Aleph. In contrast, in "Mind against Matter: The Physics of Interface in William Gibson's *The Peripheral*," *Critique: Studies in Contemporary Fiction* 60, no. 1 (2019): 34–48, Paul Piatkowski presents the novel's cybernetic peripherals as interfaces that eliminate mind/body dualism not through the absorption of human mind into cybersingularity but through leveling the hierarchy between mind and body through embodiment. This kind of reading of Gibson's work was presaged in Carl Gutierrez-Jones, "Stealing Kinship: *Neuromancer* and Artificial Intelligence," *Science Fiction Studies* 41, no. 1 (2014): 69–92. For different treatments of memory as an ontological problem, see Joel Elliot Slotkin, "Haunted Infocosms and Prosthetic Gods: Gibsonian Cyberspace and Renaissance Arts of Memory," *Journal of Popular Culture* 45, no. 4 (2012): 862–82, and Amy Novak, "Virtual Poltergeists and Memory: The Question of Ahistoricism in William Gibson's *Neuromancer* (1984)," *Journal of the Fantastic in the Arts* 11, no. 4 (2001): 395–414. For examples of how ontological discussions divert into discussions of mysticism versus empiricism or the sublime—usually configured as epistemology rather than ontology—see Lance Olsen, "The Shadow of Spirit in William Gibson's Matrix Trilogy," *Extrapolation* 32, no 3 (1991): 278–89; and Jack G. Voller, "Neuromanticism: Cyberspace and the Sublime," *Extrapolation* 34, no. 1 (1993): 28–29.
4. For a general explanation of multiverse, see Anthony Aguirre, "Multiverse: Cosmology," *Encyclopaedia Britannica*, December 19, 2018, https://www.britannica.com/science/multiverse. On many-worlds theory, see Lev Vaidman, "Many-Worlds Interpretation of Quantum Mechanics," in *Stanford Encyclopedia of Philosophy*, edited by Edward N. Zalta (Fall 2018), https://

plato.stanford.edu/archives/fall2018/entries/qm-manyworlds/. See H. Everett, "Relative State Formulation of Quantum Mechanics," *Review of Modern Physics* 29 (1957): 454–62. For a quick introduction to Wiseman and Hall's "many-interacting-worlds" theory, see https://phys.org/news/2014-10-interacting-worlds-theory-scientists-interaction.html.

5. A contestable claim, actually. In *Time Travel: The Popular Philosophy of Narrative* (New York: Fordham University Press, 2018), David Wittenberg describes the genre of time travel as a strategic suppression of social and psychological issues, supplanted by "an abiding concern with the mechanisms of time travel and with the innovative storytelling forms that such mechanisms can generate" (206).

6. William Gibson, "William Gibson on the Apocalypse, America, and *The Peripheral*'s Ending," interview by Annalee Newitz, *io9*, November 11, 2014, https://io9.gizmodo.com/william-gibson-on-the-apocalypse-america-and-the-peri-1656659382.

7. For discussions of the Subjunctive in Pynchon's work, see Amy J. Elias, "History," in *The Cambridge Companion to Thomas Pynchon*, ed. Inger H. Dalsgaard, Luc Herman, and Brian McHale (Cambridge: Cambridge University Press, 2012), 123–35; Brian McHale, "*Mason & Dixon* in the Zone, or, a Brief Poetics of Pynchon-Space," in *Pynchon and Mason & Dixon*, ed. Brooke Horvath and Irving Malin (Newark: University of Delaware Press, 2000), 43–62; and Kathryn Hume, *Pynchon's Mythography: An Approach to Gravity's Rainbow* (Carbondale: Southern Illinois University Press, 1987).

8. Thomas Pynchon, *Bleeding Edge* (New York: Penguin, 2013).

9. McKenzie Wark, *Telethesia: Communication, Culture, and Class* (Cambridge: Cambridge University Press, 2012), 30.

10. William Gibson, *Neuromancer* (New York: Ace Books, 1984), 259.

11. David Chalmers, "Ontological Anti-Realism," in *Metametaphysics: New Essays on the Foundations of Ontology*, ed. D. J. Chalmers, D. Manley, and R. Wasserman (Oxford: Oxford University Press, 2009), 77.

12. Alexander Miller, "Realism," in *Stanford Encyclopedia of Philosophy*, ed. Edward N. Zalta (Winter 2016), https://plato.stanford.edu/archives/win2016/entries/realism/.

13. For a succinct definition of correlationism in relation to speculative realism and object-oriented ontology, see Levi Bryant, "Correlationism," in *The Meillassoux Dictionary*, ed. Peter Gratton and Paul J. Ennis (Edinburgh: Edinburgh University Press, 2014).

14. For discussions of these points, see Jane Bennett, "Systems and Things: A Response to Graham Harman and Timothy Morton," *New Literary History* 43, no. 2 (2012): 225–33; Graham Harman, "An Outline of Object-Oriented Philosophy," *Science Progress* 96, no. 2 (2013): 187–99; Graham Harman,

Towards Speculative Realism: Essays and Lectures (London: Zero Books, 2010); Graham Harman, "Realism without Materialism," *SubStance* 40, no. 2 (2011): 52–72; Timothy Morton, *Realist Magic* (London: Open Humanities Press, 2013).

15. William Gibson, *Count Zero* (New York: Ace, 1986).
16. William Gibson, *Mona Lisa Overdrive* (New York: Bantam, 1988), 127.
17. Gary Westfahl, *William Gibson* (Champaign: University of Illinois Press, 2013), 108, 84.
18. See Timothy Morton, *Hyperobjects: Philosophy and Ecology after the End of the World* (Minneapolis: University of Minnesota Press, 2013).
19. William Gibson, *The Peripheral* (London: Penguin, 2014), 145.
20. Ned Beauman, "William Gibson: 'We Always Think of Ourselves as the Cream of Creation,'" *Guardian*, November 16, 2014, http://www.theguardian.com/books/2014/nov/16/william-gibson-interview-the-peripheral.
21. Sam Leith, "*The Peripheral* by William Gibson—A Glorious Ride into the Future," *Guardian*, November 19, 2014, http://www.theguardian.com/books/2014/nov/19/the-peripheral-william-gibson-ride-future. Gibson has mentioned *The Alteration* by Kingsley Amis, Keith Roberts's works, and the film *Winter's Bone* as influences. William Gibson, "William Gibson on Urbanism, Science Fiction, and Why *The Peripheral* Weirded Him Out," interview by Karin L. Kross, Tor.com, October 29, 2014, http://www.tor.com/blogs/2014/10/william-gibson-the-peripheral-interview. One commentator has noted similarities to *Timescapes*. Bryan Alexander, comments on "*The Peripheral*, by William Gibson," Goodreads, July 17, 2014, http://www.goodreads.com/book/show/20821159-the-peripheral.
22. Gibson, "William Gibson on Urbanism, Science Fiction."
23. Gibson, *The Peripheral*, 279.
24. Karin L. Kross, "The Future Is Here: William Gibson's *The Peripheral*," Tor.com, October 27, 2014, http://www.tor.com/blogs/2014/10/book-review-the-peripheral-william-gibson.
25. Gibson, *The Peripheral*, 481–82.
26. Gibson, "William Gibson on Urbanism, Science Fiction."

Chapter 10

1. William Gibson, *Pattern Recognition* (New York: Berkley, 2003), 57.
2. I take this term from Lance Olsen, but I also have in mind the Electronic Frontier Foundation. John Perry Barlow, one of the organization's founding members, metaphorically connected Gibson's vision to the Wyoming distance of his childhood, seeing it as a "frontier region, populated by the few hardy technologists who can tolerate the austerity of its savage computer interfaces" but also the "place where the future is destined to dwell." Lance

Olsen, "Virtual Termites: A Hypotextual Technomutant Explo(it)ration of William Gibson and the Electronic Beyond(s)," *Style* 29, no. 2 (1995): 296; Mitchell Kapor and John Perry Barlow, "Across the Electronic Frontier," Electronic Frontier Foundation, July 10, 1990, https://www.eff.org/pages/across-electronic-frontier.

3. William Burroughs, "The Fall of Art," in *The Adding Machine* (New York: Arcade, 1986), 60–64.
4. William Gibson, *Spook Country* (New York: Putnam, 2007), 141.
5. William Gibson, "The Net Is a Waste of Time," in *Distrust That Particular Flavor* (New York: Putnam, 2012). Gibson does still write in a way related to this figure of the surfer, toggling between a word processing application and a web browser, as if a hacker going between cyberspace and simstim.
6. Facebook, Amazon, Netflix, and Google (FANG) are four of the prime companies of what Shoshana Zuboff calls "surveillance capitalism" and Nick Srnicek calls "platform capitalism." I see both as attempts to understand the new production of space I describe here. Shoshana Zuboff, *The Age of Surveillance Capitalism: The Fight for a Human Future at the New Frontier of Power* (New York: Public Affairs, 2019); Nick Srnicek, *Platform Capitalism* (Cambridge: Polity, 2017).
7. William Gibson, *Zero History* (New York: Putnam, 2010), 179.
8. Fredric Jameson, "A Global *Neuromancer*," in *The Ancients and the Postmoderns: On the Historicity of Forms* (New York: Verso, 2015), 214.
9. Jameson does not seem invested in the technical specificity of axonometric drawing, as compared with other forms of descriptive geometry that represent three-dimensional building on two-dimensional paper (printed or virtual). The importance of the concept for Jameson is the development of types of architectural drawing whose powers of abstraction extend representation beyond mimesis.
10. Jameson, "A Global *Neuromancer*," 220.
11. Karl Marx, *Capital, Volume 1*, trans. Ben Fowkes (London: Penguin, 1976), 135.
12. Jameson, "A Global *Neuromancer*," 220.
13. William Gibson, *Mona Lisa Overdrive* (New York: Bantam, 1988), 264.
14. Ibid., 16.
15. Friedrich Kittler, "The City Is a Medium," trans. Matthew Griffin, *New Literary History* 27, no. 4 (1996): 717–29.
16. Fredric Jameson, *Postmodernism, or, The Cultural Logic of Late Capitalism* (Durham, NC: Duke University Press, 1991), see chap. 8.
17. Gibson, *Mona Lisa Overdrive*, 76; emphasis in original.
18. Henri Lefebvre, *The Production of Space*, trans. Donald Nicholson-Smith (Oxford: Blackwell, [1974], 1991).

19. Friedrich Kittler, *Optical Media*, trans. Anthony Enns (Cambridge: Polity Press, [2002] 2010), 58.
20. Ibid., 62.
21. Ibid.
22. Lefebvre, *Production of Space*, 79.
23. Kittler, *Optical Media*, 56.
24. Ibid., 65.
25. Damjan Jovanovic, "Fictions: A Speculative Account of Design Mediums," in *Speculations in Contemporary Drawing for Art and Architecture*, ed. Laura Allen and Luke Caspar Pearson (London: Riverside Architectural Press, 2016), 32; emphasis in original.
26. David Harvey, *Marx, Capital, and the Madness of Economic Reason* (New York: Oxford University Press, 2018), 189. Kim Stanley Robinson shares this view and offers the compelling metaphor "granaries for holding money"; *New York 2140* (New York: Orbit, 2017), 526.
27. Veronica Hollinger, "Stories about the Future: From Patterns of Expectation to Pattern Recognition," *Science Fiction Studies* 33 (2006): 452–55.
28. Paul Virilio, *The Information Bomb*, trans. Chris Turner (London: Verso, [1998] 2000), 1.
29. Ibid., 17.
30. Ibid.
31. Gibson, *Pattern Recognition*, 9.
32. Ibid., 21.
33. Ibid., 17–18.
34. Ibid., 12.
35. Ibid.
36. Paul Virilio, *The Futurism of the Instant: Stop-Eject*, trans. Julie Rose (Cambridge: Polity Press [2009] 2010), 10.
37. Ibid., 21.
38. Lee Konstantinou, "The Brand as Cognitive Map in William Gibson's *Pattern Recognition*," *boundary 2* 36, no. 2 (2009): 70.
39. Fredric Jameson, "Fear and Loathing in Globalization," in *Archaeologies of the Future: The Desire Called Utopia and Other Science Fictions* (New York: Verso, 2005), 386.
40. Jaak Tomberg, "On the 'Double Vision' of Realism and SF Estrangement in William Gibson's Bigend Trilogy," *Science Fiction Studies* 40, no. 2 (2013): 268.
41. Hollinger, "Stories about the Future," 463–64.
42. Tomberg, "On the Double Vision," 272. Olsen also refers to the "speed of Gibson's sentences" in *Neuromancer*; "Virtual Termites," 306.
43. Rem Koolhaas, "Junkspace," *October* 100 (2002): 175–90, http://www.jstor.org/stable/779098. Jameson does in fact compare this style to that of

cyberpunk, which seems "to revel in its own (and its world's) excess." Fredric Jameson, "Future City," *New Left Review* 21 (May/June 2003): 76.
44. Ibid., 74.
45. Gibson, *Pattern Recognition*, 1.
46. Gibson, *Zero History*, 243.
47. Gibson, *Pattern Recognition*, 9.
48. Ibid., 12.
49. Ibid., 110.
50. Gibson, *Spook Country*, 4.
51. Gibson, *Pattern Recognition*, 146.
52. William Gibson, "The Gernsback Continuum," in *Burning Chrome* (New York: Arbor House, 1986).
53. William Gibson, "Metrophagy: The Art and Science of Digesting Great Cities," in *Distrust That Particular Flavor* (New York: Putnam, 2012).
54. Joe Shaw and Mark Graham, "An Informational Right to the City?," in *The Right to the City: A Verso Report* (London: Verso, 2017).
55. Ibid.
56. Gibson, *Zero History*, 37.
57. Ibid., 183–84.
58. William Gibson, *Neuromancer* (New York: Ace, 1984), 56.
59. Ibid., 63.
60. Gibson, *Zero History*, 184.
61. Lefebvre, *Production of Space*, 101.
62. Kapor and Barlow, "Across the Electronic Frontier."

Chapter 11

1. World Health Organization, "Gaming Disorder," http://www.who.int/features/qa/gaming-disorder/en/ (accessed December 8, 2018).
2. See, for example, Ryan Avent, "Escape to Another World," *The Economist 1843*, April/May 2017, https://www.1843magazine.com/features/escape-to-another-world; and Mark Aguiar, Mark Bils, Kerwin Kofi Charles, and Erik Hurst, "Leisure Luxuries and the Labor Supply of Young Men," National Bureau of Economic Research Working Paper No. 23552 (June 2017).
3. Avent, "Escape to Another World."
4. See Louis Hyman, *Temp: How American Work, American Business, and the American Dream Became Temporary* (New York: Penguin, 2018).
5. Greta Krippner, "The Financialization of the American Economy," *Socio-Economic Review* 3, no. 2 (2005): 174.
6. Randy Martin, *Financialization of Daily Life* (Philadelphia: Temple University Press, 2002), 12.
7. Newzoo, "Newzoo's 2017 Report: Insight into the 108.9 Billion Global Games

Market," Newzoo, June 20, 2017, https://newzoo.com/insights/articles/newzoo-2017-report-insights-into-the-108-9-billion-global-games-market/.

8. William Gibson, *The Peripheral* (New York: Putnam, 2014), 3. All further citations indicated parenthetically.

9. Brendan Keogh, *A Play of Bodies: How We Perceive Videogames* (Cambridge, MA: MIT Press, 2018), 22; emphasis in original.

10. See Mackenzie Wark, *Gamer Theory* (Cambridge, MA: Harvard University Press, 2007), 006.

11. On gamification, see especially Paolo Ruffino, "Life after Gamification: How I Broke Up with Nike+ FuelBand," in *Future Gaming: Creative Interventions in Video Game Culture* (London: Goldsmiths Press, 2018), 26–44. On casual games, see especially Aubrey Anable, "Rhythms of Work and Play," *Playing with Feelings: Video Games and Affect* (Minneapolis: University of Minnesota Press, 2018), 71–102.

12. Nick Dyer-Witheford and Greig De Peuter, *Games of Empire: Global Capitalism and Video Games* (Minneapolis: University of Minnesota Press, 2009), xix.

13. Michel Foucault, *The Birth of Biopolitics: Lectures at the Collège de France, 1978–1979*, trans. Graham Burchell (New York: Palgrave Macmillan, 2008), 147, 227.

14. Ibid., 259–60. Foucault is drawing out American neoliberalism's reliance on the field of mathematics known as game theory. On this subject, see S. M. Amadae, *Prisoners of Reason: Game Theory and Neoliberal Political Economy* (Cambridge: Cambridge University Press, 2015).

15. See Wendy Brown, *Undoing the Demos: Neoliberalism's Stealth Revolution* (Brooklyn: Zone Books, 2015); Melinda Cooper, *Family Values: Between Neoliberalism and the New Social Conservativism* (Brooklyn: Zone Books, 2017); and Randy Martin, *An Empire of Indifference: American War and the Financial Logic of Risk Management* (Durham, NC: Duke University Press, 2007).

16. Brown, *Undoing the Demos*, 70.

17. Michel Feher, *Rated Agency: Investee Politics in a Speculative Age*, trans. Gregory Elliott (Brooklyn: Zone Books, 2018), 193.

18. Martin, *Empire of Indifference*, 21.

19. On the subprime, see Fred Moten, "The Subprime and the Beautiful," *African Identities* 11, no. 2 (2013): 237–45. See also Christian P. Haines, "Fictions of Human Capital, or, Redemption in Neoliberal Times," in *Neoliberalism and Contemporary American Literature*, ed. Stephen Shapiro and Liam Kennedy (Hanover, NH: Dartmouth College Press, 2019), 114–35.

20. See Christopher Paul, *The Toxic Meritocracy of Video Games: Why Gaming Culture Is the Worst* (Minneapolis: University of Minnesota Press, 2018).

21. Ivan Ascher, *Portfolio Society: On the Capitalist Mode of Prediction* (Brooklyn: Zone Books, 2016), 123.
22. Ibid., 124.
23. Wark, *Gamer Theory*, 140.
24. Ibid., 134.
25. Lisa Adkins, *The Time of Money* (Stanford, CA: Stanford University Press, 2018), 92.
26. J. Paul Narkunas, *Reified Life: Speculative Capital and the Ahuman Condition* (New York: Fordham University Press, 2018), 65.
27. Keogh, *A Play of Bodies*, 152.
28. Christopher Breu describes this outsourcing of vulnerability as avatar fetishism. See *Insistence of the Material: Literature in the Age of Biopolitics* (Minneapolis: University of Minnesota Press, 2014), 22–23.
29. Claus Pias, *Computer Game Worlds*, trans. Valentine A. Pakis (Chicago: University of Chicago Press, 2017), 18, 122–23.
30. Seb Franklin, *Control: Digitality as Cultural Logic* (Cambridge, MA: MIT Press, 2015), 27. See also Aden Evens, *The Logic of the Digital* (New York: Bloomsbury, 2015).
31. For a popular account of the digitization of finance, see Scott Patterson, *Dark Pools: The Rise of Machine Traders and the Rigging of the U.S. Stock Market* (New York: Crown, 2013). For a critical theorization, see Katherine Hayles, "Temporality and Cognitive Assemblages: Finance Capital, Derivatives, and High-Frequency Trading," in *Unthought: The Power of the Cognitive Unconscious* (Chicago: University of Chicago Press, 2017).
32. Stephanie Boluk and Patrick Lemieux, *Metagaming: Playing, Competing, Spectating, Cheating, Trading, Making, and Breaking Videogames* (Minneapolis: University of Minnesota Press, 2017), 8–9.

Afterword

1. William Gibson, *Neuromancer* (New York: Ace, 1984), 11.
2. William Gibson, *The Peripheral* (London: Penguin, 2014), 35.
3. Ibid., 47.
4. William Gibson, "The Art of Fiction No. 211," interview by David Wallace-Wells, *Paris Review*, no. 197 (Summer 2011): 110.

BIBLIOGRAPHY

Adams, Tim. "Space to Think." *Observer,* August 12, 2007, https://www.theguardian.com/books/2007/aug/12/sciencefictionfantasyandhorror.features.
Adkins, Lisa. *The Time of Money.* Stanford, CA: Stanford University Press, 2018.
Adorno, Theodor W. *Aesthetic Theory.* Edited by Gretel Adorno and Rolf Tiedemann. Translated by Robert Hullot-Kentor. Minneapolis: University of Minnesota Press, 1997.
Aglietta, Michel. *A Theory of Capitalist Regulation: The US Experience.* Translated by David Fernbach. London: Verso, 1987.
Aguiar, Mark, Mark Bils, Kerwin Kofi Charles, and Erik Hurst. "Leisure Luxuries and the Labor Supply of Young Men." National Bureau of Economic Research Working Paper No. 23552 (June 2017).
Aguirre, Anthony. "Multiverse: Cosmology." *Encyclopaedia Britannica,* December 19, 2018. https://www.britannica.com/science/multiverse.
Allan, Kathryn. *Disability in Science Fiction.* New York: Palgrave, 2013.
Amadae, S. M. *Prisoners of Reason: Game Theory and Neoliberal Political Economy.* Cambridge: Cambridge University Press, 2015.
Anable, Aubrey. *Playing with Feelings: Video Games and Affect.* Minneapolis: University of Minnesota Press, 2018.
Anderson, Perry. "Modernity and Revolution." *New Left Review* 144 (1984): 96–113.
——— . *The Origins of Postmodernity.* New York: Verso, 1998.
Arac, Jonathan. "What Good Can Literary History Do?" *American Literary History* 20 (2008): 1–11.
Ascher, Ivan. *Portfolio Society: On the Capitalist Mode of Prediction.* Brooklyn: Zone Books, 2016.
Augé, Marc. *Non-Places: Introduction to an Anthropology of Supermodernity.* Translated by John Howe. London: Verso, 1995.
Avent, Ryan. "Escape to Another World." *The Economist 1843,* April/May 2017. https://www.1843magazine.com/features/escape-to-another-world.

Azerrad, Michael. *Our Band Could Be Your Life: Scenes from the American Indie Underground, 1981–1991*. New York: Back Bay Books, 2001.

Babbage, Charles. *The Ninth Bridgewater Treatise*. London: John Murray, 1837.

———. *On the Economies of Machinery and Manufacture*. London: John Murray, 1846.

Badiou, Alain. "Thinking the Event." In *Badiou & Zizek: Philosophy in the Present*, edited by Peter Engelmann, 1–48. Cambridge: Polity, 2009.

Bakhtin, M. M. "Forms of Time and the Chronotope in the Novel: Notes toward a Historical Poetics." In *Narrative Dynamics: Essays on Time, Plot, Closure, and Frames*, edited by Brian Richardson, 15–25. Columbus: Ohio State University Press, 2002.

Beauman, Ned. "William Gibson: 'We Always Think of Ourselves as the Cream of Creation.'" *Guardian*, November 16, 2014, http://www.theguardian.com/books/2014/nov/16/william-gibson-interview-the-peripheral.

Benjamin, Walter. *Understanding Brecht*. Translated by Anna Bostock. London: Verso, 1998.

Bennett, Jane. "Systems and Things: A Response to Graham Harman and Timothy Morton." *New Literary History* 43, no. 2 (2012): 225–33.

Berlant, Lauren. "Intuitionists: History and the Affective Event." *American Literary History* 20, no. 4 (2008): 845–60.

Bishop, Katharine E. "Ecological Recentering in William Gibson's *The Peripheral*." *Polish Journal of Science Fiction* 12 (Autumn 2018): 319–34.

Bloch, Ernst. *The Utopian Function of Art and Literature: Selected Essays*. Translated by Jack Zipes and Frank Mecklenburg. Cambridge, MA: MIT Press, 1987.

Boluk, Stephanie, and Patrick Lemieux. *Metagaming: Playing, Competing, Spectating, Cheating, Trading, Making, and Breaking Videogames*. Minneapolis: University of Minnesota Press, 2017.

Bonner, Frances. "Separate Development: Cyberpunk in Film and TV." In *Fiction 2000: Cyberpunk and the Future of Narrative*, edited by George Slusser and Tom Shippey, 191–207. Athens: University of Georgia Press, 1992.

Bould, Mark. "Preserving Machines: Recentring the Decentered Subject in *Blade Runner* and *Johnny Mnemonic*." In *Writing and Cinema*, edited by Jonathan Bignell, 164–78. Harlow: Longman, 1999.

Bratton, Benjamin. *The Stack: On Software and Sovereignty*. Cambridge, MA: MIT Press, 2015.

Breu, Christopher. *Insistence of the Material: Literature in the Age of Biopolitics*. Minneapolis: University of Minnesota Press, 2014.

Briggs, Robert. "The Future of Prediction: Speculating on William Gibson's Meta-Science Fiction." *Textual Practice* 27, no. 4 (2013): 671–93.

Brinker, Felix. "Conspiracy, Procedure, Continuity: Reopening *The X-Files*." *Television & New Media* 19, no. 4 (2018): 328–44.

Brouillette, Sarah. "Corporate Publishing and Canonization: *Neuromancer* and Science-Fiction Publishing in the 1970s and Early 1980s." *Book History* 5 (2002): 187–208.
Brown, Nicholas. "One, Two, Many Ends of Literature." *Mediations* 24, no. 2 (2010): 91.
Brown, Wendy. *Undoing the Demos: Neoliberalism's Stealth Revolution.* Brooklyn: Zone Books, 2015.
Bryant, Levi. "Correlationism." In *The Meillassoux Dictionary*, edited by Peter Gratton and Paul J. Ennis, 46–48. Edinburgh: Edinburgh University Press, 2014.
Bukatman, Scott. "Gibson's Typewriter." In *Matters of Gravity: Special Effects and Supermen in the Twentieth Century*, 32–47. Durham, NC: Duke University Press, 2003.
Burges, Joel, and Amy J. Elias, editors. *Time: A Vocabulary of the Present.* New York: New York University Press, 2016.
Burroughs, William. "The Fall of Art." In *The Adding Machine*. New York: Arcade, 1986. 60–64.
Bush, George W. "Transcript of President Bush's Address." CCN.com/US, September 21, 2001. http://edition.cnn.com/2001/US/09/20/gen.bush.transcript/.
Butler, Andrew M. "Journeys beyond Being: The Cyberpunk-Flavored Novels of Jeff Noon." In *Beyond Cyberpunk: New Critical Perspectives*, edited by Sherryl Vint and Graham Murphy, 65–78. London: Routledge, 2010.
Byatt, A. S. *Possession.* New York: Vintage, 1991.
Calvert, Bronwen. "William Gibson's 'Cyberpunk' X-Files." *Science Fiction Film and Television* 6, no. 1 (2013): 39–53.
Carr, Terry. "Introduction." In Kim Stanley Robinson, *The Wild Shore*, vii–viii. New York: Ace, 1984.
Chalmers, David. "Ontological Anti-Realism." In *Metametaphysics: New Essays on the Foundations of Ontology*, edited by D. J. Chalmers, D. Manley, and R. Wasserman, 77–129. Oxford: Oxford University Press, 2009.
Chaplin, Sarah. "Report to Virtual HQ: The Distributed City." *Journal of Architecture* 2, no. 1 (1997): 43–57.
Childress, Herb. *The Adjunct Underclass: How America's Colleges Betrayed Their Faculty, Their Students, and Their Mission.* Chicago: University of Chicago Press, 2019.
Clarke, Arthur C. *2001: A Space Odyssey.* New York: Penguin, 2000.
Cohen, Patricia. "Digital Keys for Unlocking Humanities' Riches." *New York Times*, November 16, 2010, https://www.nytimes.com/2010/11/17/arts/17digital.html.
Cooper, Melinda. *Family Values: Between Neoliberalism and the New Social Conservativism.* Brooklyn: Zone Books, 2017.

Csicery-Ronay, Istvan, Jr. "Antimancer: Cybernetics and Art in Gibson's *Count Zero*." *Science Fiction Studies* 22, no. 1 (1995): 63–86.

Davies, William. "The New Neoliberalism." *New Left Review* 101 (2016): 121–34.

Debord, Guy. *Society of the Spectacle*. Sussex: Soul Bay Press, 2009. Kindle edition.

Delany, Samuel R. *Stars in My Pocket Like Grains of Sand*. Middletown, CT: Wesleyan University Press, 2004.

———. *Times Square Red, Times Square Blue*. New York: New York University Press, 1999.

Dery, Mark. "Black to the Future: Interviews with Samuel R. Delany, Greg Tate, and Tricia Rose." In *Flame Wars: The Discourse of Cyberculture*, edited by Mark Dery, 179–222. Durham, NC: Duke University Press, 1994.

Disch, Thomas. *The Dreams Our Stuff Is Made of: How Science Fiction Conquered the World*. New York: Simon and Schuster, 1998.

———. "Queen Victoria's Computers." *New York Times Book Review*, March 10, 1991, http://movies2.nytimes.com/books/98/08/09/specials/disch-gibson.html.

Dyer-Witheford, Nick, and Greig De Peuter. *Games of Empire: Global Capitalism and Video Games*. Minneapolis: University of Minnesota Press, 2009.

Easterbrook, Neil. "Alternate Presents: The Ambivalent Historicism of 'Pattern Recognition'." *Science Fiction Studies* 33, no. 3 (2006): 483–504.

———. "Recognizing Patterns: Gibson's Hermeneutics from the Bridge Trilogy to *Pattern Recognition*." In *Beyond Cyberpunk: New Critical Perspectives*, edited by Graham J. Murphy and Sherryl Vint, 46–64. New York: Routledge, 2010.

———. "William [Ford] Gibson (1948–)." In *Fifty Key Figures in Science Fiction*, edited by Mark Bould et al., 86–91. New York: Routledge, 2020.

Elias, Amy J. "The Futureless Future." *American Book Review* 36, no. 5 (2015): 12–13.

———. "History." In *The Cambridge Companion to Thomas Pynchon*, edited by Inger H. Dalsgaard, Luc Herman, and Brian McHale, 123–35. Cambridge: Cambridge University Press, 2012.

Emerson, Ralph Waldo. "The American Scholar." In *Nature and Selected Essays*, 83–105. New York: Penguin, 2003.

———. "Nature." In *Nature and Selected Essays*, 35–82. New York: Penguin, 2003.

Ernst, Wolfgang. *Chronopoetics: The Temporal Being and Operativity of Technological Media*. Translated by Anthony Enns. New York: Rowman & Littlefield, 2016.

———. "From Media History of Zeitkritik." *Theory, Culture, and Society* 30, no. 6 (2013): 132–46.

Evens, Aden. *The Logic of the Digital*. New York: Bloomsbury, 2015.

Everett, H. "Relative State Formulation of Quantum Mechanics." *Review of Modern Physics* 29 (1957): 454–62.

Feher, Michel. *Rated Agency: Investee Politics in a Speculative Age.* Translated by Gregory Elliott. Brooklyn: Zone Books, 2018.

Fiske, John. "Reading the Beach." In *Reading the Popular*, 43–76. London: Unwin Hyman, 1989.

Foucault, Michel. *The Birth of Biopolitics: Lectures at the Collège de France, 1978–1979.* Translated by Graham Burchell. New York: Palgrave Macmillan, 2008.

Franklin, Benjamin. *The Autobiography.* In *The Autobiography and Other Writings*, edited by Peter Shaw, 1–208. New York: Bantam, 2008.

———. "Epitaph." In *The Autobiography and Other Writings*, edited by Peter Shaw, 348. New York: Bantam, 2008.

Franklin, Seb. *Control: Digitality as Cultural Logic.* Cambridge, MA: MIT Press, 2015.

Freedman, Carl. *Critical Theory and Science Fiction.* Hanover, NH: University Press of New England, 2000.

Frelik, Paweł. "'Silhouettes of Strange Illuminated Mannequins': Cyberpunk's Incarnations of Light." In *Cyberpunk and Visual Culture*, edited by Graham J. Murphy and Lars Schmeink, 80–99. London: Routledge, 2018.

Fukuzawa, Yukichi. *Gakumon no Susume* (An Encouragement of Learning). Translated by David A. Dilworth. Tokyo: Keio University Press, 2012.

Galloway, Alexander. *Protocol: How Control Exists after Decentralization.* Cambridge, MA: MIT Press, 2004.

Gibson, William. "Academy Leader." In *Cyberspace: First Steps*, edited by Michael L. Benedikt, 27–29. Cambridge, MA: MIT Press, 1992.

———. *Alien III Revised First Draft Screenplay*, https://www.awesomefilm.com/script/Alien3.txt (accessed February 7, 2020).

———. "The Art of Fiction No. 211." Interview by David Wallace-Wells. *Paris Review*, no. 197 (2011): 107–49.

———. *Burning Chrome.* New York: Eos, 2003.

———. *Count Zero.* New York: Ace, 1986.

———. *Distrust That Particular Flavor.* New York: Putnam, 2012.

———. *Idoru.* New York: Berkley, 1996.

———. "An Interview with William Gibson." Interview by Jesse Hicks. *The Verge*, January 24, 2012, https://www.theverge.com/2012/1/24/2724370/william-gibson-interview.

———. *Mona Lisa Overdrive.* New York: Bantam, 1988.

———. *Neuromancer.* New York: Ace, 1984.

———. "Nostalgia for the Future: William Gibson on *The Peripheral* and His Legacy." Interview by Jonathan Sturgeon. *Flavorwire*, November 3, 2014, http://flavorwire.com/486048.

———. *Pattern Recognition.* New York: Berkley, 2003.

———. *The Peripheral.* New York: Putnam, 2014.

---. *The Peripheral*. London: Penguin, 2014.
---. *Spook Country*. New York: Putnam, 2007.
---. *Spook Country*. New York: Berkley, 2008.
---. *Virtual Light*. New York: Bantam Books, 1993. Kindle edition.
---. "William Gibson Interview: Time Travel, Virtual Reality, and His New Books." Interview by Adi Robertson. *The Verge*, October 28, 2014, https://www.theverge.com/2014/10/28/7083625/william-gibson-interview-time-travel-virtual-reality-and-the-peripheral.
---. "William Gibson on the Apocalypse, America, and *The Peripheral*'s Ending." Interview by Analee Newitz. *Io9*, November 11, 2014, https://io9.gizmodo.com/william-gibson-on-the-apocalypse-america-and-the-peri-1656659382.
---. "William Gibson on Urbanism, Science Fiction, and Why *The Peripheral* Weirded Him Out." Interview by Karin L. Kross. Tor.com, October 29, 2014, https://www.tor.com/2014/10/29/william-gibson-the-peripheral-interview/.
---. "William Gibson Talks about 'The Peripheral,' the Power of Twitter, and His Next Book Set in Today's Silicon Valley." Interview by Matt Rosoff. *Business Insider*, August 13, 2016, https://www.businessinsider.com/william-gibson-the-peripheral-interview-business-insider-2016-8.
---. "The Winter Market." In *Burning Chrome*, 124–50. New York: Ace Books, 1987.
---. *Zero History*. New York: Putnam, 2010.
Gibson, William, and Bruce Sterling. *The Difference Engine 20th Anniversary Edition*. New York: Ballantine Books, 2011.
Gibson, William, Johnnie Christmas, and Tamra Bonvillain. *Alien 3: The Unproduced Screenplay*. Milwaukie, OR: Dark Horse Comics, 2019.
Gibson, William, Michael St. John Smith, and Butch Guice. *William Gibson's Archangel*. San Diego: IDW, 2017.
Gold, Matthew K. "Day of DH." In *Debates in the Digital Humanities*, edited by Matthew K. Gold. Milwaukie: Dark Horse Comics and Minneapolis: University of Minnesota Press, 2012.
Gutierrez-Jones, Carl. "Stealing Kinship: *Neuromancer* and Artificial Intelligence." *Science Fiction Studies* 41, no. 1 (2014): 69–92.
Haines, Christian P. "Fictions of Human Capital, or, Redemption in Neoliberal Times." In *Neoliberalism and Contemporary American Literature*. Edited by Stephen Shapiro and Liam Kennedy, 114–35. Hanover, NH: Dartmouth College Press, 2019.
Harman, Graham. "An Outline of Object-Oriented Philosophy." *Science Progress* 96, no. 2 (2013): 187–99.
---. "Realism without Materialism." *SubStance* 40, no. 2 (2011): 52–72.
---. *Towards Speculative Realism: Essays and Lectures*. London: Zero Books, 2010.

Harvey, David. *The Condition of Postmodernity: An Enquiry into the Origins of Cultural Change*. Oxford: Basil Blackwell, 1989.
———. *Marx, Capital, and the Madness of Economic Reason*. New York: Oxford, 2018.
Hayles, N. Katherine. *How We Became Posthuman*. Chicago: University of Chicago Press, 1999.
———. *Unthought: The Power of the Cognitive Unconscious*. Chicago: University of Chicago Press, 2017.
Heinlein, Robert. *The Moon Is a Harsh Mistress*. New York: Tor, 1966.
Henwood, Doug. *After the New Economy*. New York: New Press, 2003.
Heppler, Jason. "What Is Digital Humanities?" https://whatisdigitalhumanities.com/ (accessed May 1, 2019).
Hindley, Meredith. "The Rise of the Machines: NEH and the Digital Humanities: The Early Years." *Humanities* 34, no. 4 (2013), https://www.neh.gov/humanities/2013/julyaugust/feature/the-rise-the-machines.
Hoberek, Andrew. "Literary Genre Fiction." In *American Literature in Transition, 2000–2010*, edited by Rachel Greenwald Smith, 61–75. Cambridge: Cambridge University Press, 2018.
Hollinger, Veronica. "Cybernetic Deconstructions: Cyberpunk and Modernism." *Mosaic* 23, no. 2 (1990): 29–44.
———. "Science Fiction and Postmodernism." In *A Companion to Science Fiction*, edited by David Seed, 232–47. Oxford: Blackwell, 2005.
———. "Stories about the Future: From Patterns of Expectation to Pattern Recognition." *Science Fiction Studies* 33, no. 3 (2006): 452–72.
Horkheimer, Max, and Theodor Adorno. *The Dialectic of Enlightenment*. Stanford, CA: Stanford University Press, 2002.
Hume, Kathryn. *Pynchon's Mythography: An Approach to Gravity's Rainbow*. Carbondale: Southern Illinois University Press, 1987.
Hutner, Gordon. "Historicizing the Contemporary: A Response to Amy Hungerford." *American Literary History* 20, nos. 1–2 (2008): 420–24.
Hyman, Louis. *Temp: How American Work, American Business, and the American Dream Became Temporary*. New York: Penguin, 2018.
Irr, Caren. *Toward the Geopolitical Novel: U.S. Fiction in the Twenty-First Century*. New York: Columbia University Press, 2014.
Jameson, Fredric. "The Aesthetics of Singularity." *New Left Review* 92 (2015): 101–32.
———. *Allegory and Ideology*. New York: Verso, 2019.
———. *The Ancients and the Postmoderns: On the Historicity of Forms*. London: Verso, 2015.
———. *Archaeologies of the Future: The Desire Called Utopia and Other Science Fictions*. London: Verso, 2005.

---. "The End of Temporality." *Critical Inquiry* 29, no. 4 (2003): 695–718.
———. "Exoticism and Structuralism in Wallace Stevens." *New Orleans Review* 11, no. 1 (1984): 10–19.
———. "Fear and Loathing in Globalization." In *Archaeologies of the Future: The Desire Called Utopia and Other Science Fictions*, 384–92. London: Verso, 2005.
———. "Foreword." In Jean-François Lyotard, *The Postmodern Condition: A Report on Knowledge*, translated by Geoff Bennington and Brian Massumi, vii–xxi. Minneapolis: University of Minnesota Press, 1984.
———. "Future City." *New Left Review* 21 (May/June 2003): 65–79.
———. *Marxism and Form: Twentieth-Century Dialectical Theories of Literature*. Princeton, NJ: Princeton University Press, 1971.
———. "Notes on Globalization as a Philosophical Issue." In *Valences of the Dialectic*, 435–55. New York: Verso, 2008.
———. "Periodizing the 60s." *Social Text* 9/10 (1984): 178–209.
———. *The Political Unconscious: Narrative as a Socially Symbolic Act*. Ithaca, NY: Cornell University Press, 1981.
———. "The Politics of Theory: Ideological Positions in the Postmodernism Debate." *New German Critique* 33 (1984): 53–65.
———. "Postmodernism, or the Cultural Logic of Late Capitalism." *New Left Review* 146 (1984): 53–92.
———. *Postmodernism, or, the Cultural Logic of Late Capitalism*. Durham, NC: Duke University Press, 1991.
———. *Signatures of the Visible*. New York: Routledge, 1990.
———. "Third World Literature in the Era of Multinational Capitalism." *Social Text* 15 (1986): 65–88.
Jones, Kristin, and Andrew Ginzel. "Metronome" http://jonesginzel.com/project/metronome (accessed December 14, 2018).
Jones, Steven. *The Emergence of the Digital Humanities*. London: Routledge, 2014.
Jovanovic, Damjan. "Fictions: A Speculative Account of Design Mediums." In *Speculations in Contemporary Drawing for Art and Architecture*, edited by Laura Allen and Luke Caspar Pearson, 28–33. London: Riverside Architectural Press, 2016.
Kaika, Maria, and Erik Swyngedouw. "Fetishizing the Modern City: The Phantasmagoria of Urban Technological Networks." *International Journal of Urban and Regional Research* 24, no. 1 (2000): 120–38.
Kapor, Mitchell, and John Perry Barlow. "Across the Electronic Frontier." Electronic Frontier Foundation, July 10, 1990, https://www.eff.org/pages/across-electronic-frontier.
Katayama, Lisa. "Man Marries Video Game Computer." Boing Boing, November 23, 2009, https://www.youtube.com/watch?v=hsikPswAYUM.

Keogh, Brendan. *A Play of Bodies: How We Perceive Videogames*. Cambridge, MA: MIT Press, 2018.

Kidd, David Comer, and Emanuele Castano. "Reading Literary Fiction Improves Theory of Mind." *Science Magazine*, October 18, 2013, 377–80.

Kirschenbaum, Matthew. *Mechanisms*. Cambridge, MA: MIT Press, 2007.

———. *Track Changes: A Literary History of Word Processing*. Cambridge: Harvard University Press, 2016.

———. "What Is Digital Humanities and What's It Doing in English Classes?" In *Debates in Digital Humanities*, edited by Matthew K. Gold. Minneapolis: University of Minnesota Press, 2012.

Kittler, Friedrich. "The City Is a Medium." Translated by Matthew Griffin. *New Literary History* 27, no. 4 (1996): 717–29.

———. *Optical Media*. Translated by Anthony Enns. Cambridge: Polity Press, 2010.

Konstantinou, Lee. "The Brand as Cognitive Map in William Gibson's *Pattern Recognition*." *boundary 2* 36, no. 2 (2009): 67–97.

Koolhaas, Rem. "Junkspace." *October* 100 (2002): 175–90, http://www.jstor.org/stable/779098.

Krevel, Mojca. "'Back to the Future': Technological Singularity in Gibson's Sprawl Trilogy." *British and American Studies* 20 (2012): 27–35.

Krippner, Greta. "The Financialization of the American Economy." *Socio-Economic Review* 3, no. 2 (2005): 173–208.

Kroker, Arthur, and Marilouise Kroker. "*Johnny Mnemonic*: The Day Cyberpunk Died." In *Hacking the Future: Stories for the Flesh-Eating 90s*, 50–51. Montreal: New World Perspectives, 1996.

Kross, Karin L. "The Future Is Here: William Gibson's *The Peripheral*." Tor.com, October 27, 2014, http://www.tor.com/blogs/2014/10/book-review-the-peripheral-william-gibson.

Langdon, David. "AD Classics: AT&T Building / Philip Johnson and John Burgee." *Arch Daily*, January 12, 2019, https://www.archdaily.com/611169/ad-classics-at-and-t-building-philip-johnson-and-john-burgee.

Lawrence, D. H. *Studies in Classic American Literature*. Edited by Ezra Greenspan, Lindeth Vasey, and John Worthen. Cambridge: Cambridge University Press, 2003.

Lefebvre, Henri. *The Production of Space*. Translated by Donald Nicholson-Smith. Oxford: Blackwell, [1974] 1991.

Leith, Sam. "*The Peripheral* by William Gibson—A Glorious Ride into the Future." *Guardian*, November 19, 2014, http://www.theguardian.com/books/2014/nov/19/the-peripheral-william-gibson-ride-future.

Levin, Harry. "What Was Modernism?" *Massachusetts Review* 1, no. 4 (1960): 609–30.

Light, Alan. "Why 1984 Was Pop Music's Best Year Ever." *Billboard*, October 24, 2014, https://www.billboard.com/articles/news/6296392/1984-best-year-of-pop-music-ever-essay.

Liu, Alan. "Transcendental Data." *Critical Inquiry* 31, no. 1 (2004): 49–82.

Martin, Randy. *An Empire of Indifference: American War and the Financial Logic of Risk Management.* Durham, NC: Duke University Press, 2007.

——. *Financialization of Daily Life.* Philadelphia: Temple University Press, 2002.

Martin, Theodore. "The Currency of the Contemporary." In *Postmodern|Postwar—and After: Rethinking American Literature*, ed. Jason Gladstone, Andrew Hoberek, and Daniel Worden, 227–39. Iowa City: University of Iowa Press, 2016.

Marx, Karl. *Capital: A Critique of Political Economy Volume 1: The Process of Production of Capital.* Marxists Internet Archive, 1999, https://www.marxists.org/archive/marx/works/1867-c1/.

——. *Capital: A Critique of Political Economy Volume 3: The Process of Capitalist Production as a Whole.* New York: International, 1977.

——. *Capital, Volume 1.* Translated by Ben Fowkes. London: Penguin, 1976.

Marx, Karl, and Frederick Engels. *Manifesto of the Communist Party.* 1848. Marxists Internet Archive, https://www.marxists.org/archive/marx/works/1848/communist-manifesto/ch01.htm#007.

McCaffrey, Anne. *The Ship Who Sang.* New York: Delray, 1985.

McCaffery, Larry. "The Fictions of the Present." In *Columbia Literary History of the United States*, edited by Emory Elliot, 1161–77. New York: Columbia University Press, 1988.

——. "An Interview with William Gibson." In *Storming the Reality Studio: A Casebook of Cyberpunk and Postmodern Fiction*, edited by Larry McCaffery, 263–85. Durham, NC: Duke University Press, 1991.

——, editor. *Storming the Reality Studio: A Casebook of Cyberpunk and Postmodern Science Fiction.* Durham, NC: Duke University Press, 1991.

McDonagh, Maitland. "Clive Barker & William Gibson: Future Shockers." *Film Comment* 26, no. 1 (1990): 60–63.

——. "New Rose Hotel." *Film Journal International* (November 2004). https://www.tvguide.com/movies/new-rose-hotel/review/134345/.

McFarlane, Anna. "'Anthropomorphic Drones' and Colonized Bodies: William Gibson's *The Peripheral*." *English Studies in Canada* 42, nos. 1–2 (2016): 115–31.

McGann, Jerome. *The Textual Condition.* Princeton, NJ: Princeton University Press, 1991.

McGurl, Mark. *The Program Era: Postwar Fiction and the Rise of Creative Writing.* Cambridge, MA: Harvard University Press, 2009.

McHale, Brian. *Constructing Postmodernism*. London: Routledge, 1992.
———. "Elements of a Poetics of Cyberpunk." *Critique* 33, no. 3 (1992): 149–75.
———. "*Mason & Dixon* in the Zone, or, a Brief Poetics of Pynchon-Space." In *Pynchon and Mason & Dixon*, edited by Brooke Horvath and Irving Malin, 43–62. Newark: University of Delaware Press, 2000.
Miller, Alexander. "Realism." In *Stanford Encyclopedia of Philosophy*, edited by Edward N. Zalta. Winter 2016, https://plato.stanford.edu/archives/win2016/entries/realism/.
Moody, Nikkianne. "Untapped Potential: The Representation of Disability/Special Ability in the Cyberpunk Workforce." *Convergence* 3, no. 3 (1997): 90–105.
Morgan, Glyn. "Detective, Historian, Reader: Alternate History and Alternative Fact in William Gibson's *The Peripheral*." *Polish Journal of Science Fiction* 12 (Autumn 2018): 307–17.
Morgan, Robert C. "Metronome." *Sculpture* 19, no. 4 (May 2000): 10–11.
Morris, Sue. "First-Person Shooters—A Game Apparatus." In *ScreenPlay: Cinema/Videogames/Interfaces*, edited by Geoff King and Tanya Krzywinska, 81–97. London: Wallflower Press, 2002.
Morton, Timothy. *Hyperobjects: Philosophy and Ecology after the End of the World*. Minneapolis: University of Minnesota Press, 2013.
———. *Realist Magic*. London: Open Humanities Press, 2013.
Moten, Fred. "The Subprime and the Beautiful." *African Identities* 11, no. 2 (2013): 237–45.
Moylan, Tom. *Becoming Utopian: The Culture and Politics of Radical Transformation*. New York: Bloomsbury, 2020.
———. *Demand the Impossible: Science Fiction and the Utopian Imagination*. Oxford: Peter Lang, 2014.
———. "Global Economy, Local Texts: Utopian/Dystopian Tension in William Gibson's Cyberpunk Trilogy." *Minnesota Review* 43/44 (1995): 182–97.
———. *Scraps of the Untainted Sky: Science Fiction, Utopia, Dystopia*. Boulder, CO: Westview, 2001.
———. "Utopia Is When Our Lives Matter: Reading Kim Stanley Robinson's *Pacific Edge*." *Utopian Studies* 6, no. 2 (1995): 1–24.
———. "Witness to Hard Times: Robinson's Other Californias." In *Kim Stanley Robinson Maps the Unimaginable: Critical Essays*, edited by William J. Burling, 11–47. Jefferson, NC: McFarland, 2009.
Narkunas, J. Paul. *Reified Life: Speculative Capital and the Ahuman Condition*. New York: Fordham University Press, 2018.
Newzoo. "Newzoo's 2017 Report: Insight into the 108.9 Billion Global Games Market." Newzoo, June 20, 2017, https://newzoo.com/insights/articles/newzoo-2017-report-insights-into-the-108-9-billion-global-games-market/.
Nilges, Mathias. "The Realism of Speculation: Contemporary Speculative Fiction

as Immanent Critique of Finance Capitalism." *CR: The New Centennial Review* 19, no. 1 (2019): 37–60.

———. *Right-Wing Culture in Contemporary Capitalism: Regression and Hope in a Time without Future*. London: Bloomsbury, 2019.

———. "William Gibson." In *Oxford Bibliographies in American Literature*, edited by Sherryl Vint. New York: Oxford University Press, 2019.

Nixon, Nicola. "Cyberpunk: Preparing the Ground for Revolution or Keeping the Boys Satisfied?" *Science Fiction Studies* 19, no. 2 (1992): 219–35.

Novak, Amy. "Virtual Poltergeists and Memory: The Question of Ahistoricism in William Gibson's *Neuromancer* (1984)." *Journal of the Fantastic in the Arts* 11, no. 4 (2001): 395–414.

Olsen, Lance. "The Shadow of Spirit in William Gibson's Matrix Trilogy." *Extrapolation* 32, no 3 (1991): 278–89.

———. "Virtual Termites: A Hypotextual Technomutant Explo(it)ration of William Gibson and the Electronic Beyond(s)." *Style* 29, no. 2 (1995): 296.

Osborne, Peter. *Anywhere or Not at All: Philosophy of Contemporary Art*. London: Verso, 2013.

Parikka, Jussi. *A Geology of Media*. Minneapolis: University of Minnesota Press, 2015.

———. "Media Archaeology as a Trans-Atlantic Bridge." In *Digital Memory and the Archive*, 1–36. Minneapolis: University of Minnesota Press, 2012.

———. *What Is Media Archaeology?* Cambridge: Polity, 2012.

Patterson, Scott. *Dark Pools: The Rise of Machine Traders and the Rigging of the U.S. Stock Market*. New York: Crown, 2013.

Paul, Christopher. *The Toxic Meritocracy of Video Games: Why Gaming Culture Is the Worst*. Minneapolis: University of Minnesota Press, 2018.

Pias, Claus. *Computer Game Worlds*. Translated by Valentine A. Pakis. Chicago: University of Chicago Press, 2017.

Piatkowski, Paul. "Mind against Matter: The Physics of Interface in William Gibson's *The Peripheral*." *Critique: Studies in Contemporary Fiction* 60, no. 1 (2019): 34–48.

Pier, John. "Narrative Levels (revised version)." In *The Living Handbook of Narratology*, edited by Peter Hühn et al, Hamburg University. Last modified October 10, 2016, http://www.lhn.uni-hamburg.de/article/narrative-levels-revised-version-uploaded-23-april-2014.

Poole, Stephen. "Nearing the Nodal." *Guardian*, October 30, 1999, https://www.theguardian.com/books/1999/oct/30/sciencefictionfantasyandhorror.williamgibson.

Pordzik, Ralph. "The Posthuman Future of Man: Anthropocentrism and the Other of Technology in Anglo-American Science Fiction." *Utopian Studies* 23, no. 1 (2012): 142–61.

Proust, Marcel. *Remembrance of Things Past, Volume 1: Swann's Way.* Translated by C. K. Scott Moncrieff and Terence Kilmartin. New York: Random House, 1981.
Public Art Fund. "Metronome." https://www.publicartfund.org/view/exhibitions/5961_metronome (accessed November 30, 2018).
Puiu, Tibi. "Neil DeGrasse Tyson Explains Why 'We Stopped Dreaming.'" *ZME Zine*, March 13, 2012, https://www.zmescience.com/space/neil-degrasse-tyson-why-we-stopped-dreaming-13032012/.
Pynchon, Thomas. *Bleeding Edge.* New York: Penguin, 2013.
Ramsay, Stephen. "Who's In and Who's Out." In *Defining Digital Humanities*, edited by Melissa Terras, Julianne Nyhan, and Edward Vanhoutte, 239–42. New York: Routledge, 2013.
Rancière, Jacques. "In What Time Do We Live?" *Politicacomun* 4 (2013). doi: 10.3998/pc.12322227.0004.001.
Related Companies Ltd. "One Union Square South." https://www.relatedrentals.com/apartment-rentals/new-york-city/union-square/one-union-square-south (accessed November 30, 2018).
"Relax (Song)." Wikipedia, https://en.wikipedia.org/wiki/Relax_(song) (accessed February 7, 2020).
Rickels, Laurence A. "American Psychos: The End of Art Cinema in the '90s." *Art/Text*, no. 67 (2000): 58–63.
Robinson, Kim Stanley. *New York 2140.* New York: Orbit, 2017.
———. *The Novels of Philip K. Dick.* Ann Arbor, MI: UMI Research Press, 1984.
———. *The Wild Shore.* New York: Ace, 1984.
Rosen, Jeremy. "Literary Fiction and the Genres of Genre Fiction." *Post45*, August 7, 2018, post45.research.yale.edu/2018/08/literary-fiction-and-the-genres-of-genre-fiction/.
Ross, Andrew. *Strange Weather: Culture, Science and Technology in the Age of Limits.* New York: Verso, 1991.
Rothman, Joshua. "How William Gibson Keeps Science Fiction Real." *New Yorker*, December 9, 2019, https://www.newyorker.com/magazine/2019/12/16/how-william-gibson-keeps-his-science-fiction-real.
Ruffino, Paolo. *Future Gaming: Creative Interventions in Video Game Culture.* London: Goldsmiths Press, 2018.
Russ, Joanna. "When It Changed." In *Again, Dangerous Visions*, edited by Harlan Ellison, 253–60. New York: Doubleday, 1972.
Schulson, Michael. "William Gibson: I Never Imagined Facebook." *Salon*, November 10, 2014, https://www.salon.com/2014/11/09/william_gibson_i_never_imagined_facebook/.
Shaviro, Steven. *Connected, Or, What It Means to Live in the Networked Society.* Minneapolis: University of Minnesota Press, 2003.

Shaw, Joe, and Mark Graham. "An Informational Right to the City?" In *The Right to the City: A Verso Report*. London: Verso, 2017. Kindle edition.

Shelley, Mary. *Frankenstein: The 1818 Text*. New York: Penguin, 2018.

Siivonen, Timo. "Cyborgs and Generic Oxymorons: The Body and Technology in William Gibson's Cyberspace Trilogy." *Science Fiction Studies* 23, no. 2 (1996): 227–44.

Slight, Graham. "Review of Pattern Recognition by William Gibson." *New York Review of Science Fiction* 15, no. 9 (May 2003): 8–9.

Slotkin, Joel Elliot. "Haunted Infocosms and Prosthetic Gods: Gibsonian Cyberspace and Renaissance Arts of Memory." *Journal of Popular Culture* 45, no. 4 (2012): 862–82.

Smith, Gavin. "Dealing with the Now." *Sight and Sound* 7, no. 4 (1997): 6–9.

Smith, Rachel Greenwald, editor. *American Literature in Transition, 2000–2010*. Cambridge: Cambridge University Press, 2018.

Snow, C. P. *The Two Cultures*. Cambridge: Cambridge University Press, 1993.

Sponsler, Claire. "Cyberpunk and the Dilemmas of Postmodern Narrative: The Example of William Gibson." *Contemporary Literature* 33, no. 4 (1992): 625–44.

Springer, Claudia. "Psycho-cybernetics in Films of the 1990s." In *Alien Zone II: The Spaces of Science Fiction Cinema*, edited by Annette Kuhn, 203–18. London: Verso, 1999.

Srnicek, Nick. *Platform Capitalism*. Cambridge: Polity, 2017.

Stanford, Angelina. "Immanuel Kant on Benjamin Franklin." Circe Institute Podcast Network, February 11, 2016, https://www.circeinstitute.org/blog/immanuel-kant-benjamin-franklin.

Starosielski, Nicole. *The Undersea Network*. Durham, NC: Duke University Press, 2015.

Sterling, Bruce. "Preface." In William Gibson, *Burning Chrome*, ix–xii. New York: Eos, 2003.

Suvin, Darko. *Metamorphoses of Science Fiction: On the Poetics and History of a Literary Genre*, edited by Gerry Canavan. Dublin: Ralahine Utopian Studies, 2017.

———. "On Gibson and Cyberpunk." *Foundation: The Review of Science Fiction* 46 (1989): 40–51.

Swanstrom, Lisa. "External Memory Drives: Deletion and Digitality in Agrippa (A Book of the Dead)." *Science Fiction Studies* 43, no. 1 (2016): 14–32.

Tatsumi, Takayuki. *Young Americans in Literature: The Post-Romantic Turn in the Age of Poe, Hawthorne and Melville*. Tokyo: Sairyusha, 2018.

Terdiman, Richard. "From City to Country: An Outline of 'Fluvio-Critique.'" *NOVEL* 41, no. 1 (2007): 53–72.

Todorov, Tsvetan, "The Typology of Detective Fiction." In *The Narrative Reader*, edited by Martin McQuillan. New York: Routledge, 2000.

Tomberg, Jaak, "On the 'Double Vision'" of Realism and SF Estrangement in

William Gibson's *Bigend* Trilogy." *Science Fiction Studies* 40, no. 2 (2013): 263–85. https://www.depauw.edu/sfs/pioneers/tomberg%20120.html.

Vaidman, Lev. "Many-Worlds Interpretation of Quantum Mechanics." *Stanford Encyclopedia of Philosophy*, edited by Edward N. Zalta. Fall 2018. https://plato.stanford.edu/archives/fall2018/entries/qm-manyworlds/.

Van Bakel, Rogier. "Remembering Johnny." *Wired*, June 1, 1995, https://www.wired.com/1995/06/gibson-4/.

Varoufakis, Yanis. *The Global Minotaur: America, Europe and the Future of the Global Economy*. London: Zed Books, 2015.

Vint, Sherryl. *Bodies of Tomorrow: Technology, Subjectivity, Science Fiction*. Toronto: University of Toronto Press, 2007.

———. "Introduction to The Futures Industry." *Paradoxa* 27 (2016). http://paradoxa.com/volumes/27/introduction.

———. "Promissory Futures: Reality and Imagination in Fiction and Finance." *The New Centennial Review* (special issue on Speculative Finance and Speculative Fiction, edited by David Higgins and Hugh O'Connell) 19, no. 1 (2019): 11–36.

———. "The World Gibson Made." In *Beyond Cyberpunk: New Critical Perspectives*, edited by Graham J. Murphy and Sherryl Vint, 228–33. New York: Routledge, 2010.

Virilio, Paul. *The Futurism of the Instant: Stop-Eject*. Translated by Julie Rose. Cambridge: Polity Press, [2009] 2010.

———. *The Information Bomb*. Translated by Chris Turner. London: Verso, [1998] 2000.

Vogel, Ezra F. *Japan as No. 1: Lessons for America*. Cambridge, MA: Harvard University Press, 1979.

Voller, Jack G. "Neuromanticism: Cyberspace and the Sublime." *Extrapolation* 34, no. 1 (1993): 28–29.

Wark, McKenzie. *Capital Is Dead: Is This Something Worse?* London: Verso, 2019.

———. *Gamer Theory*. Cambridge, MA: Harvard University Press, 2007.

———. *Telethesia: Communication, Culture, and Class*. Cambridge: Cambridge University Press, 2012.

Wegner, Phillip E. "The British Dystopian Novel from Wells to Ishiguro." In *A Companion to British Literature, Volume 4: Victorian and Twentieth-Century Literature, 1837–2000*, edited by Bob DeMaria, Heesok Chang, and Samantha Zache, 454–70. Hoboken, NJ: Wiley-Blackwell, 2014.

———. *Imaginary Communities: Utopia, the Nation, and the Spatial Histories of Modernity*. Berkeley: University of California Press, 2002.

———. Introduction to Robert C. Elliott, *The Shape of Utopia: Studies in a Literary Genre*, xiii–xxx. Oxford: Peter Lang, 2013.

———. *Invoking Hope: Theory and Utopia in Dark Times*. Minneapolis: University of Minnesota Press, 2020.

———. *Life between Two Deaths, 1989–2001: US Culture in the Long Nineties*. Durham, NC: Duke University Press, 2009.
———. *Periodizing Jameson: Dialectics, the University, and the Desire for Narrative*. Evanston, IL: Northwestern University Press, 2014.
———. "Recognizing the Patterns." *New Literary History* 38, no. 1 (2007): 183–200.
———. *Shockwaves of Possibility: Essays on Science Fiction, Globalization, and Utopia*. Oxford: Peter Lang, 2014.
Weick, Karl E. "Enacted Sensemaking in Crisis Situations." *Journal of Management Studies* 25, no. 4 (1988): 305–17.
Westfahl, Gary. "'The Gernsback Continuum': William Gibson in the Context of Science Fiction." In *Fiction 2000: Cyberpunk and the Future of Narrative*, edited by George Slusser and Tom Shippey, 88–108. Athens: University of Georgia Press, 1992.
———. *William Gibson*. Champaign: University of Illinois Press, 2013.
White, Hayden. "Anomalies of Genre: The Utility of Theory and History for the Study of Literary Genres." *New Literary History* 34 (2003): 597–615.
Whitehead, Colson. *Zone One*. New York: Random House, 2011.
Whitson, Roger. *Steampunk and Nineteenth-Century Digital Humanities: Literary Retrofuturisms, Media Archaeologies, Alternate Histories*. London: Routledge, 2017.
———. "There Is No William Blake: @autoblake's Algorithmic Condition." *Essays in Romanticism* 21, no. 1 (2016): 69–87.
Wittenberg, David. *Time Travel: The Popular Philosophy of Narrative*. New York: Fordham University Press, 2018.
Wood, Gordon. *The Americanization of Benjamin Franklin*. New York: Penguin, 2004.
World Health Organization. "Gaming Disorder." http://www.who.int/features/qa/gaming-disorder/en/ (accessed December 8, 2018).
Yenisey, Zeynep. "This Dude Married His Computer, and Is Now Suing Alabama for Not Recognizing His 'Machinist' Sexuality." *Maxim*, September 8, 2017, https://www.maxim.com/news/man-marries-computer-2017-9.
Zieger, Susan. *The Mediated Mind: Affect, Ephemera, and Consumerism in the Nineteenth Century*. New York: Fordham University Press, 2018.
Žižek, Slavoj. "Afterword: Lenin's Choice." In V. I. Lenin, *Revolution at the Gates: Selected Writings of Lenin from 1917*, edited by Slavoj Žižek, 165–336. New York: Verso, 2002.
Zuboff, Shoshana. *The Age of Surveillance Capitalism: The Fight for a Human Future at the New Frontier of Power*. New York: Public Affairs, 2019.
Zwirtz, Elizabeth. "Man, 35, Reportedly Marries Computer Hologram." Fox News, November 24, 2018, https://www.foxnews.com/world/man-35-reportedly-marries-computer-hologram.

INDEX

9/11, 45, 49
1984, 22–23, 26–27
2001: A Space Odyssey (Clarke), 118

Adkins, Lisa, 205–06
Adorno, Theodor, 80; and Max Horkheimer, 112–13
advertising, 154, 155, 160, 161, 164–65
Alberto, Maria: and Elizabeth Swanstrom, 8
Alien franchise, 99–100
Allan, Kathryn, 119
allegory, 25–26
alternate history, 133–34, 147
Anderson, Perry, 23, 220n23
apocalypse, 43–44, 168
Arac, Jonathan, 78–79
art, 14, 25, 161–62
artificial intelligence, 170–74
Ascher, Ivan, 204
Augé, Marc, 98–99, 101, 104, 108
Avent, Ryan, 196
Azerrad, Michael, 23

Babbage, Charles, 137; in *The Difference Engine*, 81, 84, 137
Back to the Future 3 (Zemeckis), 83
Badiou, Alain, 78
Bakhtin, M. M., 55, 56
Benjamin, Walter, 15, 73, 148, 149
Berlant, Lauren, 216n12
biopunk, 83
Bloch, Ernst, 78
Boluk, Stephanie: and Patrick Lemieux, 209
Bould, Mark, 108
Bratton, Benjamin, 133, 139, 140–41, 144, 148, 149
Briggs, Robert, 216n12
Brouillette, Sarah, 42
Brown, Nicholas, 79
Brown, Wendy, 201–02
Burges, Joel: and Amy J. Elias, 51–53
Burroughs, William S., 131–32
Bush, George W., 45. *See also* 9/11
Butler, Andrew M., 4

Carr, Terry, 42
Chaplin, Sarah, 97–98
cognitive mapping, 25, 32–33, 40
Cold War, 44, 83
comics, 11
computers, 116–18

Index

cyberpunk, 2, 36, 71, 125; and the body, 119–20, 121; and feminism, 218n26; in film, 1, 98, 102; and Gibson's short fiction, 68; and New Wave, 42; and postmodernism, 27, 42; as realism, 30; Samuel R. Delany on, 221n51; and *Stars in My Pocket Like Grains of Sand* (Delany), 41; and steampunk, 3, 82–83
cyberspace, 15, 97–98, 107, 180–81, 185–87

data, 132, 141
Debord, Guy, 154–55, 159, 160, 161–62, 236n30
Delany, Samuel R., 36, 38–39; and cyberpunk, 41; on cyberpunk, 221n51; *Stars in My Pocket Like Grains of Sand*, 26–27, 36–40
The Difference Engine (Gibson and Sterling), 3, 15–16, 81–85, 87, 90–92, 93, 94, 131, 132, 134, 135–39, 143, 147. See also Gibson, William; Sterling, Bruce
digital humanities, 8, 113–15, 121–23, 143, 231n11
dystopia, 45, 71

Easterbrook, Neil, 7, 58
Elias, Amy J., 15; and Joel Burges, 51–53
Emerson, Ralph Waldo, 92, 93–94
Ernst, Wolfgang, 132–33, 135–36, 138

fantasy, 11
Feher, Michel, 202
finance, 165–66, 196–97, 201, 208
Foucault, Michel, 201–02
Franklin, Benjamin, 84–85, 87–88, 89–90
Franklin, Seb, 208
Freedman, Carl, 10, 27
Frelik, Paweł, 103

Fukuzawa, Yukichi, 85, 92; in *The Difference Engine* (Gibson and Sterling), 90–92

gaming, 199, 200; disorder, 195–97; and finance, 197, 201; in *The Peripheral* (Gibson), 197–98, 199–200, 202–03
genre turn, 9–13, 217n20
Gernsback, Hugo, 100
Gibson, William: *Agency*, 6, 144; *Agrippa (A Book of the Dead)*, 4–5; *Alien III*, 99–100; Blue Ant trilogy, 5, 153, 157, 160, 161–62, 179, 180–81, 185–87; Bridge trilogy, 3, 55–57, 144; *Burning Chrome*, 2, 67, 68; *Count Zero*, 172; on cyberpunk, 10, 143; *Distrust That Particular Flavor*, 54, 57; "The Gernsback Continuum," 14, 69–73, 77–78, 190; *Idoru*, 12–13; *Mona Lisa Overdrive*, 112, 172, 182–83; *Neuromancer*, 1, 11, 13, 26–27, 30–31, 32–33, 34–36, 42–43, 55, 112, 116, 122, 171, 181, 193; *Pattern Recognition*, 5, 14, 22, 49–50, 57, 58–60, 69, 112, 155–57, 160, 164–65, 186–87; *The Peripheral*, 60, 61–64, 65, 132, 133, 139, 141–43, 144–48, 168–70, 172–73, 174–76, 178, 197–200, 204, 205–10; and postmodernism, 12, 26–27; on science fiction, 9; screenwriting, 4; short fiction, 2–3, 14, 68, 76; *Spook Country*, 163, 187; Sprawl trilogy, 2, 168, 172; on temporality, 61, 64; *Virtual Light*, 55–56; "The Winter Market," 119–21; *Zero History*, 157, 158–59, 180, 189, 192–93. See also Sterling, Bruce
globalization, 24, 159
Gold, Matthew K., 113
Google, 191

Haines, Christian P., 16
Harvey, David, 185

Hayles, N. Katherine, 118–19, 120
Heinlein, Robert, 117, 118
Hoberek, Andrew, 9, 11–12, 218n26
Hollinger, Veronica, 7, 27, 58, 188

ideology, 33–34, 148

Jameson, Fredric: on cyberpunk, 27; on ideology, 33; on *Neuromancer* (Gibson), 13, 30–31, 32–33, 34, 181–82; *The Political Unconscious*, 135, 145; *Postmodernism*, 12, 13, 30, 40, 41, 181; on postmodernism, 23–24, 25
Japan, 3; in *The Difference Engine* (Gibson and Sterling), 90–93
Johnny Mnemonic (Longo), 101–03
Jones, Steven, 143
Jovanovic, Damjan, 185

Kant, Immanuel, 85
Keogh, Brendan, 199, 207
Kippner, Greta, 196
Kirschenbaum, Matthew, 132
Kittler, Friedrich, 183, 184–85
Konstantinou, Lee, 7, 188
Koolhaas, Rem, 189
Korsnack, Kylie, 16
Kroker, Arthur: and Marilouise Kroker, 101–02
Kross, Karin L., 176

labor, 34–35, 137, 140, 157, 182, 195–96
Lacan, Jacques, 33
Lawrence, D. H., 88
Le Guin, Ursula K., 30, 39, 43, 67
Lefebvre, Henri, 183–84, 193
Lukács, Georg, 33

many-worlds interpretation, 168, 238n4
Martin, Randy, 196, 201, 202

Marx, Karl, 182; *Capital*, 140, 149; theory of labor, 140, 182
McCaffrey, Anne, 117–18
McCaffrey, Larry, 28, 30, 31, 217n14
McDonagh, Maitland, 104
McGann, Jerome, 139
McGurl, Mark, 28
McHale, Brian, 28, 99
McInerney, Jay, 26, 36
media archaeology, 133–35
Metronome (Jones and Ginzel), 50–51
modernism, 30
Morgan, Glyn, 61
Morgan, Robert C., 50
Moylan, Tom: on *Neuromancer*, 34; on Kim Stanley Robinson, 222n73

Narkunas, J. Paul, 206
neoliberalism, 201–02
New Rose Hotel (Ferrara), 103–04
New Wave science fiction, 21–22, 27; and cyberpunk, 42, 43
New York City, 26, 38–39
Nilges, Mathias, 14

ontology, 15, 168, 171–72, 178
Osborne, Peter, 75

Parikka, Jussi, 133, 136
Pease, Aron, 14–15
Pias, Claus, 208
Pier, John, 61
postmodernism, 27, 42
punk, 23, 36
Pynchon, Thomas, 170

Rancière, Jacques, 52–53, 60, 64–65
Reagan, Ronald, 83, 89
realism, 5, 14, 30, 31–32, 69
Robinson, Kim Stanley, 43, 44–47
Rosen, Jeremy, 9

Ross, Andrew, 36
Russ, Joanna, 21

science fiction studies, 10–11, 217n20
Shaviro, Steven, 102, 104
Shaw, Joe: and Mark Graham, 191
Shelley, Mary, 84; *Frankenstein*, 84, 85–87
Siivonen, Timo, 7
Snow, C. P., 115
Sponsler, Claire, 217n14
steampunk, 3, 82–83
Sterling, Bruce, 67–68, 100, 131, 134. *See also* Gibson, William
Suvin, Darko, 7, 45, 216n13

Tatsumi, Takayuki, 3
television, 11; cyberspace in, 107
Terdiman, Richard, 75, 78
The Time Machine (Wells), 61
time travel, 6, 61, 169; in *The Peripheral* (Gibson), 197–98, 205–06

Todorov, Tsvetan, 18, 19
Tomberg, Jaak, 153–54, 188, 216n13

utopia, 35, 44–45

video games, 197, 199. *See also* gaming
Vint, Sherryl, 14
Virilio, Paul, 186, 187

Wark, McKenzie, 170, 204
Wegner, Phillip E., 10, 11, 71, 133, 147
Westfahl, Gary, 100, 172
White, Hayden, 22, 74
Whitson, Roger, 15–16

The X-Files, 104–07, 108

Yu, Charles, 11, 17

Žižek, Slavoj, 41–42

THE NEW AMERICAN CANON

Half a Million Strong: Crowds and Power from Woodstock to Coachella
by Gina Arnold

Violet America: Regional Cosmopolitanism in U.S. Fiction since the Great Depression
by Jason Arthur

The Meanings of J. Robert Oppenheimer
by Lindsey Michael Banco

Neocolonial Fictions of the Global Cold War
edited by Steven Belletto and Joseph Keith

Workshops of Empire: Stegner, Engle, and American Creative Writing during the Cold War
by Eric Bennett

Places in the Making: A Cultural Geography of American Poetry
by Jim Cocola

The Legacy of David Foster Wallace
edited by Samuel Cohen and Lee Konstantinou

Race Sounds: The Art of Listening in African American Literature
by Nicole Brittingham Furlonge

Postmodern/Postwar—and After: Rethinking American Literature
edited by Jason Gladstone, Andrew Hoberek, and Daniel Worden

After the Program Era: The Past, Present, and Future of Creative Writing in the University
edited by Loren Glass

Hope Isn't Stupid: Utopian Affects in Contemporary American Literature
by Sean Austin Grattan

It's Just the Normal Noises: Marcus, Guralnick, No Depression, *and the Mystery of Americana Music*
by Timothy Gray

Wrong: A Critical Biography of Dennis Cooper
by Diarmuid Hester

Contemporary Novelists and the Aesthetics of Twenty-First Century American Life
by Alexandra Kingston-Reese

American Unexceptionalism: The Everyman and the Suburban Novel after 9/11
by Kathy Knapp

Visible Dissent: Latin American Writers, Small U.S. Presses, and Progressive Social Change
by Teresa V. Longo

Pynchon's California
edited by Scott McClintock and John Miller

Richard Ford and the Ends of Realism
by Ian McGuire

*William Gibson and the Futures
of Contemporary Culture*
edited by Mitch R. Murray
and Mathias Nilges

*Poems of the American Empire:
The Lyric Form in the Long
Twentieth Century*
by Jen Hedler Phillis

Reading Capitalist Realism
edited by Alison Shonkwiler
and Leigh Claire La Berge

*Technomodern Poetics:
The American Literary Avant-Garde
at the Start of the Information Age*
by Todd F. Tietchen

*How to Revise a True War Story:
Tim O'Brien's Process of Textual
Production*
by John K. Young